SQL Server 2012

AlwaysOn

Joes 2 Pros®

A Tutorial for Implementing High Availability and Disaster
Recovery using AlwaysOn Availability Groups

By

Balmukund Lakhani

Founder of SQLServer-Help.com

Vinod Kumar

Founder of blogs.ExtremeExperts.com

ISBN: 978-1-939666-23-9

Special Thanks

Dedicated to my wife Palak (a.k.a. Gunjan) – the most caring woman in my life and my adorable daughter Samriddhi - For their endless support and for those times when my concentration needed to be at its best they just knew not to disturb me.

– Balmukund Lakhani

To my ever supporting father, G.M.Sundaram and my wife Satya who have been pillars of strength while I worked long hours to get the perfection I needed in building this content.

– Vinod Kumar

Table of Contents

Chapter 4.   Understanding Quorum Models 70

Chapter 5.   AlwaysOn Availability Groups 85

Chapter 6.   Availability Group (AG) Actions on the Secondary .. 98

About the Authors

Balmukund Lakhani

Balmukund is a husband, father, blogger, mentor, speaker (on SQL Server technologies), and an MSDN SQL forums moderator. He has spoken at various external events including TechEd, SQL Saturday, and to the Bangalore SQL User Group. He has delivered many internal enterprise trainings and external webcasts.

He completed his graduation in 1999 from the Government Engineering College, Jabalpur (MP). In 2001 he got a post-graduate degree from the Indian Institute of Science (IISc), Bangalore. He has been passionate to learn about any upcoming SQL Server technology since his first job at Ramco Systems in Chennai. He has worked as a developer, DBA, and an on-site technical consultant for a client at Ahmedabad. He joined the Microsoft SQL Server Customer Support Service Team in 2005 as a Support Engineer. There he did work over phone to assist customers in solving their toughest problems related to the product. Later (for a span of 18 months) he joined the Premier Field Engineering team and worked with customers face-to-face to provide training and performed health checks on their SQL Server. His current role of Technical Lead revolves around troubleshooting and fixing issues related to any SQL Server feature. He works closely with the SQL Server Escalation Services team to provide faster resolutions to issues reported by customers. During his free time, he loves helping other people on issues related to the SQL Server suite via MSDN forums. He believes - "there's a solution to every problem and a reason for everything".

Recently, he has become part of an AlwaysOn Support team based out of Bangalore.

Balmukund grew up in a Gwalior (MP) and currently resides in Bangalore, along with wife and a daughter. In his spare time at home, he enjoys playing Xbox with his family.

You can keep up with Balmukund at his blog at http://SQLServer-Help.com or on Twitter at twitter.com/blakhani or on facebook at facebook.com/blakhani.

Vinod Kumar M

Vinod Kumar has worked with SQL Server extensively since joining the industry over a decade ago. He has worked on various versions of database technologies, from SQL Server 7.0 to Oracle 7.3. Vinod now works with the Microsoft

Technology Center (MTC) as a Technology Architect. With an extensive database, BI, and applications background he currently helps customers maximize on the investments in technologies to solve real world business and technology integration problems. He has worked in various roles and projects involving development, migration, deployment, networking, architecture, testing, packaging, and RND for services and product based companies. He holds 26+ Microsoft Certifications on various technologies at the present time. Before joining Microsoft, he was a Microsoft MVP (in SQL Server) for more than 3 years.

In his previous role inside Microsoft as a Technology Evangelist (SQL Server), he was a well-known top rated speaker at technical conferences (like Microsoft TechEd, MSDN, TechNet, and GIDS). He is also a regular speaker at many SQL Server User Groups. Vinod has more than 13+ years of expertise in computers and database systems since earning his Engineering degree from the College of Engineering of Guindy (Chennai). He has published numerous articles on SQL Server on multiple sites and currently writes most of his learning material (technical and nontechnical) on his site and blog at: http://blogs.ExtremeExperts.com. He also runs the popular local user groups in Bangalore, the SQL Server Bangalore Chapter (Facebook: SQLBangalore) and has been with Bangalore .NET user group (Facebook: BDotnet) since 2003.

Feel free to follow him on Twitter (@vinodk_sql). He is also an author of the book: *"SQL Server Interview Questions and Answers for all Database Developers and Database Administrators"*.

ISBN-13 - 9781466405646

ISBN-10 - 1466405643

Besides juggling all of his activities, Vinod loves to watch movies, read books (technical and management), explore various foods, and he enjoys spending time with his father (G.M.Sundaram) and supportive wife (Satya).

Acknowledgements

Authors are a bit like astronauts, when launch time comes they get all the glory and grace the cover of each printed book that records their heroic effort. Extraordinary talents are in people everywhere around us. For every need we've encountered, talented and motivated people have come out of the woodwork and shown up at just the right moment to support this effort. In this section, we want to pay tribute to core people who made the process happen:

Editors: Sandi Howard, Tony Smithlin
Content Review: Rick A. Morelan,
Technical Editor: Ryan M. Lence MCM

We also want to take this opportunity to thank a number of people within Microsoft for their unconditional support, encouragement and faith in us to deliver this book with quality. We would like to specifically express our gratitude to Aniruddha Deswandikar (Director - MTC), Sri Krishna Jagannath (Team Manager - SQL Support), Rahul Jacob (Team Manager - SQL Support), Xavier S Raj (Escalation Manager - SQL Support), Ranjan Bhattacharjee (Group Manager - Developer Support) and Govind Kanshi (Technical Director, MTC) who have patiently waited as we completed the book.

Introduction

If we think for a moment on activities that we do daily and start exploring simple ways to complete them, we just made our life more exciting. In this process we will need to reinvent our understanding of these concepts. For instance let us take an example of how we work and get started with computers.

Today we are sure that each one of us is at ease once we get to our work stations our office. We automatically press the power button to start our computers. It is now second nature for all of us. Over the years there have been a few changes to the way this process happens. Nowadays we see people bringing their laptops and docking them at their work stations and opening it to start working. Though the fundamental concepts of working with computers have not changed, the methods we use to work with them have surely changed over the years. We think the next generation is where the tablets, touch based computers, all-in-one computers, and many others are going to change the way we will work.

All of us have had our own bad luck at work while there are people surrounding us. They are asking for answers about why the software failed or why things are not working. For these few moments of anxiety with all eyes on us, we need answers from somewhere. We try all the possibilities to come up with a solution.

I still remember a situation in one of the companies I worked for as System Administrator. Our CEO called me in for some help. She said she had lost her Outlook PST file and it contained close to 10 years of her emails. During a recent rebuild of her machine it has gone missing. We kept scrambling to find where it was and after close to 15 minutes of searching I was slowly running out of ideas. This is when my colleague suggested checking if the file was hidden. It worked like a magic. The file suddenly appeared and we were back in business. What a sigh of relief! Later my colleague said he had read about it somewhere and had seen the same behavior on another manager's laptop.

Our actions are based on what we have learned from our experiences in the past. Sometimes it can also mean we need to learn some new tricks to keep ahead of the technology curve. Technologies change, behaviors change, understandings change, and implementations change. This IT world lives up to the adage that "change is the only constant".

To these changing times, this book is geared toward the DBAs who are looking at understanding and implementing SQL Server 2012 AlwaysOn Availability Groups in their respective organizations. It is difficult to get all the information about Availability Groups in one place, so this book has been turned into a guide for everyone who wants to learn and practice Availability Groups.

PS: Quick note, AlwaysOn must be written as one word. To help others, please try to use the same naming convention whenever we communicate about AlwaysOn.

Skills Needed for this Book

This book assumes at least an intermediate knowledge of SQL Server and readers are aware of the various High Availability (HA) and Disaster Recovery (DR) mechanisms available in the SQL Server 2008 R2 version. This can be from a combination of knowledge from experience or training. You need to already have knowledge of basic administration operations and scripting (PowerShell, using Management Studio and T-SQL). If you are new to the field of administration then all you need to do is complete the first two SQL Administration books from Joes 2 Pros (*SQL Administration 2012 Joes 2 Pros Volume 1* and *SQL Administration 2012 Joes 2 Pros Volume 2*).

This book also assumes an intermediate level of coding and development in writing queries, stored procedures, and using functions. If you are new to the field of SQL coding then all you need to do is complete the first four SQL Queries books from Joes 2 Pros (*SQL Queries 2012 Joes 2 Pros Volume 1 - 4*). With the knowledge in those books, most of the prerequisites are covered. This book will guide you to deploy SQL Server AlwaysOn Availability Groups.

About this Book

This book is based on many firsthand experiences from author Balmukund Lakhani during his vast experience in a support role for customers all over the world. Some of the experiences of Vinod Kumar have been added as concepts and explanation as we expand the scope of the whole book.

Ask DBAs what their most dreaded situation would be. You will find they are very cautious in their production environments. For most people it would be the fear of production servers failing. A seasoned organization always performs mock drills to simulate disasters and they failover to the DR (Disaster Recovery) site to check their infrastructure resilience. It is a very common practice to perform these types of drills. There are documents DBAs have called recovery procedures which are used by the team.

SQL Server 2012 brought in some great new features and one of the important ones is scalability and performance via AlwaysOn. AlwaysOn is a superset feature and is a combination of many things you will learn about. As the language suggests, this technology achieves a SQL Server infrastructure that can be "always on". For businesses that run 24x7 downtime means the loss of business. This type of risk is out of the question for these businesses. This book discusses in detail the concepts of SQL Server AlwaysOn starting from the basics.

How we organized this Book

When we are learning something new, we look for a guide or someone to help us understand the concepts better. In the same way, this book discusses in detail the basics. This includes installation, monitoring, troubleshooting, and possible deployment options in quite some detail. We want to call out what you can expect from each chapter before you start reading.

Chapter 1: High Availability and Disaster Recovery Concepts: This chapter sets up the different concepts required when it comes to High Availability and Disaster Recovery. We will also define the basics of various recovery SLAs in this chapter.

Chapter 2: Existing High Availability and Disaster Recovery options: This chapter discusses the various HA/DR options available in SQL Server 2008 R2. This is a recap of the previous widespread deployments people are comfortable with.

Chapter 3: What is AlwaysOn?: In this chapter we introduce the AlwaysOn basics. This chapter also discusses the deployment of the Failover Cluster Instance (FCI) and the enhancements made to FCI in SQL Server 2012.

Chapter 4: Understanding Quorum Models: As we start learning in detail about Availability Groups (AG), we need to know about quorum models. Although the basics of quorums are the same for an FCI (Failover Cluster Instance), this builds the base of what you need to know.

Chapter 5: AlwaysOn Availability Groups: This chapter concentrates on AlwaysOn Availability Groups. We discuss the various terms and features introduced in an Availability Group.

Chapter 6: Availability Group Actions on the secondary: In this chapter we look at the various interesting additions made to secondary nodes like active secondary, readable secondary, and backups on the secondary.

Chapter 7: Deploying AlwaysOn Availability Groups: In this chapter we take a step-by-step approach to installing and configuring an Availability Group. This will get us to the typical AlwaysOn Availability Group deployment.

Chapter 8: Features of AlwaysOn Availability Groups: This chapter concentrates on the specific additional features available with Availability Groups. These are an extension to the configurations we can add when deploying an Availability Group.

Chapter 9: AlwaysOn Monitoring and Troubleshooting: No solution can be complete without a manual for troubleshooting or getting started. This chapter brings to light the basic tools available for monitoring and troubleshooting an AlwaysOn deployment. This is part 1 of 3 parts on monitoring.

Chapter 10: AlwaysOn Diagnostics: SQL Server 2012 introduces the new diagnostics command for SQL Server and this can also double up for monitoring a SQL Server AlwaysOn deployment. This is part 2 of 3parts on monitoring.

Chapter 11: AlwaysOn Advanced Monitoring: The need to know more about the internals of monitoring is critical. This chapter talks about the integration with System Center, understanding some AlwaysOn wait types, and the AlwaysOn Health session. As the chapter says, these are advanced monitoring and troubleshooting techniques. This is part 3 of 3 parts on monitoring.

Chapter 12: Deployment Variations of AlwaysOn: Even in previous SQL Server versions the HA/DR deployment variations are abundant. With an AlwaysOn configuration the number of deployment choices is very large. In this chapter we show some of the most used deployment options with AlwaysOn.

Chapter 13: AlwaysOn Common Issues: With the number of options and choices available for deployment in AlwaysOn, there are some common errors we will encounter. This chapter brings out some of these common errors with the steps to solve them.

Chapter 14: Availability Group Failover: Once we build an AlwaysOn Availability Group deployment we need to know we can do a failover during disaster. This chapter shows the various options for manual and automatic failovers.

Chapter 15: Migrating from previous High Availability scenarios: Not all deployments are a fresh install of HA (High Availability). This chapter shows what would be the concept workflow needed when moving to AlwaysOn from Log Shipping and Database Mirroring deployments.

Chapter 16: AlwaysOn Availability Group Maintenance Activities: All the previous chapters showed how to add databases and create an Availability Group. In this chapter we will show how to remove databases, remove an Availability Group, drop a Listener, and remove a secondary database.

Chapter 17: AlwaysOn FAQ: We have helped customers (almost daily) and there are some frequently asked questions that keep coming up. We have summarized the common questions with answers to all of them. We cover 75+ questions in this chapter to give you a complete view.

Chapter 18: SQL Server 2014: *AlwaysOn Enhancements Teaser* – This chapter covers the basic enhancements that were introduced with SQL Server 2014. When this book was released, SQL Server 2014 was in CTP1.

Chapter 1. High Availability and Disaster Recovery Concepts

Life is full of interesting twists even as we tend to plan each and every move. Our plans are made so that we don't get any surprises at a later time. Once these plans are in place, we must make sure to stick to them to achieve our goals. Think of a movie like The Matrix or Mission Impossible. The movie's plot is based on strategies and plans made by the team. As the movie progresses, we see that there is a sudden unexpected event and the plan goes haywire. The team then resorts to plan B. In the database world the same type of plans have to be made. Ask a DBA what part of their work is the toughest or what situations they dread the most. Then ask them what plans they have for disasters and what plans they have to monitor their servers.

In the current world of 24x7x365 online ecommerce sites and mission critical applications, people use the same applications across the globe. Any downtime can impact a business with big financial losses. With so much at stake, database engines are expected to be available as much as possible to serve the critical client applications. Availability is commonly defined as the percentage of uptime in a given period of time (like a year, quarter, month, or day).

READER NOTE*: This chapter provides many diagrams to demonstrate the important concepts that are needed for AlwaysOn. In this chapter there will be no need to have your machine configured to follow along. The tutorial steps begin in Chapter 7.*

Uptime Requirements

Imagine we were just about to retire an older server that has been in operation for 15 years. During those 15 years the server was down for a total of 2 minutes. This is an amazing achievement but can we say this server achieved 100% uptime? How good can we rate this server? If this server's goal was to be up 99% of the time then it could be down for one full day out of every 100 days. Or it could be down for almost four full days per year before it falls below the 99% mark. Another way to state that is this server did achieve two 9s of uptime (two 9s is 99%). What is three 9s? That means 99.9% of the time the server was available. So for every 1,000 days of service it could be down 1 day (24 hours) or less to achieve three 9s.

Our 15 year old server being down for just 2 minutes easily went well beyond the three 9s mark. Since no server can be up 100% of the time, we talk about server uptime in the number of 9s. If we needed six 9s it means we need the server to be up 99.9999% of the time. So how many seconds of downtime does six 9s allow?

Availability is most commonly calculated as a ratio of actual uptime over expected uptime. The following table is the simple calculation to show the annual downtime allowed based on the "number of 9s" school of thought.

Number of 9s	% Uptime	% Downtime (100 - % Uptime)	Downtime (Annual)		
			Minutes	Hours	Days
1	90.0 (not 9.0)	10	52416	873.6	**36.4**
2	99	1	5256	87.6	**3.65**
3	99.9	0.1	525.6	**8.76**	0.365
4	99.99	0.01	**52.56**	0.876	0.0365
5	99.999	0.001	**5.256**	0.0876	0.0037
6	99.9999	0.0001	**0.526 (35 SEC)**	0.00886	0.0004

Table 1.1 Amount of maximum downtime on a system and its impact on applications.

Measuring availability based on the number of 9s doesn't quite reflect the real availability of the system. For example, if there is a network outage connecting to the SQL Server then the uptime of the SQL Server would seem high but availability of the application using SQL Server could be lower. The SQL Server was never down but the company still lost business. Hence the application's overall availability is another point of view when measuring the availability which also includes the databases availability.

As we define the scenarios of availability, we must also understand there are maintenance downtimes, scheduled downtimes, and administration downtimes to be taken into account. Outside of these scenarios, additional downtime can be experienced. Consider a scenario where a DBA is performing an offline rebuild of the indexes during business hours. This can cause blocking within the SQL Server. In this particular scenario, the application's access to a table will be blocked and unavailable for the time that it takes for the index rebuild operation to complete.

For industries that need 24 hour service (like call centers or financial institutions) there is no way applications can afford system failures. Downtime can be further classified into planned and unplanned downtime. Planned downtime can be defined as a period of scheduled downtime for maintenance. Typical scheduled downtimes include applying service packs, cumulative updates on SQL Server, or updates to the operating system. Unplanned downtime is generally caused by human error, software bugs, power failure, or natural disaster. Planned downtime is always preferable to unplanned downtime because users can be informed well in advance about the downtime. Even though downtime is planned, it still counts against your number of 9s of availability.

Understanding RTO and RPO

Imagine that we are a data entry operator who reads sheets of feedback forms to enter as data into the system. When we hit the save button it generates the auto number for the system from our form. If it takes 15 minutes to fill out a form and computer losses all of our data at the end then we could lose up to 15 minus of work. This is really no downtime at all but to our system causes us to redo some work. We want to prevent downtime and data loss.

As we define availability from a business context, there are two concepts that get questioned. They are the Recovery Point Objective (RPO) and the Recovery Time Objective (RTO). RPO is the amount of time for which work might need to be redone after a disaster. Recovery Point Objective (RPO) is defined as the amount of acceptable data loss or the point-in-time up to which the data can be recovered. Recovery Time Objective (RTO) is defined as the time taken to restore normal operations after a failure or planned failover. In other words, RTO is the amount of time the business can be without the service (for example 5 minutes).

Now, what would happen if we had a major incident, like a fire, at the data center? The Business Continuity team would send notifications and start working toward resuming the services as fast as possible. The team informs us that it will take at least two hours to get the systems up and running. Once this is up and running we need to re-enter the data which we entered for at least the last 15 minutes before the incident. In this example, our RTO time is 2 hours and our RPO is 15 minutes.

High Availability vs. Disaster Recovery

All of us have a habit of making our very own availability plans in our daily lives. For example, based on the time available we might use a car or a bicycle to get to work. If we choose the car then the bike stays in a standby mode. In another scenario, when the vehicle runs out of gas we know we have the bike ready to get us to work. This is a typical High Availability scenario.

Let's assume another scenario, where the city is impacted by heavy rains and it might not be safe to drive to work. We have an important meeting to attend. We might have to use public transportation as a backup plan. This is a typical Disaster Recovery scenario.

In the computer industry, both High Availability and Disaster Recovery are used interchangeably but there are fundamental differences between them. Disaster Recovery is a process to resume operations of business after a disaster. A disaster at the primary data center could be an earthquake, fire, or a power failure. In case of such natural disasters there would be a loss of service at our primary site. We might need to bring up secondary servers and make a switch-over of the applications to a DR (Disaster Recovery) site.

There are human errors that can occur. A junior DBA could have executed a delete or truncate command on one of the critical transaction tables. This can also be categorized as a Disaster Recovery situation.

On the other hand, High Availability provides the capability to continue operations even when one of the hardware components fails to function. A typical hardware failure includes CPU, Memory, Disk system, or Network card failures. Most of the organizations use clustering as a method to implement High Availability supported by a SAN backend to mitigate the chances of any disk failures. Organizations also consider a table's availability during a re-indexing operation as part of High Availability and therefore the feature of online re-indexing was introduced starting with SQL Server 2005. Since online re-indexing keeps the SQL Server available it is a very basic part of the High Availability features.

Until SQL Server 2008 R2 versions (before SQL 2012), the options of High Availability and Disaster Recovery have been confusing and organizations needed to combine various different features to meet their needs. Each solution has its own limitations. As DBAs we have to come up with innovative deployments to meet the challenges of any given deployment goal. Chapter 2 will show the existing High Availability solutions as of SQL Server 2008 R2 while showcasing all the advantages and disadvantages of each. After doing that we will soon see that AlwaysOn seems to have all the advantages of these existing High Availability solutions.

By the end of this book, we should all be able to install, configure, troubleshoot, and perform administrative tasks with the SQL Server 2012 AlwaysOn feature.

Summary

Organizations place their business in the trust of a few critical applications and business users. They expect these systems to be available 24x7 for reporting, analytics, and transactional needs. Given the data explosions in the industry, it is critical for DBAs to have these databases always available to serve these demanding needs from the business. SQL Server has always provided different solutions for DBAs as choices based on those business needs. SQL 2012 introduces the AlwaysOn feature which pulls from all the advantages and almost none of the limitations of past solutions.

Points to Ponder - High Availability and Disaster Recovery Concepts

1. We measure uptime in terms of the number of 9s.

2. A 5 9s (99.999%) of uptime means not more than 5.256 minutes of downtime annually is acceptable.

3. A 3 9s (99.9%) of uptime means up to 8.76 hours of downtime annually is allowed.

4. Planned downtime can be defined as a period of scheduled downtime for maintenance.

5. Unplanned downtime is generally due to human error, software bugs, power failures, or natural disasters.

6. Disaster Recovery is a process to resume operations of business after a human caused error or a natural disaster.

7. High Availability provides the capability to continue operations even when one of the hardware components fails to function.

8. SQL Server 2012 introduces the AlwaysOn capability as a High Availability and Disaster Recovery solution.

9. Recovery Point Objective (RPO) is defined as the amount of acceptable data loss or the point-in-time up to which the data can be recovered.

10. Recovery Time Objective (RTO) is defined as the time taken to restore normal operations after a failure or planned failover.

Review Quiz - Chapter One

1.) A downtime of 0.01% translates to how many minutes annually?

O a. 525.6
O b. 52.56
O c. 5.256
O d. 0.5256

2.) Which of the following is categorized under Disaster Recovery scenario? Choose all that apply.

□ a. Earthquake
□ b. Fire at primary data center
□ c. Power Failure
□ d. Online Indexing

3.) Which solution can provide real time reporting from a secondary server?

O a. Log Shipping
O b. Database Mirroring
O c. SQL Server Failover Clustering
O d. None of the above

Answer Key

1.) 0.01% translates to 99.9%, this means (a) 525.6, (c) 5.256 and (d) .5256 are all wrong. Hence the correct answer is (b) 52.56 minutes annually.

2.) Since Online Indexing doesn't cause any downtime (d) is the wrong answer. (a) Earthquake, (b) Fire and (c) Power Failure are all correct and defined under Disaster Recovery scenario.

3.) None of the options (a) Log Shipping, (b) Database Mirroring, or (c) SQL Server Failover Clustering can give real time reporting capability. Option (d) None of the above, is the correct answer.

[NOTES]

Chapter 2. Existing High Availability and Disaster Recovery Options

It is second nature for us to look for options in everything we do. For example let's think about how we choose our clothes at the store. A typical mall has multiple floors and a number of store options. The choice will sometimes depend on the reasons why we are buying. Is it casual wear? Is it for the holiday season, a party, or our friend's wedding? We decide on where to shop based on the reason we are shopping. The options of High Availability or Disaster Recovery and what we choose depends on our intended use.

The value of most businesses is in the data. Our SQL Server has many databases and each database has many objects. If a critical server with two databases goes down, what happens? Let's say one database ran our ecommerce site and the other was just a test database with no immediate revenue importance. Knowing this ahead of time, we might have decided on a database level High Availability option rather than spending extra resources to protect the entire server. If all the databases on our SQL Server have an SLA (service level agreement) to stay up with five 9s then we want an instance level High Availability option.

In either case do we want the system to detect its own failure and run the redundant system automatically or can we just get an alert and tell our DBA to make the switch-over? Some of our HA (High Availability) options allow for automatic failover and some require that the failover process be done manually. These are good options to put before the stakeholders of the company.

With SQL Server the selection of High Availability and Disaster Recovery technology choices start with looking over the requirements. In addition to that we must be aware of any limitations of the High Availability technologies before making the final decision.

Before we do a deep dive into AlwaysOn we will briefly discuss the various High Availability and Disaster Recovery solutions that were available before SQL Server 2012 was released. These options are still available inside of SQL Server 2012 and can still be used.

READER NOTE: *This chapter provides many diagrams to demonstrate the important concepts that are needed for AlwaysOn. In this chapter there will be no need to have your machine configured to follow along. The tutorial steps begin in Chapter 7.*

Failover Clustering Concepts

A lot work and research has gone into making storage systems for servers fast and nearly foolproof. Naturally we are hinting at high speed disk arrays, where if one or more drives go down then the other drive (with the same data) keeps running. The most common type of reliable high speed storage system is the shared disk resource called SAN (Storage Area Network).

This SAN is often so reliable that unless there is a natural disaster or a power failure to the SAN it will keep running. A few times a year we might need to reboot the SQL Server that is using the SAN. This reboot of a few minutes could be costly downtime. In addition to the few reboots, there is a chance of a CPU or memory failure that would cause even longer downtime. With clustering we can bring in another server that connects to the same SAN and is up and running before we bring the first server down. The Node 2 server will talk with the SAN and keep all operations going while the Node 1 server is down. This configuration of two servers is known as a Failover Cluster.

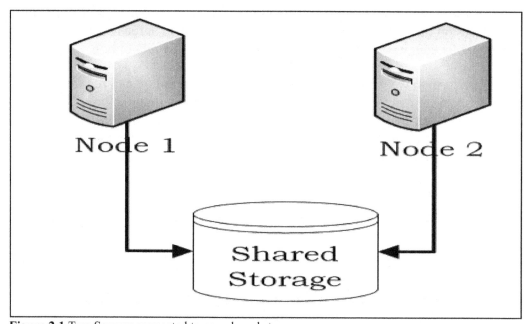

Figure 2.1 Two Servers connected to one shared storage area.

The Failover Cluster will even work if one server goes down unexpectedly. This is the reason that failover clustering is one of the oldest and most commonly used High Availability options. This solution provides for instance level High Availability. To install a SQL Server Failover Cluster, we need to have a

Windows Cluster created with at least one free shared disk resource (often a SAN) to store the database files.

In this age of IT, the need to provide 24x7 support is something we are getting used to. Assume we bought a laptop from a vendor and it has been working for a year without any problems. With a critical customer visit scheduled tomorrow, we suddenly find that our laptop has been shutting down abruptly. Since this is a critical situation for us we would call the customer support line immediately. We only need one person from the support team to do the troubleshooting for us. When the support professional is done with their working hours, they will pass on the phone to the next available support professional. From an end customer experience, the phone line is seamlessly transferred from one support engineer to another with little or no delay. The 24 hour help line that we call is really a cluster of support professionals. One support professional ending their shift while another takes their place is a process called failover. The support professionals in this Failover Cluster example are the nodes.

In a cluster configuration, multiple machines form a single entity for the application to access data (see Figure 2.2). The applications connect to this cluster set using a Virtual Server Name. The Virtual Server Name is a network resource with an IP address resource dependency. In this typical setup, the IP address would be owned by one node in the cluster and this ownership is seamless to the client application that tries to connect.

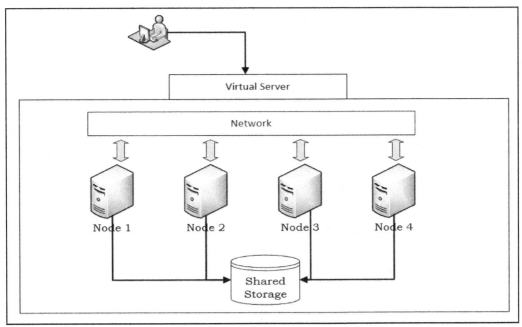

Figure 2.2 Typical four node SQL Server Cluster configuration.

In the case of planned or unplanned downtime the active node's resources (the databases) would be moved over to the next node automatically and the clients reconnect to the same Virtual Server Name. This would give the clients access to the resources. This process is called a failover. As in the case of clustering, we need to make sure that the database files are kept on a shared storage array that all nodes in the cluster can access. Any problem with the shared storage array would affect the cluster. If the storage goes offline the availability can't be protected using the clustering topology. The storage is a single point of failure for this type of deployment.

What if we had two SQL Server instances that needed the protection of clustering? Do we need two clusters (one for each server) or can we have two SQL instances on one cluster? As part of clustering we hear a concept called multi-instance cluster. This terminology is used to describe a deployment where we have multiple instances of SQL Server installed on each machine participating inside a cluster configuration.

Clustering technologies used by other products (like Windows or application servers) are implemented for increased processing power by using load balancing for better performance. SQL Server Clustering is not implemented for performance gains; it is purely a High Availability feature at an instance level.

SQL Server Clustering has been changed in the SQL Server 2012 release and is now known as the AlwaysOn Failover Cluster Instance. Health checks and failure responses have been changed and we will discuss them in more detail in later chapters.

Log Shipping Concepts

If we walk back in history, rivers (like the Mississippi or the York River) have a history of transporting timber downstream from the forest to factories or paper mills. The river provided a free and easy transportation mechanism and helped communities to be built around the river. The metaphor of Log Shipping is synonymous with the concept of Log Shipping inside SQL Server. The transaction logs are shipped from one server to one or more servers waiting downstream. This is one of the most common longstanding methods of High Availability within SQL Server.

We know any changes to the database need be saved to the database. These changes are sent to the transaction log first and then the checkpoint process saves these changes to the data file (mdf). If we backed up the log and all its changes then that backup file would have the latest database information. What if we restored the log backup to another server with the same database? That server would have the same data. Having our data in two places is always considered to be some level of HA (High Availability).

To better understand Log Shipping we need to know the basics of transaction log backups. Let's outline some of the key facts about transaction logs.

- Log backups can be taken from the database when the recovery model is set to full or bulk-logged.
- In the simple recovery model, transaction log backups are not allowed because every checkpoint flushes the transaction logfile so there is nothing to backup.
- In the full or bulk-logged recovery models a checkpoint does not flush the log but log backups will flush the log.
- All transaction log backups form a chain and they must be restored in sequence. Missing any file part of the sequence would cause an error message during a restore.

In Log Shipping; backup, copy, and restore activities are done automatically and periodically by SQL Agent service jobs.

Figure 2.5 shows a Log Shipping configuration with three destinations (three secondary databases). Since we can log ship to multiple servers, the backup location is shared by the three secondary servers. All secondary servers can get a copy of the log backup to perform the restore.

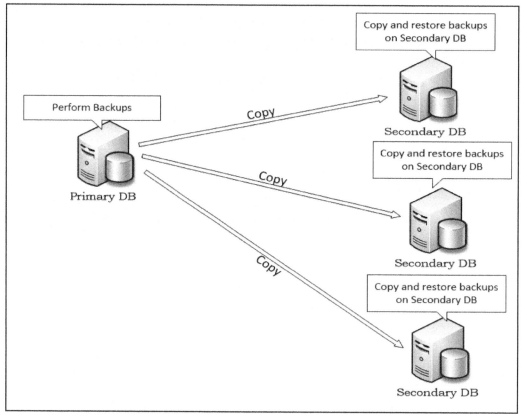

Figure 2.3 Log Shipping to three destinations.

The source server (the primary DB) in technical terms is called the primary server. The receiving server has the secondary database and is called the secondary server. The secondary server does the copy and restore of the log backups from the primary server.

The secondary databases on the secondary servers can be in one of two possible states. In one state the secondary databases get restored and recovered which allows queries to be run against them. In the other state the data is restored but not recovered and queries will not run on the secondary.

Generally the secondary database is in an unrecovered state. We can choose to keep the secondary server's database in a standby state. The standby state allows read only queries to access the secondary database(s). In the standby state we can have reporting applications benefit by using the secondary databases. This way read only traffic will not affect the performance of the primary server.

It takes time for the logs to get shipped and processed. The latency of the secondary server is defined by the interval at which the transaction log backups are taken on the primary server and how fast it gets copied and restored onto the secondary server.

Monitor Server

In production environments, DBAs are like doctors who need to take corrective actions for any abnormal event happening on the database servers. In real life, when we get into an emergency health situation our instinct is to call 911. In the same way, when the database server health is abnormal an alert has to be sent to our doctor (the DBA). The DBA will take corrective actions based on the nature of the situation.

It is possible that a secondary might have a problem and it will stop getting logs from the primary. When this happens we will want to know about that delay but we don't want to have to watch for the delays ourselves. We can set up a server to watch for any unexpected delays in the Log Shipping process for us.

The process of backing up, copying, and restoring (when coupled with multiple servers) can be a tough task to monitor. We have a concept known as a monitor server. The monitor server is responsible for checking the health of the copy, backup, and restore jobs. If the jobs are not running properly then the secondary server would get too far behind the primary server. This defeats the purpose of a Log Shipping Disaster Recovery solution.

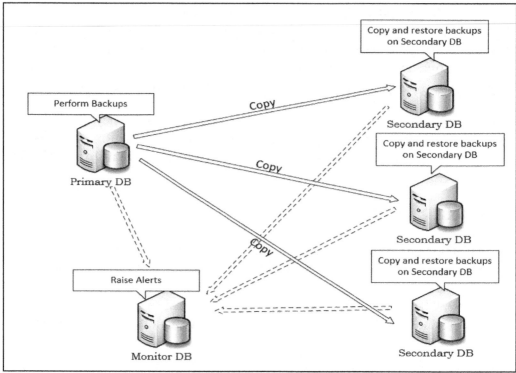

Figure 2.4 Log Shipping with one primary and three secondary servers.

How far behind is too far behind? Based on the various thresholds defined, the monitor server can raise alerts so that corrective actions can be taken by us. It is advisable to use a server other than the primary or the secondary to detect problems on either of the server types. One monitoring server can monitor multiple primary-secondary server pairs.

Log Shipping SQL Agent Jobs

In summary, Log Shipping is made up of four operations, which are handled by dedicated SQL Server Agent jobs: The jobs are the backup job, the copy job, the restore job and the alert job.

The backup job is created on the primary server and as the name suggests it performs a transaction log backup of a database. Additionally, this job can also delete the old backup files and history information based on the defined retention period.

The copy job is created on every secondary server to copy the log backup of the primary server from the designated shared backup location.

The restore job is created on each secondary server and it performs restores of the current backup and then it deletes any old backup history information based on the defined retention period.

The alert job should be created on the monitor server to raise alerts if a backup, copy, or restore operation did not complete successfully in the specified period of time. In the absence of a monitor server, local jobs are created on the primary server (for a backup alert) and on the secondary server(s) (for a copy and a restore alert).

SQL Server Replication Concepts

SQL Server Replication technology is the process of moving data between databases (usually to another SQL Server). SQL Server Replication technology is one of the most commonly used techniques by DBAs and Application Developers for scale-out technologies. SQL Server Replication uses "publish" and "subscribe" terminology in its implementation. The easiest way to understand the various terms of replication is by comparing it with the newspaper or magazine industry. Every publication has several articles. They publish these articles because they know people will subscribe to them. They operate on a publisher-subscriber model. Newspaper publishers are like the publisher database. Instead of publishing the whole database, they will publish various articles (like tables, or stored procedures). In the newspaper world a publication (set of articles) is sent to its destination which is the newspaper distributer. For SQL Server the publication is sent to the subscriber database via a distributer database.

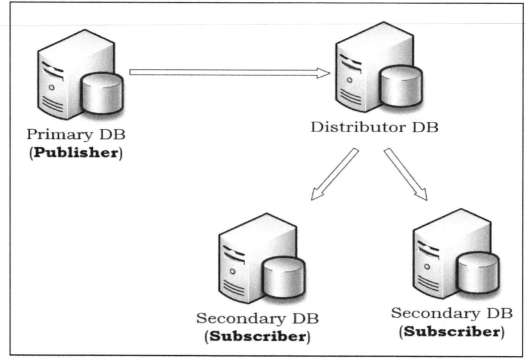

Figure 2.5 Topology for replication to subscribers via a distributor.

Not all forms of replication are like the newspaper example. When we vote on a reality TV show for our favorite dancer or singer, we (at home) are sending data to the TV network database.

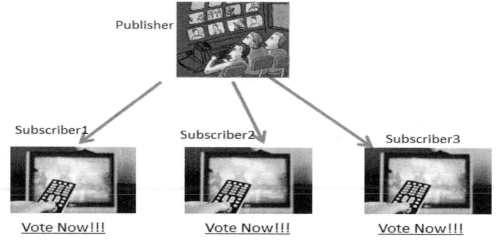

Figure 2.6 In some cases the subscriber's data is collected.

Once the data is compiled we also get to see the results later. In this case the subscriber is performing a type of merge replication. The subscriber is in effect sending data and receiving data from the publisher.

Replication Types

There are four fundamental implementation types of replication available with SQL Server. They are called Transaction replication, Merge replication, Snapshot replication and Peer-to-Peer replication.

Transaction Replication

This is the most commonly used replication type. In this replication type, objects are selected for replication. As transactions happen on the publisher they are sent to the subscriber in the same order. The subscriber receives the changes in the same transaction scope and therefore this implementation is used for applications that require very low latencies between the publisher and the subscriber.

Merge Replication

In this replication type the transactions made on the publisher and subscribers are recorded to the publisher. Once these changes are accrued they are later sent back to all subscribers on the next connection session. This means Subscrber1 can make changes to the publisher and later Subscriber2 can get this data. The subscribers will never send changes directly to each other. There is a chance that two subscribers will change the same data differently on their own machine and replicate them to the publisher. This is known as a data conflict. The DBA or the application logic needs to manage conflict resolutions when multiple subscribers change the same data via different servers.

Snapshot Replication

A snapshot of the database is created to setup the other replication types. So what is Snapshot replication? As the name suggests, a snapshot is like an image of a database at a particular point in time. Consider this method as a process of taking an entire snapshot of data and applying it to all the subscribers. This replication is ideal when the changes are minimal and applications can accept a copy which is little older than what is on the publisher.

Peer-to-Peer Replication

In this replication all transactions are propagated to all the nodes. Peer-to-peer replication also has the ability to decide on conflict resolution. Applications get a unique opportunity to update any of the nodes in case the nearest node goes down for some reason.

Replication Uses

The most widely used replication for High Availability is transactional replication as it provides low latency and high throughput with less overhead. Transaction replication can replicate specific objects (selected during setup) which are part of the publication configuration. Since the publication is a subset of the database, the subscriber does not have all of the objects of the database. Therefore, if the database on the publisher becomes unrecoverable and the subscriber only has some of the data then Transaction Replication is not providing database level or instance level protection.

Transaction replication can be setup in different ways. For example Peer-to-Peer (P2P) replication is a special type of transactional replication where each machine would act as a publisher as well as a subscriber. Since every node has the same copy of the data, it provides redundancy of the data and no single point of failure. This means P2P replication ensures a form of High Availability. Two nodes might make changes to the same record and then try to publish both of them. As part of the synchronization across nodes, it is important for applications be designed in such a way to minimize any conflicts in data getting updated from two nodes at the same time. P2P replication does have an option to work on conflict resolution and we can override data updated from any of the nodes based on conflicts.

Database Mirroring Concepts

The other day someone told me there was an ink smear on my face. It was not there this morning when I looked in the mirror but it is there now. Mirrors are something we use almost every day of our life. Mirrors are used to show exactly how we look and it reflects the current state as-is. Database Mirroring is a software-based solution for High Availability that is set at the database level. In other words the whole database is mirrored and not just some of its objects. The process of Database Mirroring allows us to keep another copy of the database, up-to-date with changes, from the primary database (the primary copy of database).

SQL Server Database Mirroring was introduced in SQL Server 2005 and became fully supported with SQL Server 2005 Service Pack 1. Unlike Failover Clustering, Database Mirroring does not require any special hardware or shared storage. Database Mirroring can be setup between two different instances of SQL Servers (even on same machine).

During Database Mirroring discussions, there are common terms such as Principal, Mirror, Witness and log records. We will now talk about what these terms mean.

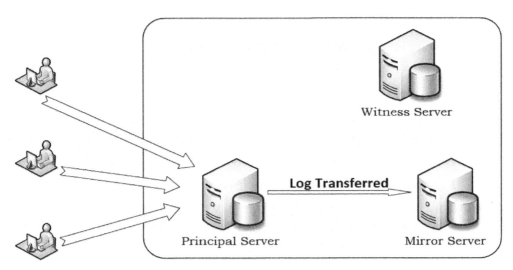

Figure 2.7 Database Mirroring topology.

The database server sending the data is called the principal server. The database server receiving the data is known as the Mirror server. Notice we only have one Mirror server (Figure 2.7).

Unlike Log Shipping, mirroring cannot have multiple servers on the receiving end. The third server is called a Witness server. The Witness server is often optional depending on the operating mode of the SQL Server Database Mirroring configuration. The Witness server is only required for configurations that need automatic failover. Let's explore some of the highlights of each of the roles.

Principal

- This is the database where the client or the applications connect to.
- This database allows modifications in a read/write fashion.

Mirror (Instant standby)

- This is the standby database that clients cannot access normally.
- This applies changes to its copy of the database as they occur on the Principal.
- This server can switch roles with the Principal and become the new Principal using automatic or manual failover.

Witness

- This is an optional server and can be used on an instance with any edition of SQL Server (including SQL Server Express Edition).
- This monitors the two servers in topology (the Principal and the Mirror).
- This can be used for automatic failover.
- If we have many mirror sets in our network we don't need to have many witness servers. A single witness server can be used for multiple database principal-mirror pairs (Figure 2.8).

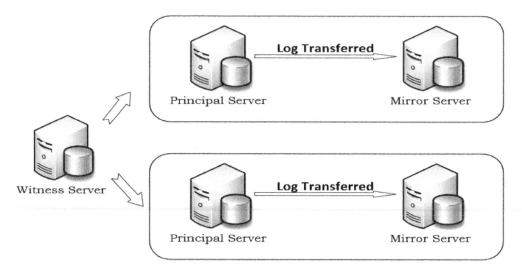

Figure 2.8 One Witness can handle many Mirror sets.

While choosing Database Mirroring as a High Availability solution, we need to keep a few things in mind. If our application depends on more than one database then mirroring is not a good choice since it would require custom code to failover multiple databases together. Out of the box Database Mirroring works at a database level. Also, if our database relies on entities that are not part of the database (like logins in master database, jobs in msdb database, alerts configured, file shares or system OS settings) then mirroring will not protect them.

People may say that with Database Mirroring we can read the data using a snapshot but as the name suggests, snapshot is a point-in-time of the data of when it was taken. In a synchronous mirror the secondary is closer to real time with data than with an asynchronous mirror. Irrespective of synchronous or asynchronous Database Mirroring, reading from the secondary (via a snapshot) will always be a delayed reading.

As per the announcement made in SQL Server 2012 Books Online, the Database Mirroring feature was deprecated and will be removed in a future version of Microsoft SQL Server. It is highly recommended to use the new AlwaysOn Availability Group feature which is richer in functionality as compared to Database Mirroring from SQL Server 2012. Database Mirroring can be replaced with AlwaysOn Availability Groups.

Database Snapshots

Our life is filled with memories and these memories not only reside within us but are also shared from pictures taken with a camera. It is sort of a ritual that we take a picture when we go out with our family during a holiday event. The photos taken capture our presence or state at that moment of time and it brings to life that special day when the picture was taken.

The same concept applies to database snapshots. Database snapshots are a readonly point-in-time copy of the database. Database snapshots work using a copy-on-write mechanism. This means when the snapshot is created the files used by the database would be empty. As soon as pages are modified in the source database, the old copy of the page is pushed to the snapshot data file. Since database snapshots are readonly, it doesn't make sense to have transaction log file(s) to support the database snapshot.

To better understand the copy-on-write concept of database snapshots, let us have a look at the Figure 2.9. In this illustration, the source database has a total of six pages and a snapshot is created with no pages in it at the beginning. If pages 2, 3, and 5 are modified, then the old copy of pages 2, 3, and 5 are sent to the snapshot file. If an application queries the snapshot database to read the unmodified page (let's say page 6) then the request would be redirected to the data file of original database. In other words a query needing data from these six pages would pull 1, 4 and 6 from the source database and 2, 3, and 5 from the snapshot database. If the source database were down then this query could not be completed since half of its data is not available.

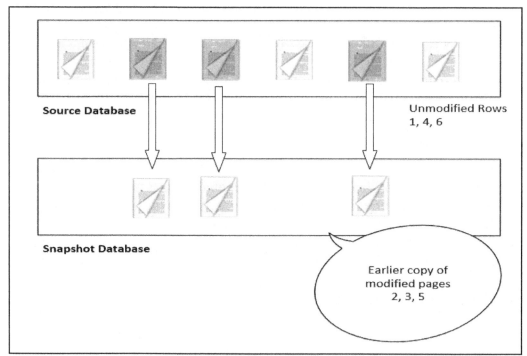

Figure 2.9 Copy-on-write mechanism of database snapshots.

As shown in Figure 2.9, database snapshots are dependent on the source database. This means we cannot drop the source database if any snapshots associated with it. We have included this concept as part of a High Availability technique in this book because if something minor goes wrong with the source database we can perform some data retrieval from the database snapshot. If the source database is down, the snapshot database is of no use. This technique is not a replacement for proper backup strategies. Additionally, the restore from a snapshot brings the source database data to when the snapshot was taken. It doesn't include the updates done after the snapshot.

Choosing the best High Availability Technique

There are multiple choices when it comes to High Availability and each technique has its own advantages and limitations. To provide an accurate answer on what choice to use, DBAs need to understand the business needs for High Availability, how fast the failover should happen, how many replicas are required and if reads can happen on the secondary. Each SQL Server High Availability technology gets an edge compared to the others in some of the feature dimensions. Likewise each SQL Server High Availability technology has shortcomings on a different dimension. Here is a quick table for reference:

Feature	Failover Clustering	Database Mirroring	Log Shipping	Transactional Replication
Storage redundancy?	✗	✓	✓	✓
No need for special hardware?	✗	✓	✓	✓
Role change automatically?	✓	✓	✗	✗
No need for additional server?	None	Witness	Monitor*	Distributor*
Reports read data from secondary?	NA	No	Readonly	Yes
Scope of availability	Instance level	Complete Database	Complete Database	Database Objects
Multiple secondary	NA	No	Yes	Yes
Client Auto Redirection after failover?	Yes	No: Need Custom Solution	No: Need Custom Solution	No: Need Custom Solution
Recovery Model?	Any	Full	Full or bulk-logged	Any

Table 2.1 Compare and contrast multiple HA/DR options with common requirements.

We now have solutions that can take all the advantages from each of the solutions without the restrictions or limitations. This would be a complete solution that allows real-time reporting and multiple secondary servers. This is exactly what *SQL Server 2012 AlwaysOn* brings to the table. Some of the notable features include the following:

- Synchronous data movement (real-time data) to the secondary server(s) (just like synchronous mirroring).

- Real-time or near to real-time reporting (just like Log Shipping).

This makes SQL Server AlwaysOn technology a strong candidate to be implemented as a High Availability and Disaster Recovery solution. With organizations investing in some hardware for secondary servers the AlwaysOn solution can provide an active secondary. This means we can use our existing investment in hardware and have a better HA solution. Later chapters will expand on each of these benefits and what advantages AlwaysOn brings to the table.

Summary

High Availability and Disaster Recovery requirements to some businesses are non-negotiable. These businesses need to keep running 24x7. With such growing needs to do a number of activities on the same database, we need to look at what existing techniques fit the bill based on the business requirements. Though all the existing techniques work in SQL Server 2012, it is a good idea to evaluate how they compare to the new method of AlwaysOn.

Here are some typical facts about High Availability:

- Database Mirroring can provide fast failover but can have only one secondary.
- SQL Clustering allows many secondary servers but has a limitation whereby the secondary is a passive server and unusable for reporting needs.
- Log Shipping allows many redundant servers for reporting but would always have latency based on the previous restore. Latency means there is a delay and the most recent data is not on all the servers.
- None of these available solutions by themselves so far can provide us *real-time* reporting from a secondary server.

Points to Ponder – Existing High Availability and Disaster Recovery Options

1. Failover Clustering is a solution that provides SQL Server instance level High Availability.

2. For a SQL Server Failover Cluster, we need a Windows Cluster created with at least one free shared SAN (Storage Area Network) to store database files.

3. In SQL Server Clustering the single point of failure is the shared storage.

4. Log Shipping uses log backups which must come from databases using the full or bulk-logged recovery models.

5. In Log Shipping terms, the source server is called the primary server and all the receiving servers are called secondary servers.

6. Log Shipping is made up of four operations, which are handled by dedicated SQL Server Agent jobs: backup job, copy job, restore job and alert job.

7. SQL Server Replication uses publish and subscribe terminology in its implementation.

8. There are three fundamental types of replication available inside SQL Server: Transaction replication, Merge replication and Snapshot replication.

9. There is a special option with transactional replication called Peer-to-Peer (P2P) where each machine would act as a publisher as well as a subscriber.

10. Database Mirroring is a software-based solution for High Availability which works at the database level.

11. In mirroring terminology, the sending database server is called a Principal server and the receiving database server is known as the Mirror server.

12. Database Snapshots are a readonly point-in-time copy of a database.

13. A restore from a snapshot brings the source database data to when the snapshot was taken. The code for this is as follows:

    ```
    RESTORE DATABASE database_name
    FROM DATABASE_SNAPSHOT = database_snapshot_name
    ```

14. Log Shipping provides database level protection.

15. Log Shipping allows us to have multiple copies of a database on different SQL instances.

16. Replication can provide flexibility to send filtered data from the publisher to the subscriber which is not possible in Log Shipping and Database Mirroring.

Review Quiz - Chapter Two

1.) Which of the following gives SQL Server resilience from instance level failure?

O a. Failover Clustering
O b. Log Shipping
O c. Transactional Replication
O d. Database Mirroring

2.) Which of the following gives SQL Server resilience from complete database level failure? Choose all that apply.

☐ a. Failover Clustering
☐ b. Log Shipping
☐ c. Transactional Replication
☐ d. Database Mirroring

3.) Which of the following gives SQL Server resilience for only specific database objects? Choose all that apply.

☐ a. Failover Clustering
☐ b. Log Shipping
☐ c. Transactional Replication
☐ d. Database Snapshot

4.) Which of the following techniques provide an automatic failover option inside SQL Server? Choose all that apply.

☐ a. Failover Clustering
☐ b. Log Shipping
☐ c. Transactional Replication
☐ d. Database Mirroring

5.) Which of the following are false? Choose all that apply.

☐ a. There can be multiple snapshots of a database.
☐ b. There can be multiple secondary databases in Log Shipping.
☐ c. There can be multiple mirror databases in Database Mirroring.
☐ d. There can be multiple copies of a database in a two node Failover Clustering.

Answer Key

1.) (b) Log Shipping, (c) Transactional Replication, and (d) Database Mirroring are all wrong. (a) is the correct answer.

2.) Option (a) Failover Clustering is a wrong answer. The options of (b) Log Shipping, (c) Transactional Replication, and (d) Database Mirroring are all correct answers. When all database objects are included inside Transactional replication, it can be considered as database resilience.

3.) Because (a) Failover Clustering and (b) Log Shipping are wrong answers, the correct answer is (c) Transactional Replication and (d) Database Snapshot. We can query from a snapshot database to bring back dropped tables if required.

4.) Option (a) Failover Clustering and (d) Database Mirroring are the correct answers. Hence the options (b) Log Shipping and (c) Transactional Replication are all wrong answers.

5.) Options (a) There can be multiple snapshots of a database and (b) There can be multiple secondary databases in Log Shipping are true statements. Hence options (c) There can be multiple mirror databases in Database Mirroring and (d) There can be multiple copies of a database in a two node Failover Clustering are false and are the correct answer.

[NOTES]

Chapter 3. What is AlwaysOn?

Keeping systems running is something we have focused on over the ages. Now that we are very good at it we start assuming things will always work that way. A typical example is how we assume our refrigerators will always be running 24x7 every single day. The refrigerators function is to make sure all the ingredients inside are kept in good condition. Over the years we have a tendency to keep upgrading our equipment to get better and newer features. In the SQL Server example, organizations expect their databases to always available and online. Businesses are getting complex and most of their decisions are based on analysis of these systems. With every release of a new SQL Server version there have been incremental features added to the Disaster Recovery and High Availability areas. SQL Server 2012 is no exception and this release brings the AlwaysOn feature.

In the past we had to choose between things like having multiple secondary's or live automatic failover (that is seamless to the clients). Database Mirroring does automatic failover but only has one redundant secondary server. In the past we had to decide which feature we needed more than the other. What if we wanted all the feature advantages of every type of a High Availability solution? Past versions of SQL Server did not have a way for this and we would've had to spend money on special software and equipment like a Windows Cluster to get closer to our goal. Even then the Windows Cluster is doomed in the case of a flood or data center level failure.

AlwaysOn is a new integrated, flexible, and cost effective HA and DR solution which can provide redundancy of data within and across data centers. AlwaysOn is a bigger umbrella which covers two feature sets:

- The AlwaysOn Failover Cluster Instance (FCI) (instance level protection)
- The AlwaysOn Availability Group (AG) (database level protection)

There have been a few enhancements made in the traditional SQL Server Failover Clustering and it has been rebranded as AlwaysOn FCI. Some of the enhancements which we will cover in detail are named:

- Flexible failover policy
- Multisite clustering across subnet
- Improved Diagnostics

READER NOTE: *This chapter provides many diagrams to demonstrate the important concepts that are needed for AlwaysOn. In this chapter there will be no* *need to have your machine configured to follow along. The tutorial steps begin in Chapter 7.*

Introduction to FCI and AG

One of the common questions asked is, why SQL Server in an Availability Group uses the Windows Failover Cluster? The short answer is to detect problems and make adjustments automatically. If we recall how the SQL Server Database Mirroring feature is implemented, to perform automatic failover we need to have a third SQL Server instance called Witness. The role of the witness was to detect the health of the system, and if needed initiate the failover. In Availability Groups, the Windows Cluster performs inter-node health detection and it also performs the failover. You could say that the Windows Failover Cluster is acting like our witness.

The Windows Failover Cluster is also used for failover coordination. One node (server) can act as a primary replica at any given point in time. The secondary replicas stay up to date (sometimes in real-time) with the changes on the primary replica. Using the Availability Group architecture we have the capability of having synchronous replicas (real-time) and asynchronous replicas (almost real-time) for our databases.

As a prerequisite of creating AlwaysOn Availability Groups using SQL Server 2012 Enterprise edition, we need to use the Windows Server Failover Cluster running on Windows Server 2008 SP2 or Windows Server 2008 R2 SP1 (along with a few hotfixes which are mentioned in Books Online).

READER NOTE: *Here is the link which has the list of hotfixes we need to install for the Windows Server 2008 cluster* http://msdn.microsoft.com/en-us/library/ff878487(v=SQL.110).aspx.

Many people think AlwaysOn is just equivalent to the AlwaysOn Availability Group. In reality it covers this and more. We can think of AlwaysOn as a superset of the SQL Server Failover Cluster instances (traditional Failover Clusters which have been around for years) and the new AlwaysOn Availability Groups (Figure 3.1).

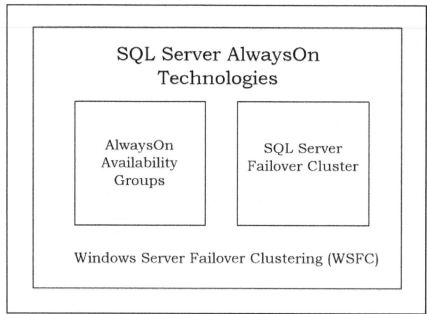

Figure 3.1 SQL Server AlwaysOn consists of two feature sets.

If someone says they are using AlwaysOn then the first thing we need to find out is which feature set they are using (AG, FCI, or both).

AlwaysOn Availability Groups

Some applications will need data from one database. There are many applications that pull for multiple databases. It is common for business logic to require multiple databases to work as a single unit because the application is dependent on multiple databases for its complete functionality. For example, let's say we have an application which stores user's information in an Admin database and real operational data is residing on an HRMS (Human Resource Marketing Services) database. As soon as a user logs in to the application their login credential would be validated against the Admin database. Once validation passes the security layer, it can then perform its tasks. This application also needs HR related tasks in the HRMS database. The login has permission to both databases on this server and the query context runs.

This login would not have permissions to any databases that are on another server. As long as both of these databases are on the same server and the login has the needed permissions the application should work.

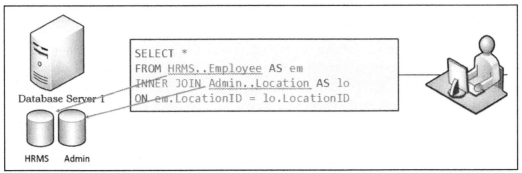

Figure 3.2 The login connection to SQL Server is accessing two databases in one query.

Using the currently available technology (up to SQL Server 2008 R2) we can do Database Mirroring for both databases to one Mirror server. We might hope that either Server 1 has the Principal Role for both databases or Server 2 has them. It could be that Server 1 has the Principal Role for the HRMS database and Server 2 has the Principal Role for the Admin database (Figure 3.3).

There is no guarantee that both databases would be in the Principal Role on the same server all the time. In certain situations the Admin database could be in the Principal Role and the HRMS database could be in the Mirror Role on Server 1 (as shown in Figure 3.3). In this scenario the application will not work. Since Database Mirroring works at the database level, there is no guarantee to change the role of two databases simultaneously.

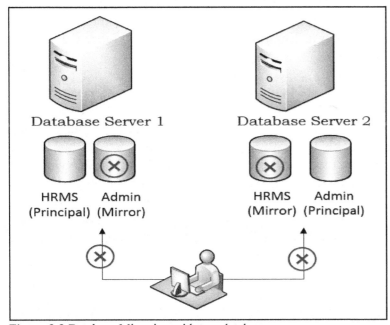

Figure 3.3 Database Mirroring with two databases.

To overcome this limitation, SQL Server AlwaysOn Availability Groups provide us the capability to group two or more databases (Admin and HRMS in our example) and perform a failover of both servers as a logical unit. Another famous example of using Availability Groups would be SharePoint which has multiple databases working together to make the application work. Think of a group of databases that an application needs as an application does a failover to a new server. We don't call them application groups; we call them Availability Groups (AG).

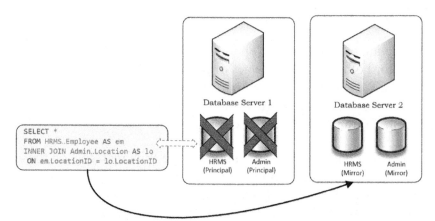

Figure 3.4 SQL Server AlwaysOn has two feature sets.

READER NOTE: *While writing this book, SharePoint 2010 supported AlwaysOn Availability Groups. Refer to whitepaper available on TechNet* http://technet.microsoft.com/en-us/library/hh913923.aspx *(Configure and manage SQL Server Availability Groups for SharePoint Server).*

AlwaysOn Availability Groups are tightly coupled with Windows Server Failover Clustering (WSFC). This means to utilize an AlwaysOn Availability Group, we must enable Windows Server Clustering. One common misunderstanding about a Windows Cluster is that people think we need a costly shared storage (quorum disk or SAN). The reality is, there are various types of models available with Windows Clustering, some use a shared disk and some do not need that. We will discuss these models in Chapter 4. In our explanations in this book for AlwaysOn Availability Groups, we would use one of the nodes models so we don't need to have a shared storage. We can also use nodes with a file share model which also does not need a special shared storage array.

AlwaysOn Failover Cluster Instance

The ideas used in the world of AlwaysOn are something we experience almost daily. It happens so seamlessly that we take it for granted. Recently my family and I were watching an amazing thriller movie at home. All of a sudden we got an unexpected power outage. Under normal circumstances, this would have been the most frustrating time because we would've missed the highlight of the movie and our minds would have wandered all over the place dreaming of every possible outcome. Even worse, we would need to watch that movie again when the electricity came back on. Luckily for us we had a UPS device at home and we were able to watch the entire movie. The UPS gave us a perception that the power never went out and it gave us the feeling of being "AlwaysOn".

SQL Server Clustering provides instance level data protection by having the database on shared storage between two (or more) nodes. This is one of the proven techniques by administrators to deploy SQL Server and provide instance level redundancy. The AlwaysOn Failover Cluster Instance (FCI) has the same core concepts as SQL clustering in SQL 2008 R2 but with a few feature enhancements.

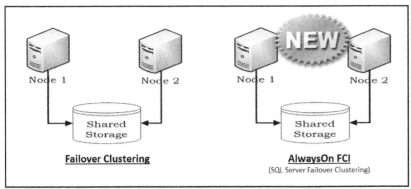

Figure 3.5 SQL 2008 Failover Clustering is now called AlwaysOn FCI in SQL 2012.

In Failover Clustering for SQL 2008 R2 and FCI in SQL 2012 each node is independent and self-sufficient with its own memory and CPU. FCI therefore also uses a "share nothing" architecture. This means two or more SQL Server nodes use no shared resources (except for the storage).

In this section we will discuss the Failover Clustering enhancements available in the SQL Server 2012 release now called FCI.

Placing tempdb on the Local Drive

Before buying a new vehicle, it is customary to do a test drive so we know if we will be comfortable with the car model, spaciousness, features, and the driving experience. There are test drive cars available for every model in every showroom for test drive purposes. In a similar way the SQL Server tempdb is like the temporary staging area where interim work is done. There is one tempdb per SQL Server instance that is being used by all the databases. Often times tempdb is the location for storing temporary content for a SQL Server instance to use (like sorting, creating indexes, version store, and worktables).

One of the major enhancements in SQL Server 2012 for tempdb is the ability for us to keep the tempdb database files on the local drive rather than on the shared storage for a clustered environment. This should be a consideration for applications which heavily use the tempdb. This can give us better overall performance and save money because SAN storage is always costlier than local disks.

READER NOTE: *Tempdb is mostly random I/O, unless the local disk is on a high end SSD, then tempdb will be slower on the local disk than the SAN Array in most cases. Really I would push to keep it on the SAN, unless you have a high end SSD for the local disk. If performance is critical for applications, then we can consider placing the tempdb files on the fastest local drive or even a solid state disk (SSD).*

The tempdb database gets recreated when the SQL Service is restarted. The SQL Service knows what folder the tempdb is stored in. On the new node, the same service is running and expecting the same location for the databases. One of the critical tasks DBAs need to ensure is that the same folder structure exists on all the nodes and the SQL Server service account should have permission to perform read and write operations on those folders.

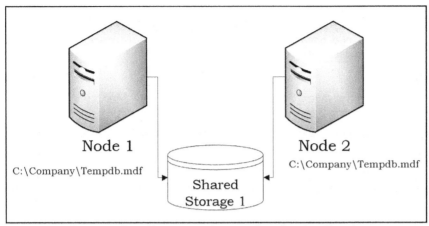

Figure 3.6 The Tempdb.mdf must use the same location for all nodes.

There are two ways to achieve putting the tempdb on the local drive. We can either specify the tempdb path to the local drive during installation or (if SQL is already installed) we can use an ALTER DATABASE statement to modify the path of the database files for the tempdb database. The ALTER DATABASE command would show the following message:

Messages
Msg 5191, Level 10, State 1 Local directory '%.*ls' is used for tempdb in a clustered server. This directory must exist on each cluster node and SQL Server service has read/write permission on it.

READER NOTE: *The topic on how to alter a database and add or change data file locations is covered in SQL Administration 2012 Joes 2 Pros Volume 1.*

Not having access to the tempdb will stop the other nodes from being able to take over during a failover. SQL Server resources will only come online in the Failover Cluster Manager once everything is set up correctly. If a node does not have access to the Tempdb.mdf file than the typical error log would contain the following message:

Messages
Clearing tempdb database. Error: 5123, Severity: 16, State: 1. CREATE FILE encountered operating system error 3(The system cannot find the path specified.) while attempting to open or create the physical file 'C:\SQLData\TempDB.mdf'.

Messages
Error: 17204, Severity: 16, State: 1. FCB::Open failed: Could not open file C:\SQLData\TempDB.mdf for file number 1. OS error: 3(The system cannot find the path specified.).

Messages
Error: 5120, Severity: 16, State: 101. Unable to open the physical file "C:\SQLData\TempDB.mdf". operating system error 3: "3(The system cannot find the path specified.)".

Messages
Error: 1802, Severity: 16, State: 4. CREATE DATABASE failed. Some file names listed could not be created. Check related errors. Could not create TempDB. You may not have enough disk space available. Free additional disk space by deleting other files on the tempdb drive and then restart SQL Server. Check for additional errors in the event log that may indicate why the tempdb files could not be initialized.

Multi-site Clustering

Since Windows Server 2008, we can have nodes in the same cluster reside in different network subnets and communicate across network routers rather than to directly attached cables. This is known by many names. The following four terms mean the same thing:

- Stretch cluster(ing)
- Multi-site cluster(ing)
- Multi-subnet cluster(ing)
- Geo cluster(ing)

Since nodes are often located in two different data centers at geographically dispersed locations, there is no shared storage between the nodes in a multi-site cluster. Clustering across two different data centers provides a higher level of availability and protection at the storage level as we have more than a single copy of the data.

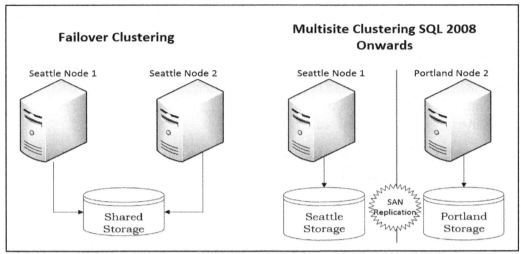

Figure 3.7 Two node in two different location is possible since SQL 2008.

For SAN replication technology implemented in such clusters, the main activity is to keep data replicated between the sites. Typically, if we have nodes on two different sites, we would have two different network infrastructures and the nodes would be in different subnets. In such cases, if we are on a SQL Server version before 2012, we need to use third party VLAN (Virtual LAN) technology so that one IP address travels between two sites. This is called wide-IP. Companies hesitate with this solution because of the need to buy a third party solution to deploy the VLAN. Using VLAN technology means the same IP address would failover to the remote site in case of a local site disaster. Network administration might consider this as an overhead to maintenance and an extra piece of the networking component that needs to be secure.

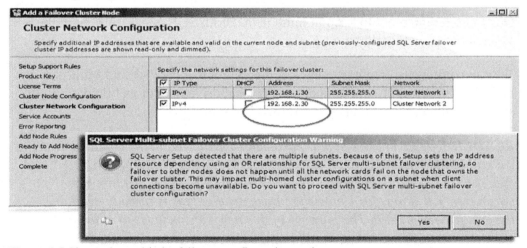

Figure 3.8 Shows the multi-site failover configuration option.

With SQL Server 2012 we do not need to use stretch VLAN technology but SAN replication is still needed for multi-site clustering. The OS version for this can be from Windows Server 2008 R2 and above. In this deployment, we can have a SQL virtual network name having an "OR" dependency on two different IP addresses. One address would be representing each subnet. With the "OR" dependency, if IP1 or IP2 is online we just use the network name. This is one of the Enterprise Editions only features.

FCI: Multisite Clustering in SQL Server 2012

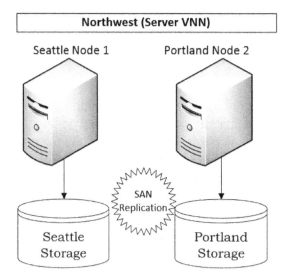

Figure 3.9 A VNN is used with two underlying IP addresses (one for each site).

One more requirement to keep in mind is that both SQL nodes must be in the same active directory domain.

We can combine two enhancements: tempdb on the local disk and Multi-site Failover Clustering. Using tempdb on the local drive in conjunction with multi-site clustering can save money on storage and replication costs.

READER NOTE: *There is a new parameter introduced in the connection string called MultiSubnetFailover. If our application is using .Net framework 3.5 SP1 then we need to apply the patch specified in KB 2654347 to get this new parameter. KB stands for Knowledge Base article. This is already available with the .Net framework 4.0. The purpose of this new parameter is to allow faster client connection by sending initial requests in parallel to all IP addresses registered in DNS for the Virtual Server Name. We will again revisit this parameter in Chapter 8 – "Connection Strings related to AlwaysOn" section.*

Failover Routine Checks

As we grow up, we have a regular routine to do medical checks once a year to make sure our vitals are fine. On the same lines, similar checks are being done in the SQL Server Cluster as health checks.

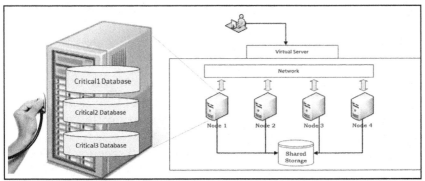

Figure 3.10 The primary node will need frequent automatic health checks.

Going back in time, if we ever put a profiler trace on a SQL Server 2008 R2 (or earlier) clustered instance we can see the Select @@SERVERNAME query running at regular intervals. Have you ever wondered who would be running such a weird query? Well, it is run by a SQL resource DLL as a part of its health check routine.

Types of Health Checks

The movie Weekend at Bernie's had a man named Bernie who died just before an important event. The other characters needed him to look alive for his meeting so they put sunglasses on his eyes and dressed him up in a suit and put him at the table. He did not move but he looked like he was alive. Naturally if any doctor checked his pulse or temperature they would know he was not alive. A quick look at Bernie made us think he was alive but another check showed he was not really available. SQL also has different ways to check if a server is alive.

In SQL Server 2008 R2 (and earlier) there were two checks to determine the health of SQL Server. These checks were called LooksAlive and IsAlive. A quick introduction on what they mean is listed here:

- LooksAlive is a light-weight check (tip to remember – both "LooksAlive" and "light-weight" start with the letter "L"). LooksAlive checks if the SQL Service is running in the active node (the node which owns the resource).

- The IsAlive check is an intensive check (hint, both IsAlive and "intensive" start with the letter "I"). IsAlive makes a connection to SQL Server and executes a Select @@SERVERNAME query and waits for the results.

Flexible Failover Policy

Failover is a process where one (or more) clustered resource(s) goes offline. This happens because of a failure of one or more predefined sets of health checks. After the failover is detected the cluster comes back online to a different node.

Node1 might try the LooksAlive and IsAlive checks every 60 seconds but we might want that to be every 30 seconds. In versions prior to SQL Server 2012, the end user had no control over the failover conditions. In SQL Server 2012, the health detection logic has been changed which gives better flexibility to the end user to decide the failover condition levels. This is where it gets the name *flexible failover policy*. More about this type of failover diagnostic will be explained in Chapters 9, 10 and 11 with various monitoring and troubleshooting techniques.

If a response is received from the IsAlive check then the ping is successful and no failover would be performed. This is a kind of polling mechanism because the connection is made at regular intervals and based on the health of the query processor a decision is made. If there is an issue with connectivity (due to the network) or the query did not run (may be due to worker thread exhaustion) then a failover is initiated. The default time interval for the LooksAlive check and the IsAlive check is 5 seconds and 60 seconds respectively. There are no checks performed on the individual databases health. There is no guarantee that all user databases are available or they are performing within acceptable performance and response time requirements. The Flexible Failover Policy does not address the heath checks for the individual databases.

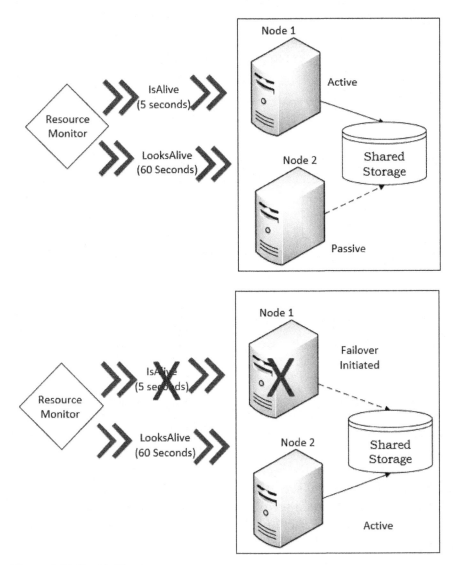

Figure 3.11 Health Checks

How does the Cluster come up?

Since we are discussing clustering, one important thing to understand is that clustering is not a load balancing solution. We have seen DBAs use the term "Active/Active clustering" which gives an impression that SQL Server can take connections and be operational on both the nodes. This is not possible in a Failover Cluster. At any given point of time, only one node for a SQL instance can be functional and accessible.

During failover, the Windows Cluster service starts the SQL Server service for that instance on the new node. Since this is a restart of the SQL Server service, we have to perform the recovery process to start the databases to maintain consistency.

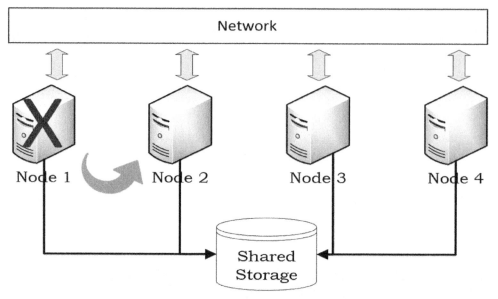

Figure 3.12 Upon detecting a failure we start the failover process to a new node.

As soon as the service is started, the master database is brought online. Once the master database is online the cluster configuration knows that this node is online. This means the SQL Server resource is considered to be up. In the Failover Cluster Manager interface we will see its status is online. After this step, each user database will go through the normal recovery process. During recovery, any committed transactions in the transaction log are rolled forward, and any uncommitted transactions are rolled back.

Broader Storage Support

As an enhancement to meet the changes happening in the IT industry, SQL Server 2012 has made enhancements to its storage options as well. Prior versions of SQL Server supported two kinds of shared storages; fiber channel and iSCSI target. With rapid improvements in network components, the network bandwidth has increased. Keeping this in mind, SQL Server 2012 supports database file(s) on a common connected file system called SMB (Server Message Block). The SMB protocol deals with access to a file share so that clients may make requests to a file server. There are a few advantages of having files on the SMB as seen in the following list:

- Centralized storage for many instances of SQL Server 2012.

- Allows us to use Fileservers on Windows Server 2008 and above.

- Drive letter limitation (A to Z) would not be applicable while installing SQL Server Failover Cluster instances. This means that we can go beyond 26+ instances in a single Windows Server Failover Cluster.

- SQL Server 2012 added support for System DB on SMB file shares.

- SQL Server 2012 added support for SQL Server clusters using SMB file shares.

READER NOTE: *When using an SMB file share, please make sure to apply the windows patch mentioned in KB 2536493. Without this hotfix, we would notice significantly slow performance for the kind of I/O operation done by SQL Server.*

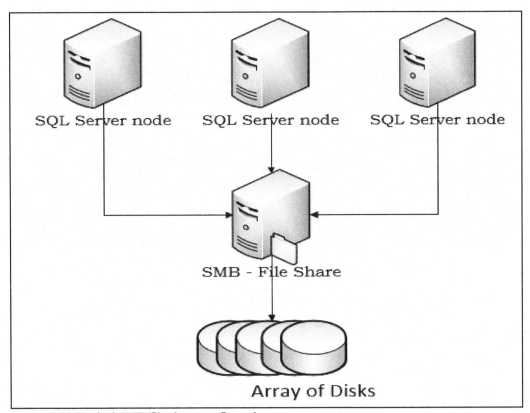

Figure 3.13 Typical SMB file share configuration.

Introduction to PowerShell

Windows PowerShell is a powerful interactive shell and scripting language provided by Microsoft. If we look at the PowerShell prompt for the first time, it looks like a command prompt (like the cmd). Watching the Windows PowerShell in action proves that it really has much more power than the cmd. PowerShell can be launched by these steps:

Start > **Run** > **PowerShell.exe**.

SQL PowerShell is a snap-in provided to Windows PowerShell since SQL Server 2008. It can be launched by typing **SQLPS** from the PowerShell prompt or the following steps

Start > **Run** > **SQLPS**

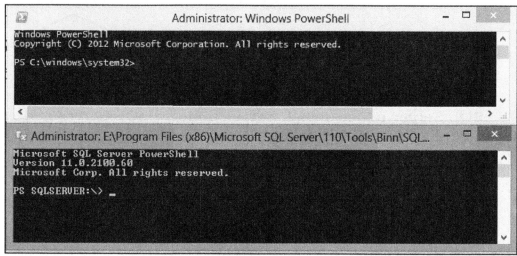

Figure 3.14 Windows PowerShell and SQL PowerShell prompts.

Another great way of launching SQL PowerShell is to use SQL Server Management Studio. We can right-click on any node in the Object Explorer and choose **Start PowerShell**. The good part by launching this way is that the context is automatically set to the place where we did the right-click.

Summary

In this chapter we took a quick tour of understanding how AlwaysOn brings two flavors of implementation, the FCI and the Availability Groups. We also saw the enhancements made to the SQL Failover Cluster implementation like the local drive for tempdb, Multi-site Clustering, Flexible Failover Policy and extended Storage support with SMB.

Points to Ponder – What is Always On?

1. AlwaysOn is a bigger umbrella which covers two feature sets:

   - AlwaysOn Failover Cluster Instance (FCI) (instance level protection)
   - AlwaysOn Availability Group (AG) (database level protection)

2. AlwaysOn is a superset of SQL Server Failover Cluster instances and AlwaysOn Availability Groups.

3. SQL Server Failover Clustering has been rebranded as AlwaysOn FCI. Some of the features enhanced are as follows:

   - Flexible failover policy
   - Multi-site clustering across subnet
   - Improved diagnostics

4. SQL Server AlwaysOn Availability Groups provide us the capability to group databases and perform failovers as a logical unit.

5. AlwaysOn Availability Groups is tightly coupled with Windows Server Failover Clustering (WSFC).

6. SQL Server 2012 allows us to keep the tempdb database files on a local drive rather than on shared storage for a clustered environment.

7. For multi-site clustering in SQL Server 2012 onwards we do not need to use stretch VLAN technology but SAN replication is still needed.

8. In SQL Server 2012, the health detection logic has been changed which gives better flexibility to the DBA to decide the failover condition levels, therefore it is called Flexible Failover Policy.

9. Whenever there is a failover of a SQL instance, it stops and starts the needed SQL Service. This means existing connections would be broken on the stopped SQL Server service and any uncommitted transactions on the started SQL Server service would be rolled back.

10. SQL Server 2012 supports database files on SMB file share storage.

Review Quiz - Chapter Three

1.) Which of the HA / DR solutions provides database level protection?

   O a. AlwaysOn Failover Cluster Instance
   O b. AlwaysOn Availability Group

2.) Which of the following use Windows Server Failover Clustering? Choose all that apply.

   □ a. AlwaysOn Failover Cluster Instance
   □ b. AlwaysOn Availability Group
   □ c. Database Mirroring
   □ d. Log Shipping

3.) SMB Support for SQL Server is applicable from which version of Windows Server? Choose the lowest version supported.

   O a. Windows Server 2003 SP2
   O b. Windows Server 2008
   O c. Windows Server 2008 R2
   O d. Windows Server 2012

4.) Which was the first version of SQL to introduce SQL PowerShell?

   O a. SQL Server 2005
   O b. SQL Server 2008
   O c. SQL Server 2008 R2
   O d. SQL Server 2012

Answer Key

1.) AlwaysOn Failover Cluster Instance is wrong answer as it is instance level protection. Hence, (b) AlwaysOn Availability Group is the correct answer.

2.) Database Mirroring and Log Shipping are wrong. (a) AlwaysOn Failover Cluster Instance and (b) AlwaysOn Availability Group are the correct answers.

3.) The SQL Server allows us to use Fileservers on Windows Server 2008 and above. The correct answer is (b) Windows Server 2008. Options (a), (c) and (d) are wrong.

4.)   SQL Server PowerShell was introduced with SQL Server 2008. So the correct answer is (b) SQL Server 2008 and all other options are wrong.

[NOTES]

Chapter 4. Understanding Quorum Models

In a democratic country the most important and touted right is the right to vote for our leaders who will run our government. It is surprising how this concept differs from country to country. The most commonly accepted age for voting is 18 years. A majority of countries accept this age minimum. Interestingly enough there are countries like Ecuador, Cuba, and Austria who have the age minimum at 16. On the other extreme are countries like Singapore, Malaysia, Fiji, Cameroon, and a few others who have the minimum age for voting at 21. Adding to the confusion there are countries with different minimum ages like Indonesia is 17, South Korea is 19 and Japan is 20 years. A simple concept of voting and the minimum age for voting is not the same all over the world. They have different voting models.

Governments are elected based on the number of candidates won in an election and each candidate wins based on the number of votes they got in comparison to their opponents. The mantra remains simple, higher is better and to get the majority, one needs to have more than 50% of the votes get elected. We can take this example to the AlwaysOn world. There is a concept called a quorum which is like a majority vote requirement in an election. The quorum helps us decide which server will be the primary.

What if none of the nodes can reach the current primary? It could be down or offline. In that case which server should take over the primary role? In order to decide on the next primary we need to have a voting mechanism to establish the fact that the current primary is not reachable by a majority of voters before another secondary can automatically take over that primary role.

In this chapter we will discuss the basics of various quorum models. We will be using this concept when configuring an AlwaysOn Availability Group configuration later.

> **READER NOTE:** *This chapter provides many diagrams to demonstrate the important concepts that are needed for AlwaysOn. In this chapter there will be no need to have your machine configured to follow along. The tutorial steps begin in Chapter 7. You will see some screen shots or code steps just to give you a visual awareness of the tutorial steps that will begin in Chapter 7.*

Quorums

As per the dictionary, a quorum is defined as "the number (as a majority) of officers or members of a body that when duly assembled is legally competent to transact business". In other words, anything over half is a majority and considered a quorum.

Split-Brain Cluster Concepts

Someone may ask why we need votes in Windows Clustering? To make this concept clear, we will look at the concept of a *split-brain* in a cluster. Let's assume that there are two cluster nodes. Each node is in a different data center a few miles apart. Due to network failure between the data centers, these two nodes are not able to talk to each other. Each node might think that the other one is not available and it should take over the responsibility and become the primary to serve all the requests.

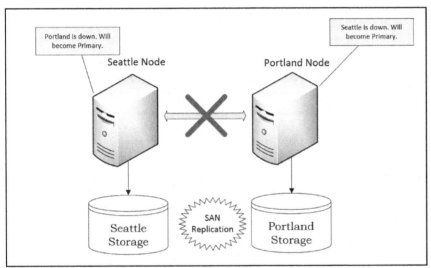

Table 4.1 Two nodes acting as the primary is a problem known as a split-brain cluster.

In this situation both nodes have become the primary and are serving the client requests. This has caused a cluster to split into two parts. In this situation, both the servers are operating independently and are not visible to each other. This can cause a data loss scenario that the business cannot accept. This is not a desirable situation of a HA solution and must be avoided.

Quorum Models

To avoid split-brain problems in Windows Clustering, a voting mechanism was built in. The vote is taken to elect the owner of the resource by a majority vote. Along the same lines, in parliament if there are too few members present (half or less) then the parliament does not have a quorum. The formula for required minimum number of votes is (nodes/2) + 1. If there are fewer votes then we cannot hold an election.

In the case of two nodes in a cluster, a tie breaker vote should be cast by a witness or arbitrator. This is how split-brain is avoided in a Windows Cluster. It would be important to note that if a quorum is not maintained, the cluster service would be stopped.

There are four quorum models available in Windows Server 2008 onwards and they are based on the number of cluster voting elements.

Node Majority

In this model, each node gets a vote. It is not mandatory for each node to have a vote and this will be discussed later in the chapter under "How to Adjust Quorum votes". More than 50% of the nodes must be available to form a healthy quorum. This quorum model is recommended if we have an odd number of nodes in the Windows Cluster.

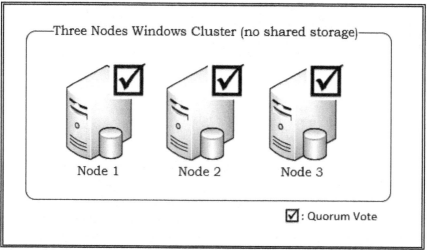

Figure 4.1 Shows quorum with Node Majority.

Node and Disk Majority

In this model, each node and shared disk gets a vote. This quorum model needs a shared storage between the nodes. This allows us to lose up to half the nodes, provided the witness disk is available. This is best suited for a cluster with an even number of nodes. This model was introduced in Windows Server 2008. For a cluster to function we need two out of three votes in Figure 4.2.

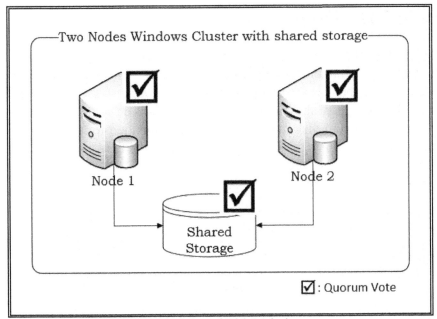

Figure 4.2 Shows quorum with node and Disk Majority.

Node and File Share Majority

This model is the same as "Node and Disk Majority" but the shared disk is replaced by the File Share Witness. Since the Shared Disk Witness is not required, we can use this quorum without any SAN requirements. This is generally recommended for multi-site clusters, no-shared-storage clusters or even nodes clusters.

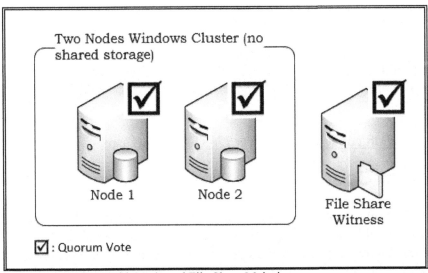

Figure 4.3 Quorum with Node and File Share Majority.

No Majority: Disk Only

As the name suggests, "Disk Only" is enough to form a quorum and the number of available nodes doesn't matter. In this quorum model, the cluster will continue to run if at least one node has access to the shared storage because the quorum's only vote is from the storage as shown in Figure 4.44. This is a traditional Windows Server 2003 quorum disk model and not recommended for a Windows 2008 cluster because the disk is a single point of failure. If the disk goes bad, the whole cluster would not be functional.

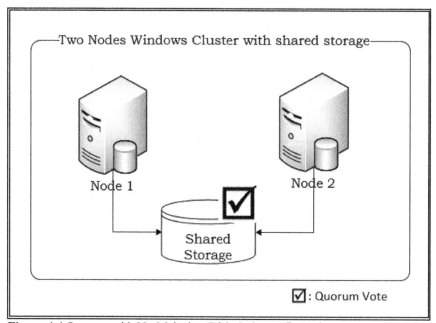

Figure 4.4 Quorum with No Majority: Disk Only configuration.

In those quorum models where there is no shared disk, the quorum related information is stored on each node. For a detailed explanation of each model and the recommended configuration, we would advise more reading with the following article:

http://technet.microsoft.com/en-us/library/cc770830(WS.10).aspx

View Quorum Configuration

Just like in our election example, we need to know how we can vote. Where can we change the electoral location information in case of a location change? Likewise, the next logical question is in understanding the health of our quorum and how to find out the current quorum configuration. How can we modify the quorum? There are various ways available to view and change the quorum model. These will be detailed in the next few pages.

What does a professional photographer do as they prepare for a shoot? They seem to want everything perfect; like the position, lighting and the angle. Well, this is not quite true for wild life photography because their subjects are not humans who can be asked to change their position for a better shot. In the Windows Cluster world, we are allowed to look at a quorum model from various points of view. For UI lovers, the Failover Cluster Manager exists. For scripting/command-line lovers Cluster.exe and PowerShell are the options. Let's have a look at all of these options.

To look at the quorum model, we can launch the Failover Cluster Manager with the following steps:

Start > All Programs > Administrative Tools > Failover Cluster Manager.

Alternatively, we can also use this shortcut to the utility:

Start > Run > Cluadmin.msc.

From Figure 4.5 we can see Quorum Configuration is set to Node Majority.

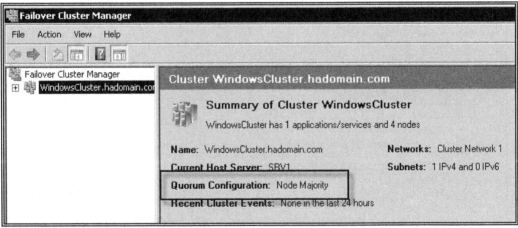

Figure 4.5 View Quorum Configuration in Failover Cluster Manager.

We can also use the cluster.exe command with the quorum switch line to view the information as shown in the following example:

C:\Windows\system32>**cluster /quorum**

Witness Resource Name	Path	Type
(Node Majority)		Majority

With the cluster.exe command the cluster name can also be provided. For the PowerShell geek, the following code is the equivalent way to get this information:

PS C:\Windows\system32> **import-module FailoverClusters**
PS C:\Windows\system32> **Get-ClusterQuorum**

Cluster	QuorumResource	QuorumType
WindowsCluster		Node Majority

Modifying Quorum Configuration

Driving a hybrid car these days is a common environmentally friendly step. The use of a fuel based engine coupled by an electric motor adds to the efficiency of the drive. The manufacturers have mastered this in many ways and to the end user the switch between the two modes is almost non-existent. In a similar way, there is a need to switch between the various quorum models from time-to-time in any cluster-enabled environments.

If we are using the Failover Cluster Manager we can connect to the Windows Cluster and choose the action called **Configure Cluster Quorum Setting** as shown in Figure 4.6.

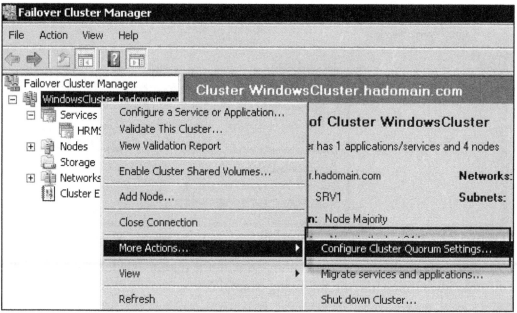

Figure 4.6 Modifying Quorum configuration.

Once we choose this option, we see a screen where the required quorum configuration can be selected as in Figure 4.7.

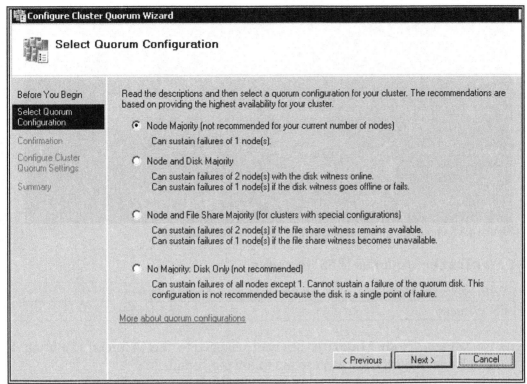

Figure 4.7 Configure Cluster Quorum Wizard.

The same thing can be done by cluster.exe and PowerShell as well. Below are the parameters for use with the cluster.exe command-line utility:

```
/QUORUM /NODE[MAJORITY]
/QUORUM:witness-resource-name
/QUORUM:disk-witness-resource-name [/PATH:path]
/QUORUM:disk-resource-name [/PATH:path] /DISK[ONLY]
```

Here is the sample command to add the File Share Witness resource and modify the quorum configuration to use the File Share Witness along with the nodes (i.e. Node and File share majority):

```
C:\Windows\system32>cluster /quorum
```

Witness Resource Name	Path	Type
(Node Majority)		Majority

```
C:\>cluster /cluster:WindowsCluster.hadomain.com res "FS
Witness" /create /group:"Cluster Group" /type:"File Shar
Witness" /priv SharePath=\\DC\FileShareWitness
```

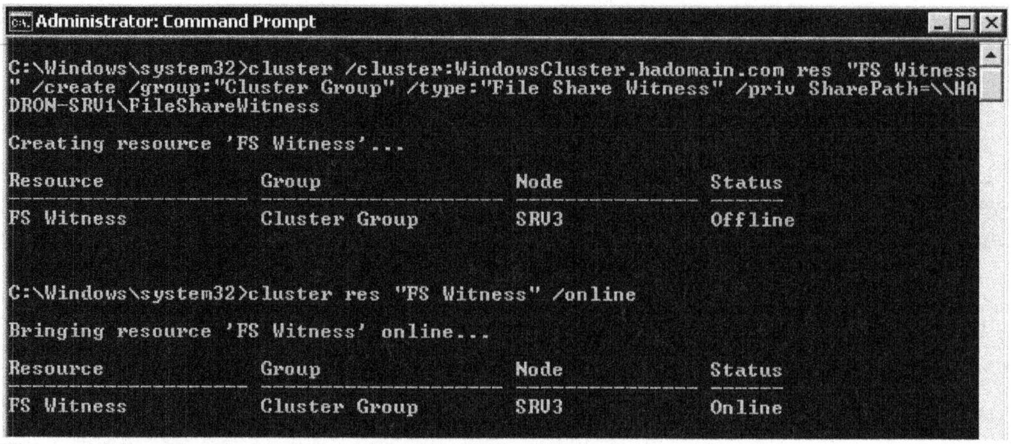

Figure 4.8 Sample command to add the File Share Witness resource.

C:\>`cluster /quorum:"FS Witness"`

Witness Resource Name	Path	Type
FS Witness		Majority

As we can see, "**Node Majority**" has been changed to "**FS Witness**". To bring it back to Node Majority, we can use the following command:

C:\>`cluster /quorum /Node`

Witness Resource Name	Path	Type
(Node Majority)		Majority

Let's also do this with a PowerShell command-line. For this example we will convert the quorum configuration to from **Node Majority** to **Node and File Share Majority**, then bring it back to again **Node Majority**.

PS C:\> `Get-ClusterQuorum`

Cluster	QuorumResource	QuorumType
WindowsCluster		Node Majority

PS C:\> `Set-ClusterQuorum -NodeAndFileShareMajority` `\\DC\FileShareWitness`

Cluster	QuorumResource	QuorumType
WindowsCluster	File Share Witness	NodeAndFileShareMajority

PS C:\> `Get-ClusterQuorum`

Cluster	QuorumResource	QuorumType
WindowsCluster	File Share Witness	NodeAndFileShareMajority

```
PS C:\> Set-ClusterQuorum -Node Majority
```

Cluster	QuorumResource	QuorumType
WindowsCluster		Node Majority

Notice with PowerShell it involves fewer steps than the cluster.exe command shown before.

How to Adjust Node Votes

While using multi-site clustering, it is recommended that a remote site (meant for Disaster Recovery) should not have any votes. The reason behind this is simple – if there is a network outage for a small time, the remote site nodes would not be able to participate in a quorum (even if they are healthy). To achieve such a requirement, we might need to adjust the vote of a cluster node.

READER NOTE: In some cases your cluster might not allow you to turn off the voting for a note. After we apply the KB 2494036 hotfix we would be able to configure a cluster node that does not have quorum votes. This hotfix adds a new property called NodeWeight for each node, which can be adjusted by PowerShell or Cluster.exe.

Let's look at a few examples of adjusting the node votes. The following PowerShell snippet returns the vote setting for each node in the cluster where our Cluster Name is WindowsCluster:

```
Import-Module FailoverClusters
$nodes = Get-ClusterNode -Cluster WindowsCluster
$nodes | Format-Table -property NodeName, State, NodeWeight
```

Using PowerShell in the following example we are setting NodeWeight to 0 for **SRV2**:

```
Import-Module FailoverClusters
$node = "SRV2"
(Get-ClusterNode $node).NodeWeight = 0
```

Another command-line way is using cluster.exe. Here is the example of setting NodeWeight to 0 (zero) for **SRV2** in a Windows Cluster named **WindowsCluster**:

Cluster.exe **WindowsCluster** node **SRV2** /prop NodeWeight=0

It would be important to note that the File Share Witness (if available to vote in given quorum model) would always have a vote and can't be adjusted.

In Windows Server 2012, NodeWeight can be viewed and adjusted by the UI. To change the quorum witness configuration, we can right-click the name of the cluster in the far left pane, choose **More Actions**, and select **Configure Cluster Quorum Settings**.

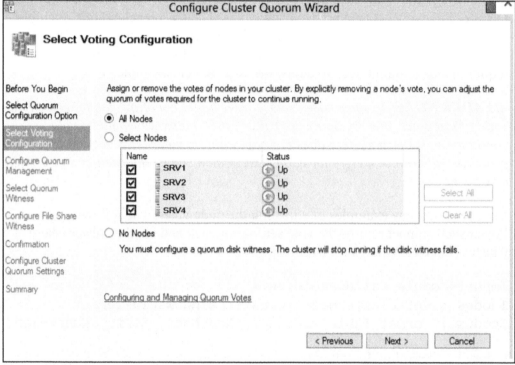

Figure 4.9 Cluster Quorum wizard.

Summary

Quorums are an important concept and are critical configuration options when it comes to AlwaysOn deployments. Understanding the distinctions and properly giving weights for quorum nodes will help us with automatic failures.

Points to Ponder – Understanding Quorum Models

1. There are 4 Quorum Models available:
    *   Node Majority
    *   Node and Disk Majority
    *   Node and File Share Majority
    *   No Majority: Disk Only

2. Under Node Majority each nodes gets a vote. More than 50% of the nodes must be available to form a quorum.

3. The Node Majority quorum model is recommended if we have an odd number of nodes in the Windows Cluster.

4. In a Node and Disk Majority model, each node and shared disk gets a vote. This quorum model needs a shared storage between the nodes.

5. The Node and Disk Majority model was introduced in Windows Server 2008.

6. The Node and File Share Majority is the same as the Node and Disk Majority but the shared disk is replaced by the File Share Witness. Since the Shared Disk Witness is not required, we can use this quorum without SAN requirements.

7. In a No Majority: Disk Only model the disk is enough to form a quorum and the number of available nodes does not matter.

8. In the No Majority: Disk Only model the disk is a single point of failure. If disk goes bad, whole cluster would not be functional.

9. The Cluster service on all the nodes would stop by itself if a quorum is not available in any of the quorum models.

10. Starting in Windows 2012 the NodeWeight can be set by the UI. Traditionally, Cluster.exe or PowerShell was used to adjust the NodeWeight.

Review Quiz - Chapter Four

1.) On Windows Server 2012, where is the UI to change the quorum weight?

O a. Add-Remove Programs
O b. Cluster UI
O c. SQL Server Management Studio

2.) Which model has a single point of failure?

O a. Node Majority
O b. Node and Disk Majority
O c. Node and File Share Majority
O d. No Majority: Disk Only

3.) Which of the following is the traditional Windows Server 2003 quorum model? Choose all that apply.

□ a. Node Majority
□ b. Node and Disk Majority
□ c. Node and File Share Majority
□ d. No Majority: Disk Only

4.) Which of the following got introduced with Windows Server 2008? Choose all that apply.

□ a. Node Majority
□ b. Node and Disk Majority
□ c. Node and File Share Majority
□ d. No Majority: Disk Only

Answer Key

1.) Options (a) Add-Remove Programs and (c) SQL Server Management Studio are wrong answers. On Windows Server 2012 we can change the NodeWeight using the UI in the Cluster Manager, so (b) Cluster UI is the correct answer.

2.) Answers (a) Node Majority, (b) Node and Disk Majority and (c) Node and File Share Majority are wrong. In (d) "No Majority: Disk Only" the single point of failure would be the disk making (d) is the correct answer.

3.)   Option (d) "No Majority: Disk Only" is the quorum model used in traditional Windows Server 2003 which makes it the correct answer. Options (a) Node Majority,(b) Node and Disk Majority and (c) Node and File Share Majority are all wrong.

4.)   Windows Server 2008 introduced the (b) "Node and Disk Majority" quorum model. Options (a) Node Majority, (c) Node and File Share Majority and (d) No Majority: Disk Only are wrong answers.

[NOTES]

Chapter 5. AlwaysOn Availability Groups

In our college days we have our own group of people to hang around with. This is a group of people who love to spend most of their time together; at every place, every party, and every event. These concepts of being together in groups have obviously transcended into the software world too. For example, Facebook, G+ or LinkedIn all have a concept of groups or grouping our friends. This is a great advantage because we can target our communications to just this small focused group when we want. These groups allow easy access to the selected group via the web, on a mobile phone or from our tablet devices.

READER NOTE: This chapter provides many diagrams to demonstrate the important concepts that are needed for AlwaysOn. In this chapter there will be no need to have your machine configured to follow along. The tutorial steps begin in Chapter 7. You will see some screen shots or code steps just to give you a visual awareness of the tutorial steps that will begin in Chapter 7.

Application Failover

In the same context, in the SQL Server world to understand AlwaysOn Availability Groups we will consider a typical example. Consider two applications, an Employee timesheet application and a Finance application. In reality both of these applications are using two different databases and are developed by two different teams. During the month end cycle it might be a requirement that in order to process an employee's salary we will need to query the Employee Timesheet database. Such cross-dependent databases do exist in many businesses. Now consider a situation where one of the databases had a failover to the secondary server.

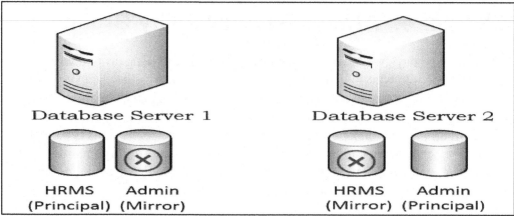

Figure 5.1 Server 1 has the principal role for the HRMS database and Server 2 has the principal role of the Admin database.

In this scenario, when the other dependent database is not available, our application will most likely break. Therefore the concept of databases being together is critical in a business sense for the Employee Timesheet database and the Finance database. This is exactly what AlwaysOn Availability Groups do. To learn the finer details of AlwaysOn Availability Groups we must get to know some of the key technical terms and their meanings.

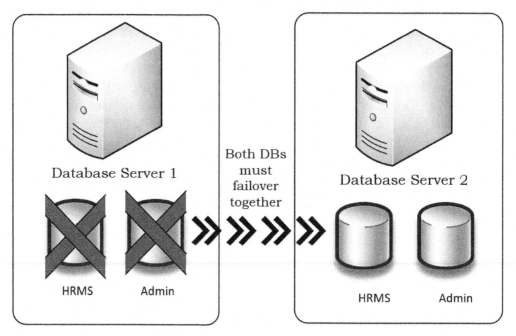

Figure 5.2 We need both databases in this group to be primary on the same server. AlwaysOn Availability Groups can do this.

Availability Group (AG)

As per the dictionary, the term "Group" is a set of objects. We use groups in various places like the choir group, the rugby group, or the bikers group. If we ask teens over the years about a group, the answers will vary from the Fantastic Four, to the Spice Girls or even the Beatles. The list can go on and on. There is something about a group that causes us to remember them for a long time.

In the SQL Server AlwaysOn world, an AlwaysOn Availability Group is a set of databases. In other words, an AlwaysOn Availability Group is a container of one or more highly available user databases that would be able to failover together as a unit. In the Windows Cluster configuration an Availability Group is a new cluster resource available in the Failover Cluster Manager interface once we configure an AlwaysOn Availability Group.

In Figure 5.3 we have opened the Failover Cluster Manager (**Start>Run>Cluadmin.msc**) and opened the Properties window of an Availability Group that was already created named HRMS. This resource was formed when someone created an Availability Group and gave it the name of HRMS in SQL Server 2012. If we notice the resource type, it is a SQL Server Availability Group.

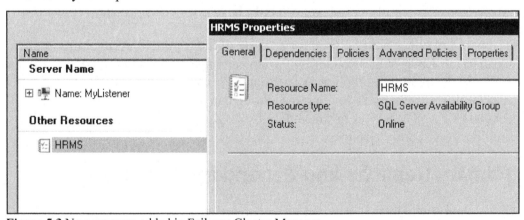

Figure 5.3 New resource added in Failover Cluster Manager.

*   **READER NOTE:** *To start the Failover Cluster Manager on the server we can do the following:* **Start** > **All Programs** > **Administrative Tools** > **Failover Cluster Manager.**

We will be covering the complete steps of creating an Availability Group in Chapter 7.

In SQL Server 2012 AlwaysOn, Availability Groups can be hosted by only one of the nodes in a Windows Cluster but it has the capability to failover to other nodes either automatically or manually based on the configuration settings. Each AlwaysOn Availability Group could be optionally associated with a virtual network name resource and an IP address resource which are used to connect from applications.

Availability Replica

When someone asks you to list all of your employers they know you probably only have one current employer. The other employers are companies you have worked for in the past. If you did leave your active employer and go back to one of your other companies to work then that new company would be your active employer.

It is interesting and realistic to assume that at any point-in-time we can be working with only one company as a full-time employee. We can have a number of other companies still listed under our name but we might not be working with them anymore. This is the same in the case of Facebook or G+ profiles. These sites allow only one primary employer. This example appropriately represents what an Availability replica is inside an AlwaysOn Availability Group. In an AlwaysOn Availability Group we can only have one active primary replica.

The word "replica" is often used for a "copy of the original". Availability replica means each AlwaysOn Availability Group can have one or more readonly replicas and only one read/write replica. A user database can only participate in one Availability Group. Each Availability Group can host only one copy of a user database on a SQL Server instance. Finally, SQL Server instances can host multiple Availability Groups.

Primary Replicas and Secondary Replicas

The instance which hosts the read/write copy of the database is known as the primary replica. Those instances which are hosting readonly copies are secondary replicas. SQL Server 2012 allows a total of up to four secondary replicas.

Synchronous and Asynchronous Configurations

Let's look at an example of how we ship gifts to our loved ones. We carefully pack the parcel and give it to FedEx or UPS. Our transaction ends there (theoretically) since we don't really need to accompany the package to the desired destination. This activity happens in the background and we know it will reach the destination in time. This can be considered an asynchronous transaction.

On the other hand, this is not the interaction we have when communicating with people over an instant messenger (IM) program like Skype, MSN messenger, or G-Talk. In a real-time chat we wait for the person to say something and they look for use to say something back. The conversation is almost real-time with an immediate reaction from other side. This can be considered a synchronous transaction.

Synchronous data movement guarantees that if a commit confirmation has been received by the client, the log record has been hardened to the primary replica as well as the secondary replica. Logically, we can think of it as a two-phase commit. This means the secondary has 100% of the data that the primary has. If the secondary needed to take over, it has all the needed data. This gives us the capability of zero data loss and comes with little overhead of increased transaction latency. This also gives the option of an automatic failover to the secondary replica because the data is already present. On the other hand, asynchronous data movement doesn't guarantee zero-data loss because log records for a transaction might arrive a bit later.

Remember we can have one primary replica and four secondary replicas. Out of the four secondary replicas, we can have two set up in a synchronous configuration. Either of these synchronous secondary replicas can take over the primary role with no data loss. Only one of these synchronous replicas can be designated as the automatic failover partner.

If we have worked with Database Mirroring then we can easily understand the advantage of the AlwaysOn Availability Group. In Database Mirroring, we were forced to choose either synchronous (high safety mode) or asynchronous (high performance mode). In AlwaysOn Availability Groups, we have the option to choose a maximum of two synchronous secondary replicas and the rest would need to be asynchronous replicas.

SQL Server 2012 allows for a total of four secondary replicas. The synchronous secondary replica is generally used for High Availability scenarios where we can take advantage of automatic failover. The asynchronous replicas are used for Disaster Recovery scenarios where there secondary is located at geographically dispersed location.

Primary and Secondary Interactions

If we have set a synchronous secondary replica and there is no connection between the primary replica and the secondary replica (i.e. they are in a disconnected state), what would happen to the transactions? Will they continue to commit on the primary replica? Yes, they will. Since they are in a disconnected state, the primary replica would no longer wait for confirmation from the secondary replica. Such a state is technically called an exposed state. In this situation, only a manual failover can be performed, with possible data loss.

It is usually assumed that the primary replica contacts the secondary replica for each commit transaction and it hardens the log on the secondary before committing. If we check Figure 5.4, we have deliberately made the arrow go from the secondary as a pull action. In reality the secondary replica requests the log from the primary for the changes to get flushed and the log scanner on the primary checks and acknowledges the log block after it is completed.

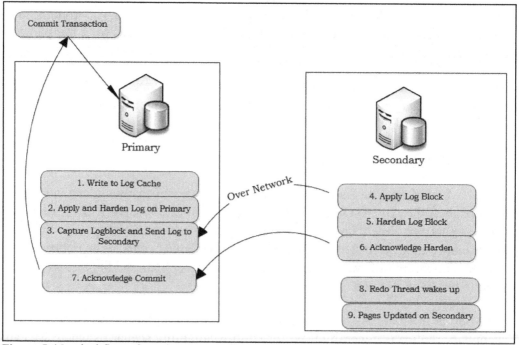

Figure 5.4 Logical flow of synchronous mode.

Logically this makes complete sense because the primary replica is already doing too many activities currently from a read/write workload. It would add more overhead on the primary replica if it had to track the LSN sent to the secondary replica(s). Therefor this mechanism of pulling really helps considering how the primary replica can be made efficient with less workload overhead.

The process is almost the same for the asynchronous secondary replica with one small exception. In this mode the primary replica commits the transaction after hardening into the local log file but it does not wait for the hardening into secondary replica. The secondary is hardened asynchronously. The advantage of this configuration is that the primary replica does not have to wait for confirmation from an asynchronous secondary. The disadvantage of this configuration is that the secondary replica can be lagging behind the primary.

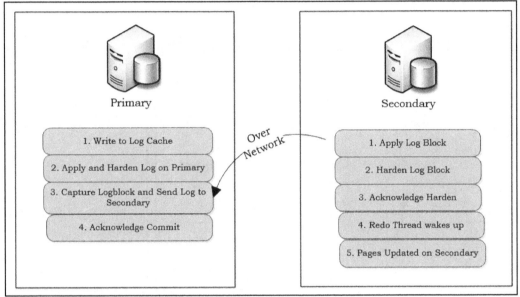

Figure 5.5 Logical flow of asynchronous mode.

Availability Group Listener

One the most cherished days in our life would be our college days. We sometimes get reminded about those days whenever we meet up with an old friend. As our normal job pulls us in all directions we do have this wonderful tool of using social networking sites to keep in touch with all of our longtime friends. Our group was called the Kappa's. I have never met anyone named Kappa, it was like a virtual network name (VNN) for our group.

Recently, in one such conversation we found a friend who has been in touch with every one of our college Kappa gang. It was such a pleasant surprise and it became simple to just call this person to get updates about the various individuals.

In the AlwaysOn world this friend (who has information and contacts of the rest of the group) is called the "Listener".

With a primary replica and multiple secondary replicas available in an AlwaysOn configuration, how can we make sure we connect to the correct replica at any given time? The AlwaysOn Availability Group Listener is a virtual network name (VNN) resource in Failover Cluster Manager. It's like a computer name is created on the domain that represents all the computers in the group. The VNN has a dependency on an AlwaysOn Availability Group at the point of creation. The VNN is similar to the Virtual Server Name concept as part of SQL Server Failover Clusters.

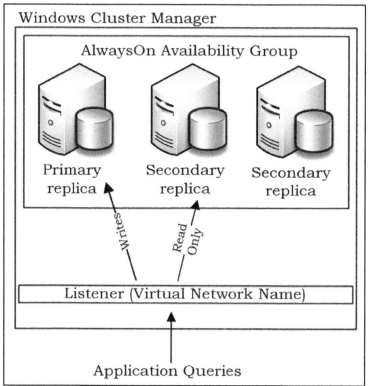

Figure 5.6 The VNN Listener for the group handles the connections for the Application Queries.

A VNN is bound to one or more IP addresses and ports, which are used to route connections to the primary or secondary replicas. The Listener gives us the flexibility to connect to either the primary or secondary replicas based on connection string parameters. The Listener failover is automatic and happens along with the Availability Group so that applications do not need to change the connection string. The connection string of Database Mirroring requires us to use a principal server and failover partner name. Using the AlwaysOn Availability

Group Listener we can give only one server name (i.e. the VNN) in the connection string and scale out our deployment. This allows the client to connect without worrying about changing the application code in case of a failover.

Whenever a Listener is created, a computer object name is created for it on the domain controller. Generally, in a controlled environment, computer accounts are pre-staged in active directory. For more details see this link http://technet.microsoft.com/en-us/library/cc731002(WS.10).aspx

Also remember that the VNN of the Listener is bound to a single Availability Group resource and can't be shared. It's almost like the VNN is the network name of our group. It would stay in the same cluster group and have the same owner as an Availability Group resource.

Summary

This chapter forms the fundamental building blocks to understand the different terms that are used with the SQL Server AlwaysOn Availability Groups. The concepts of forming a group, understanding replicas, and how the Listener works, is vital to how we will build architectures in AlwaysOn. The two core features of an active readable secondary and a backup secondary were discussed in detail with possible scenarios.

Points to Ponder - Always On Availability Groups

1. The AlwaysOn Availability Group is a container of one or more highly available user databases that would be able to failover together as a unit.

2. Each AlwaysOn Availability Group could be optionally associated with a virtual network name (VNN) resource and an IP address resource which are used to connect from applications. This is known as a Listener.

3. Each AlwaysOn Availability Group can have up to four readonly replicas and only one read/write replica.

4. The instance which hosts a read/write copy of database is known as the primary replica and those instances which are hosting the readonly copies are the secondary replicas.

5. The AlwaysOn Availability Group Listener is a virtual network name (VNN) resource in Failover Cluster Manager.

6. A VNN is bound to one or more IP addresses and ports, which are used to route connections to the primary or secondary replicas.

Review Quiz - Chapter Five

1.) How many primary replicas can you have with a SQL Server 2012 AlwaysOn Availability Group?

  O a. 1
  O b. 2
  O c. 3
  O d. 4

2.) What is the maximum number of secondary replicas possible with a SQL Server 2012 AlwaysOn Availability Group?

  O a. 1
  O b. 2
  O c. 3
  O d. 4

3.) What is the maximum number of synchronous secondary replicas possible with a SQL Server 2012 AlwaysOn Availability Group?

  O a. 1
  O b. 2
  O c. 3
  O d. 4

4.) Read this statement: "As soon as data is committed on the primary replica, it can be seen by a select statement on a synchronous secondary replica." Is this statement:

  O a. TRUE
  O b. FALSE

5.) Once the Availability Group with a Listener is created, what are the resources created in the Windows Cluster? Choose all that apply.

  □ a. Availability Group
  □ b. SQL Server Agent
  □ c. virtual network name
  □ d. IP address

Answer Key

1.) We can have only one primary (read/write) database in an AlwaysOn configuration, therefore (b) 2, (c) 3 and (d) 4 are all wrong. (a) 1 is the correct answer.

2.) (a) 1, (b) 2, and (c) 3 are all wrong. A maximum of 4 secondary replicas are possible making (d) 4 the correct answer.

3.) Options (a) 1, (c) 3, and (d) 4 are all wrong. A maximum of 2 sync replicas can be configured in an Availability Group. (b) 2 is the correct answer. BTW, there can be only 1 replica marked for automatic failover.

4.) As soon as data is committed on the primary replica the redo thread has to redo the transaction before it becomes available for reading on the secondary. The correct option is (b) False.

5.) The correct options are (a) Availability Group, (c) Virtual Network Name and (d) IP Address. These are the resources created in a Windows Cluster when an Availability Group Listener is created. Option (b) SQL Agent is not created by Availability Group creation.

[NOTES]

Chapter 6. Availability Group (AG) Actions on the Secondary

In very large cities with dense populations one of the most common travel combinations we have seen around the world is a four-wheel vehicle and an additional two-wheel vehicle (like a scooter or a motorcycle). If we need to make a quick trip to the nearby grocery store, it would be quick and easy to use the two-wheeler rather than traveling in the SUV. The concept of having a hot standby ready to use based on the situation is a great flexibility option.

We can only carry limited grocery items if we are on a two-wheeler, and we cannot drive it when it is snowing outside. Parking is much easier when compared to an SUV. Even though we have this flexibility, we need to use each option based on the situation. Therefore in this example we can see how we have to think before using each of the active secondary options.

In the AlwaysOn Availability Group configuration we do scale out multiple secondary options that can be used in a special way. In this chapter we will outline the various activities that we can do on a secondary replica.

READER NOTE: *This chapter provides many diagrams to demonstrate the important concepts that are needed for AlwaysOn. In this chapter there will be no need to have our machine configured to follow along. The tutorial steps begin in Chapter 7. You will see some screen shots or code steps just to give us a visual awareness of the tutorial steps that will begin in Chapter 7.*

Active Secondary Replicas

In the management and leadership world there is a concept called "two-in-a-box". The idea here is to complement each other's strengths and cover for each other's weaknesses when we have two people working in the same role. A lot of organizations use this technique to maintain continuity in business. Sometimes this can mean extra overhead but the benefit it gives in the long run can be amazing. This team should always be on the same page, every single time. We can call this as an "active always available secondary backup".

Organizations and businesses look for a return on investments with hardware before agreeing on solutions that involve such costs. Therefore an active secondary concept brings the best of investment rather than a cold standby server. Let's take the solutions built on SQL Server Clustering or normal Database

Mirroring, the secondary is passive and is not available for reading from reporting applications. Therefore though businesses see the importance of a standby server for High Availability needs, they look for ways to maximize their current investments in hardware for the secondary. The SQL Server AlwaysOn Availability Group implementation takes this feedback and makes the secondary servers readable.

In AlwaysOn Availability Groups, an active secondary can be used for things like redirecting the readonly workload, off-loading the backup load, and offloading the DBCC check commands. Before we get into the fine print of implementation, let's understand how people achieved this requirement prior to SQL Server 2012.

Readable Copy: Option 1 (Database Mirroring)

Let's assume that we are using a SQL Server 2008 R2 Database Mirroring solution. In this configuration, an application can make readonly reporting based queries. There are two options for this:

- Run them directly on the principal server.
- Create a snapshot of the database on the mirror server.

If we generate reports on the principal server; it would consume CPU cycles, perform extra IO operations for queries, and take locks on the underlying objects. This technique gets us real-time data with no latency or lag for reporting needs. In doing this, extra overhead exists on the live system which is a big disadvantage. Some users decide to run their reporting needs during off peak hours to overcome resource related issues.

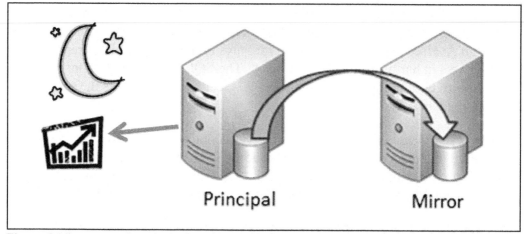

Figure 6.1 Reports on the principal server work but can slow down our production system.

The alternate way of running a readonly workload on the mirror server would be to create a Database Snapshot. The limitation of this approach would be that the data seen in the snapshot copy will be at the point when the snapshot was generated (not in real-time). So this architecture and latency limitation must be acceptable to the business. Typical reports that can accept this latency would be end-of-day reports, quarterly MIS reports, or other historical reports.

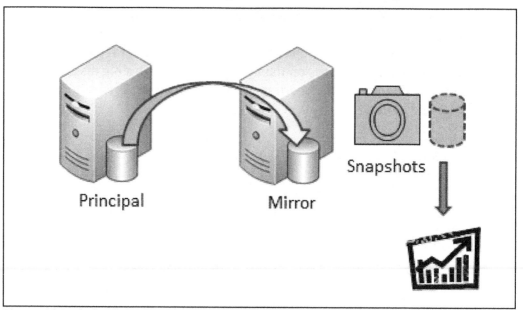

Figure 6.2 Technique to offload reporting workload to database mirror server.

Since snapshots have the limitation of longer latencies, DBAs can also create snapshots more frequently and get closer to real-time data. In reality, this might be too much administrative overhead to create frequent Database Snapshots. A new Database Snapshot often gets a new name. This means the application needs to be intelligent enough to redirect subsequent queries to the newly created snapshot database whenever it needs the latest data. Figure 6.2 shows a typical configuration.

Readable Copy: Option 2 (Database Mirroring and Replication)

Another topology commonly used is to generate reports from a subscriber database using any of the replication methods. Figure 6.3 is one typical topology which can be used to achieve High Availability using Database Mirroring. For the reporting workload we can use transactional replication to a subscriber. This means we need a third server which would act as the subscriber.

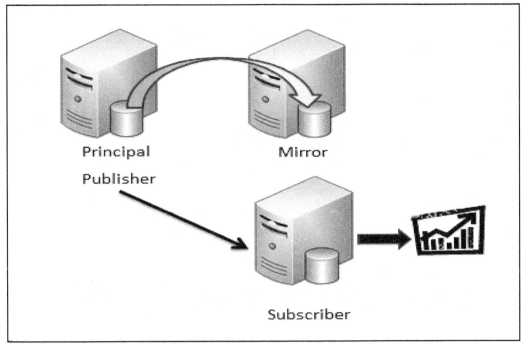

Figure 6.3 Technique to offload reporting workload to subscriber server via transactional replication.

The best part about this topology is if reporting requires just a subset of the database tables then replication can replicate only those needed. One of the disadvantages with this technique is the need for additional hardware and it might also need some design level changes to tables to accommodate replication. There are some prerequisites for transactional replication, such as every table involved must have a primary key. Sometimes it may not be feasible to make design changes to our database just to enable replication of these objects.

Readable Copy: Option 3 (Database Mirroring and Log Shipping)

Another common configuration is to use Log Shipping and accessing the secondary in Standby Mode for reporting. The only disadvantage of this method (in addition to needing three instances) is that when the restore happens on the reporting server, the client needs to be disconnected. This means the database is not accessible during this time. As discussed before, in a Log Shipping configuration the data is as current as the interval applied for the "log backup and restore" sequence. Therefore the delay in reporting data would be equal to the last successful restore time.

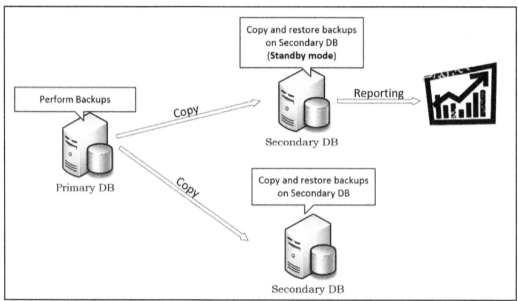

Table 6.1 Technique to offload reporting workload to subscriber server via Log Shipping.

SQL Server 2012: AlwaysOn Options

With every new release of software there are interesting new techniques that allow us to do new things. With the release of SQL Server 2012, we can use the AlwaysOn Availability Group for a reporting capability on the secondary. During the configuration we can use the primary database for a read/write workload and redirect the reporting workload to a readonly secondary database. In case of primary failover in a typical two node configuration, we can reconnect the applications without making any changes to the application connection string. This will be discussed in more depth in Chapter 8. There are a few interesting points we need to remember:

- Data available on the secondary is either real-time or close to real-time data. If there is any latency it is due to log synchronization running behind the scene.

- Reporting with an AlwaysOn Availability Group is different from using reporting for replication deployments. With Replication we can give the secondary server some custom indexes tuned for the report retrieval. We cannot create indexes on AlwaysOn secondary replicas to speed up the reports. The indexes must be created on the primary.

- Replication can be done for specific objects and can also filter records to get a subset of data from the primary. An AlwaysOn Availability Group has the scope of the whole database and replicates all of its data.

The logs of the synchronous secondary always commit before that of the primary. So let's understand the meaning of "almost real-time" that was mentioned earlier with the SQL Server AlwaysOn Availability Group. The most important question is, if a replica is configured in a synchronous mode then why should we have any latency? Even while using a synchronous replica there would be a delay because this mode guarantees that the change log is written to the transaction logfile of a secondary replica database. Such "writes" into the transaction log does not guarantee it is being applied to the datafiles for access and therefore there can be a lag.

There is a background redo thread working asynchronously behind the scene to read the log record and it applies these modifications in the database file to bring it back in sync with the primary.

Another interesting feature introduced as part of the active secondary is ability to offload the work of taking the database backup from the secondary server (with some limitations discussed later). The backup is an administrative process done during a maintenance window because it can significantly put stress on I/O and the CPU (using compression) on the servers. If we compare this feature with Database Mirroring, we can't take database backups on mirrored servers, backups are only allowed to be taken from the primary database. This means that a backup workload would impact the performance of the application workload. Using this new feature of the SQL Server 2012 AlwaysOn active secondary, we can take a backup of the database from the secondary replica. The backups can also be taken from the primary if needed.

Readable Secondary Replica

One of the key benefits we discussed about AlwaysOn Availability Groups is that we can redirect the readonly workload to the secondary servers. During the setup of the AlwaysOn Availability Group, we can define whether the connections are allowed to the server when it is in the secondary role. These settings can also be changed using T-SQL or SQL Server Management Studio. The typical options for a readable secondary are shown in Figure 6.4.

Availability Replicas					
Server Instance	Role	Availability Mode	Failover Mode	Connections in Primary Role	Readable Secondary
SRV1	Primary	Synchronous commit ▼	Automatic ▼	Allow all connections ▼	No ▼
SRV2	Second...	Synchronous commit ▼	Automatic ▼	Allow all connections ▼	Yes ▼
SRV3	Second...	Synchronous commit ▼	Manual ▼	Allow all connections ▼	Read-intent only ▼

Figure 6.4 Various options available in readable secondary.

The readability of the secondary can be set in one of three states. The first two settings of No and Yes are self-explanatory. A setting of No doesn't allow connections while a setting of Yes allows readable secondary connections. As per the UI in Figure 6.4, SRV1 is currently the primary. If SRV1 is later in a secondary role, then no connections would be allowed. Any connection attempt to this database would fail with error message 976.

```
Messages
Msg 976, Level 14, State 1, Line 1
The target database, 'MyAdventureWorks', is participating in an Availability
Group and is currently not accessible for queries. Either data movement is
suspended or the availability replica is not enabled for read access. To
allow readonly access to this and other databases in the Availability Group,
enable read access to one or more secondary availability replicas in the
group. For more information, see the ALTER AVAILABILITY GROUP statement in
SQL Server Books Online.
```

The third value of Read-intent only is interesting. This connecting application needs to specify the read-intent in its connection string property. Without the read-intent in the connection string, the connection would fail with error 978.

Messages
Msg 978, Level 14, State 1, Line 1
The target database ('MyAdventureWorks') is in an Availability Group and is currently accessible for connections when the application intent is set to readonly. For more information about application intent, see SQL Server Books Online.

This is exactly the scenario where an AlwaysOn Listener is useful as it can redirect the connection to an available secondary replica based on the "Readonly Routing" based on what we want to set up.

Impact of Readable Secondary

The need for having a readable secondary replica is obvious. In this section we will discuss a few of the overhead items associated with a readable secondary replica.

After the logs are written to the secondary replica (for an update done on the primary) there is a background redo thread working to modify the pages in the database file. It does this by bringing the pages into memory and modifying them. If we are running a heavy reporting workload on the secondary then this will consume valuable CPU and IO resources. This may impact the redo thread operation and the secondary can fall behind the pace of the primary. This might impact the RTO (Recovery Time Objective) as the recovery process might take longer.

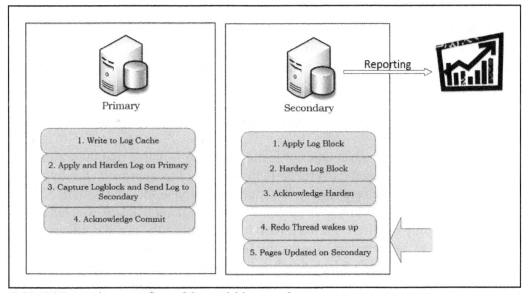

Table 6.2 Internal process flow of the readable secondary.

When we have heavy concurrent transactional users in the system, the system can have a slower reaction. It is worth understanding these behaviors before enabling the secondary.

By reading data from the secondary while data is being written to on the primary we have good concurrency. In a situation where a reporting workload reads from the secondary and locks the primary would not be good. While running under the Serializable isolation level all locks are held for the complete duration of a connection (even for Shared locks). The rows being read at a point-in-time on the secondary might also be written to the primary. Now this row is sent from the primary to the secondary and then hardened in the secondary's transaction log. The redo thread needs to modify the rows by replacing it on the secondary data file. This process of the redo thread can't do the write because there is already a shared lock taken by the currently executing read query. This would mean that the redo has to wait until the read transaction is completed. It is not a good situation to have an isolation level with heavy locking for a topology that includes synchronous secondary replicas in AlwaysOn Availability groups.

READER NOTE: *The topics on isolation levels and locks are covered in SQL Queries 2012 Joes 2 Pros Volume 3.*

AlwaysOn and Transaction Isolation

In a SQL Server AlwaysOn deployment, to solve the problems of isolation, SQL Server would map all the isolation levels to the Snapshot isolation level. This way the redo thread will not be blocked while reading reports. Even if we specify an isolation level explicitly (like Serializable) as part of the query, the transaction would be automatically mapped to the Snapshot isolation level and SQL Server would ignore any locking hints by queries on the readable secondary. Therefore SQL Server AlwaysOn makes it efficient for read-queries giving a consistent view of data while it manages the last committed value via Snapshot isolation.

Having understood the advantages of using Snapshot isolation and increasing the concurrency, there are some overhead items of using this approach. To support Snapshot isolation, each row has to have a row version associated with it. The space needed for a row version is an extra 14 bytes for each data row. This row versioning is only required when the redo thread applies the log and the data is being queried by the reporting app on the secondary (or vice versa). We do not need to enable the Snapshot isolation level explicitly to use a readable secondary, this is automatically done by SQL Server. In our above example, row version records are generated only on the readable secondary.

Since Snapshot isolation is internally used on the readable secondary replica, tempdb space would be consumed to place the copies of the row versions. So we must look at sizing and monitoring the tempdb usage on the readable secondary.

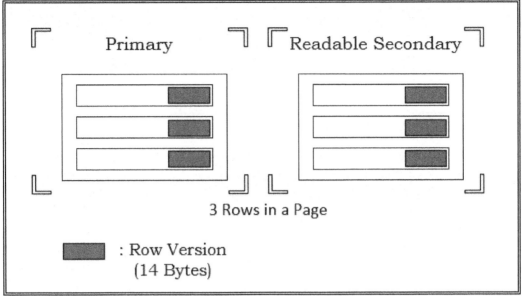

Figure 6.5 Shows the 14 byte overhead for each row on both replicas.

Blocking on Readable Secondary Replicas

In the last section, we learned that on a readable secondary, all isolation levels are mapped internally to the Snapshot isolation level and so a reader-writer conflict would not happen. When we run a read query in the Snapshot isolation level, it takes a schema stability lock to make sure there is no other process changing the definition of the tables accessed. The Snapshot isolation level means that queries use no object level locks to conflict with changes on the primary.

The next situation we are going to talk about is very rare. When we are creating a new table or performing some other design changes with DDL statements some reports will have to wait until those changes are done. If the reports are already running, then the DDL statements on the primary will have to wait. During development deployments or updates in the live system we might want to stop the reporting until the deployment is done just to be safe.

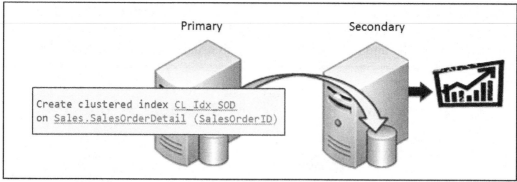

Figure 6.6 DDL statement being run on the primary.

Why would a query with no locks on the table block a DDL statement? All queries, as a minimum, issue a shared schema lock. The schema stability (Sch-S) lock is compatible with all lock modes except the schema modification (Sch-M) lock. The DDL statement requires the (Sch-M) lock to complete. The order of this is seen in Table 6.3.

primary replica	secondary replica
	Start reporting workload on table.
	Takes SCH-S lock on table.
Execute DDL operation on table and commit.	
	Received log record from the primary.
	REDO processes the DDL log record.
	Requests SCH-M lock on table.
	REDO process blocked.
	Reporting workload completes.
	REDO process unblocked.

Table 6.3 Representation of scenario where a DDL in the primary blocks the secondary reports.

Let's assume an extreme situation where a report query running for 30 minutes on the secondary takes a Sch-S lock as discussed earlier. Now assume a schema change happened on the primary replica when this happened. Once the log record is received and persisted in the transaction log of the secondary, the redo thread will try to apply this but due to a conflict of locks, it would be blocked.

The reverse is also true and the behavior will be the same. If the redo thread is performing a schema modification lock and there is a reporting workload, it would get blocked and wait for the redo thread to finish (release the locks taken).

If a reporting workload is blocked, it may not be much of a problem but blocking of the redo thread might impact our recovery time objective (RTO). For those records, SQL Server would generate an extended event lock_redo_blocked which can be used to monitor this specific situation. DBAs can use this information and can potentially write a script to kill the workload which is blocking the redo thread. The redo thread is never chosen as the deadlock victim.

Backups on Secondary Replicas

We discussed the concept of "two-in-a-box" earlier where we had two individuals working on the same job complementing each other. One of the major advantages to this concept is that when one person needs to leave because of some personal emergency, there is someone there as a backup to take over. We want to make sure our business keeps running 24x7 and it is important for us to use all the available resources.

With critical systems that need maintenance we are often given a time frame to start and complete the work. This time frame is called a "maintenance window". In the SQL Server world, it is common that we do administrative operations during the maintenance window timeframe. The reason for doing such activities during non-peak hours is because these tasks are resource intensive. Resource intensive maintenance tasks compete with resources used to run the business. Non-peak business hours can mean more freed up recourses and overall less interruption.

In prior SQL Server releases (especially with Database Mirroring) customers always wanted to take a backup on the mirror database which is functioning as a standby until the failover happens. By design backups are only possible on the primary server in a mirroring configuration.

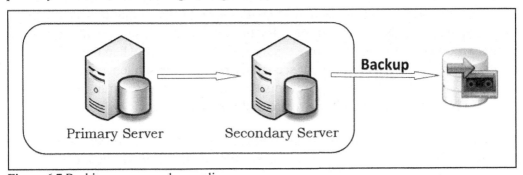

Figure 6.7 Backing up a secondary replica.

In an AlwaysOn Availability Group configuration, backups can be performed on any replica of the database (synchronous or asynchronous).

Transaction logs have a unique requirement that they be taken in sequence so that they can be restored in the same order. The best part about AlwaysOn is being able to do backups on the secondary replica. This means they can be backed up on one server and restored in sequence on another server.

Here is a summary of some of the backup operations allowed in an AlwaysOn Availability Group:

- Log backups can be done on the primary or the secondary replicas.
- Differential backups are not allowed on secondary replicas.
- Full backups are not allowed on the secondary replicas but we can back up everything by using a copy-only backup.
- All the SQL backup types are available on the primary replica.

Transaction Log Behavior on Backups

With the ability to do backups on secondary replicas it is important to understand how the log truncation and synchronization will happen. Normally transaction logfiles continue to grow until they are backed up. With backups happening on various secondary replicas, will the transaction logs on the servers we are not backing up grow out of control?

SQL Server AlwaysOn has a simple process, when a log backup starts on the secondary replica; the primary is notified that the log backup is underway. The primary replica gets the starting LSN (Log Sequence Number) so that other secondary replicas are not backing up the same log records. Once the log backup finishes, the primary replica is notified with the end LSN so that it is aware and persists in its transaction log. In turn, the primary sends this conversation to all other secondary replicas. This process makes sure that even when the transaction log backups are taken on different secondary replicas the sequence is never broken. This conversation also prevents the situation where the transaction log backup is happening on multiple replicas at the same time.

Earlier we mentioned that differential backups are not allowed on the secondary replicas. This is because the syncing of the differential bit might be too challenging and it can become highly resource intensive to communicate that across all the replicas. The only difference between a regular full backup and a copy-only backup is that SQL Server doesn't clear the differential bit.

Another question is that since log backups are allowed on all replicas, does SQL Server maintain a history of the backup in the msdb database of the primary? The quick answer is No. Each msdb database has history only for local backups taken. This information is not present centrally on the primary. To mitigate this problem there is a new interface called the Database Recovery Advisor (DRA) which can read multiple backup files together and advise us of the exact recovery sequence. We highly recommend using the recovery advisor. It would be good idea to keep all the backups from various replicas at a single location; otherwise we will need to hunt for a backup location in the interface and this might be time consuming (especially when there is a disaster situation).

Automated Backups

Doing repetitive jobs is quite boring and most importantly can become error prone. Therefore backups (as an activity) are something every DBA needs to do to meet the SLA set by businesses. One of the major tasks is to automate the process and introduce monitoring techniques to track backups. As discussed before, with a number of choices for backups on different replicas, it does add complexities to where a backup can be taken form and how to use the restore chain sequence in case of a disaster. We highly recommend storing backups in a centrally accessible location so that DBAs can easily find them in case of a disaster. In this section, we will look at various options available for database backups which are part of the SQL Server AlwaysOn Availability Group.

In the Database Mirroring configuration, DBAs used a common technique of creating backup jobs on both the principal and the mirror server and expected the backups to work on the current principal. In order to avoid errors, DBAs would even put a check in the script to query the current role and run a backup command only when the current role is the principal. Though these intelligent scripts have existed, this logic will not work in the AlwaysOn Availability Group replicas because the backup can be taken both on primary and secondary replicas. Also, we can't use the same logic to get the current role of replica as there could be more than one secondary replica.

Set Backup Preference

To view the backup preferences for the Availability Group, we can use Management Studio or a T-SQL query. We have opened the properties window for an Availability Group in Figure 6.8. We will show exactly how to get the properties window and set it in Chapter 7. For now we need to be aware of the concepts of the backup preferences.

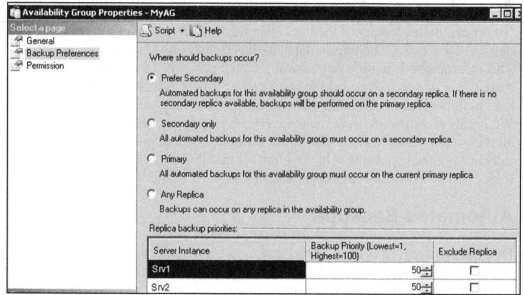

Figure 6.8 UI preference screen where automated backups should happen.

In the Figure 6.8, we can see the ability to choose our backup preference and replica Backup Priority. The dialog in the figure has two sections; one for "Where should backups occur?" and the second section for "replica backup priorities". As described, the first section scopes to an automatic backup preference location for this Availability Group. The default is to use "Prefer secondary". If there are multiple secondary servers for backups then we need another setting that can break the tie between them. This tie breaker is specified in the second section, on the lower half of the page. We need to understand that these settings are just an advisory and are not enforced as rules set in stone. This means that even if we set "Secondary only" we would not be prevented from performing backups on the primary replica.

As we see from the dialog box in Figure 6.8, there are 4 options for the backup preference.

- **Prefer secondary**: Means automated backups for this Availability Group should occur on a secondary replica. If there are no secondary replicas available, the backup will be taken on the primary replica.

- **Secondary only**: All automated backups for this Availability Group will happen only on a secondary replica.

- **Primary**: Direct automated backups for the Availability Group will take place only on the current primary replica.

- **Any Replica**: Backups can occur on any of the replicas (primary / secondary).

The same information can also be retrieved via T-SQL using the following code:

```
SELECT     automated_backup_preference_desc
FROM master.sys.availability_groups
WHERE name = 'MyAvailabilityGroup';
GO

SELECT replica_server_name, backup_priority
FROM master.sys.availability_replicas AR
INNER JOIN master.sys.availability_groups AG
ON AR.group_id = AG.group_id
AND AG.name = 'MyAvailabilityGroup';
```

automated_backup_preference_desc	replica_server_name	backup_priority
secondary	SRV1	50
	SRV2	50

Maintenance Plans using Backup Preference

Even the maintenance plan wizard is aware of the backup preference which we have selected for the Availability Group. If we launch the Maintenance Plan Wizard (using **Management Studio** > **Management** > **Maintenance plan** > **Right Click** > **New Maintenance Plan Wizard**) and select any backup task, the UI is going to ask if we want to consider the backup preference settings. The typical setting is available in Figure 6.9 for reference.

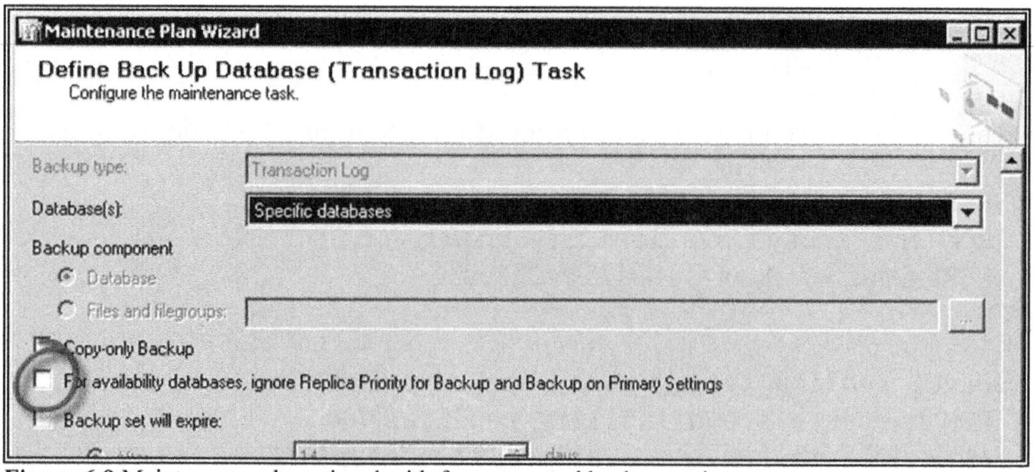

Figure 6.9 Maintenance plan wizard with for automated backup options.

Here is an interesting catch we should be aware of. If we define the backup setting as "Prefer Secondary" for the Availability Group (the default setting) and then we create a maintenance plan for the database only on the primary replica and we don't check the option which is highlighted in Figure 6.9, we would end up in a no backup situation.

As a DBA, if we want to create our own jobs to perform the backup, then a T-SQL function is available to find the preferred replica. The function fn_hadr_backup_is_preferred_replica is used to identify if the current replica is the preferred backup. If the query below returns a 1 then we can back up this database on this SQL instance:

```
SELECT sys.fn_hadr_backup_is_preferred_replica('JProCo')
```

The function returns Boolean (0 or 1) so we can easily put a check mark in the box and perform backups only on preferred replicas. As outlined before, this is already done by a maintenance plan as an out-of-box feature. The same function is used for Log Shipping jobs which are created for the databases in an Availability Group.

The process flow to identify the final preferred backup replica is as follows:

- Identify and remove the replicas which are not running. These can't be used to take a backup of an availability database.
- Remove the replicas which are not meeting the role policy (first selection in the screen). For example, if the policy is "primary only" then filter out all the secondary replicas. On the other hand, if policy is set to "secondary only" then filter out the current primary.

114

- If there is more than one replica eligible then the priority set would be considered (defined in second section of backup preference UI). The highest priority replica would be the preferred replica.
- If priority for the replicas is the same then the instance name is the tie breaker.

How Backups on the Secondary happen?

We mentioned earlier that the log backups taken on the secondary will form a chain. Therefore it is critical for a SQL Server to maintain some sort of locking to enable this behavior. As seen in Figure 6.10 the steps are simple.

1. We initiate a log backup on the secondary.
2. A backup initialization is sent to the primary replica and a lock is taken to make sure no other secondary replicas initiate another log backup.
3. Once the backup finishes, the lock placed on the primary replica is released.

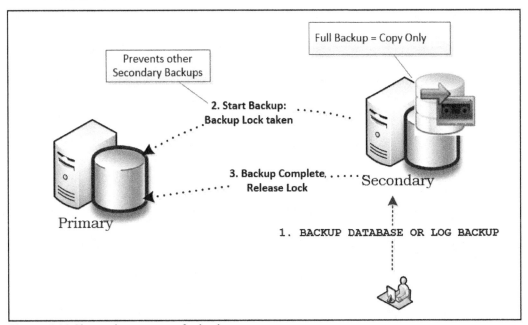

Figure 6.10 Shows the sequence for backups.

If we attempt to take a transaction log backup on another secondary when there is no primary replica (i.e. Availability Group in a resolving state) we will get the following error message:

Messages
Msg 3062, Level 16, State 1, Line 1 Cannot backup from a HADRON secondary because it is not in Synchronizing or Synchronized state.

Summary

As we start deploying multiple secondary replicas, utilizing the benefits of scale out are important. In this chapter we discussed how we can use the secondary for as a readonly scale out secondary. As we expand the use of secondary servers, using them for offloading the backup workload can be yet another use.

Points to Ponder – Availability Group (AG) Actions on the Secondary

1. In AlwaysOn Availability Groups, an active secondary can be used for redirecting a readonly workload, off-loading the backup load, and offloading the DBCC checks command.

2. Even if we specify an isolation level explicitly as part of a query, the SQL Server AlwaysOn Availability Group databases would be automatically using the Snapshot isolation level and SQL Server would ignore any locking hints by queries on the readable secondary.

3. Differential backups are not allowed on secondary replicas.

4. Regular full backups are not allowed in a secondary replica but a copy-only backup is an option.

5. Log backups can be done on any secondary replica.

6. In AlwaysOn Availability Group technology, transaction log backups taken on different replicas would form a sequence and can be restored in case of a disaster.

7. The T-SQL function fn_hadr_backup_is_preferred_replica is used to identify if the current replica is preferred as per the preferences provided in the automated backup screen.

8. As per logic defined in function fn_hadr_backup_is_preferred_replica, if there are multiple instances having the same preference of backup then the instance name is used as tie-breaker to get stable results on all replicas.

9. We cannot create indexes on AlwaysOn secondary replicas for reporting needs. We need to create indexes on the primary so all replicas can get them.

10. In SQL Server AlwaysOn Availability Group deployment, to solve problems of concurrency, SQL Server would map all the isolation levels to Snapshot isolation level on a readable replica.

11. We don't have to enable the Snapshot isolation level explicitly to use a readable secondary, this is automatically done by SQL Server.

12. To support snapshots, each row has to have a row version associated with it. The space needed for a row version is an extra 14 bytes for each data row.

13. Differential backups are not allowed on secondary replicas.

14. All the SQL backup types are available on the primary replica.

15. We can only perform backups on secondary replicas where the databases are in a synchronized or synchronizing state. We can't perform a backup while in a resolving state.

16. To perform backups on the secondary, the replica does not need to be in readable secondary mode to perform the backup.

17. Prior to SQL Server 2012, we had the option to use replication, Log Shipping, or database mirroring to offload the reporting workload from production to the reporting server.

18. The maintenance plan is aware of the setting provided in the backup preference of the Availability Group.

Review Quiz - Chapter Six

1.) What are the types of backups we can do on a primary replica in SQL Server 2012 AlwaysOn Availability Group configuration? Choose all that apply.

   □ a. Full
   □ b. Log
   □ c. Differential
   □ d. Full backup with COPY_ONLY option

2.) What are the types of backups we can do on a secondary replica in SQL Server 2012 AlwaysOn Availability Group configuration? Choose all that apply.

   □ a. Full
   □ b. Log
   □ c. Differential
   □ d. Full backup with COPY_ONLY option

3.) What is the space needed for each row when using row versioning?

   O a. 14 bits
   O b. 14 bytes
   O c. 14 MB
   O d. 14 GB

4.) To perform a backup on a secondary, it has to be configured as readonly.

   O a. True
   O b. False

5.) If we set the backup preference to "primary" and run a log backup on the secondary, what would happen?

   O a. Error Message.
   O b. Command automatically fires on primary replica.
   O c. Backup succeeds on secondary replica.

6.) What is the function we can use to determine if the current database is on the replica that is preferred for backups?

O a. sys.fn_hadr_preferred_replica_backup
O b. sys.fn_hadr_backup_is_preferred_replica
O c. sys.fn_alwayson_preferred_replica_backup
O d. sys.fn_alwayson_backup_is_preferred_replica

Answer Key

1.) There are no restrictions for backups on the primary therefore all the answers (a), (b), (c) and (d) are correct.

2.) We cannot take Full and Differential backups on a secondary. Hence answers (a) and (c) are wrong. The correct answers are (b) Log and (d) Full backup with COPY_ONLY option.

3.) The overhead for snapshot is 14 bytes for each row. Option (b) is the correct answer. Answers (a) 14 bits, (c) 14 MB, and (d) 14 GB are wrong answers.

4.) There is no prerequisite of having a readable secondary to take backups on the secondary replica. Hence the correct option is (b) False.

5.) The correct option is (c) Backup succeeds on secondary replica. Hence the options (a) Error Message and (b) Command automatically fires on primary replica are incorrect.

6.) The function is (b) sys.fn_hadr_backup_is_preferred_replica, making all other options wrong.

[NOTES]

Chapter 7. Deploying AlwaysOn Availability Groups

Information Technology (IT), as a field, is a very interesting place to work. The challenges IT overcomes is amazing. Any IT solution is geared towards solving problems that the business faces day-to-day to make the system efficient. After working in multiple IT organizations, I have seen that one of the common activities a decision maker needs to have is meetings. Meetings are a great way to plan our tasks at hand, but just holding meetings are not enough. Forecasting and understanding problems is critical for creating the right solutions.

While we need to be cognizant of the facts, it is critical that we understand what it takes to deploy these solutions. This involves laying out the finer details of implementation and what responsibilities each person has. In this chapter we will progress into what it takes to deploy the SQL Server AlwaysOn Availability Group technologies in our environment.

READER NOTE: You will need to view the video on how to setup your labs. The steps and hardware assumptions listed in the next few pages will already be part of your lab setup. By following those steps you can do the tutorials of this chapter.

This chapter assumes a SQL Server standalone instance has already been installed on all machines which are going to become replicas in the AlwaysOn Availability Group. If we follow the setup videos our virtual environment will have all of these items. Let's review this deployment environment of the AlwaysOn Availability Group. The following describes the environment we will be working on:

- Our setup environment consists of 5 servers.
- We have one Domain Controller (called DC) and four member servers (SRV1, SRV2, SRV3 and SRV4). These four member servers all have SQL Server 2012 RTM (11.00.2100) or above installed.
- All member servers are part of the same domain (hadomain.com) and all SQL Services are running under the hadomain\demouser account.

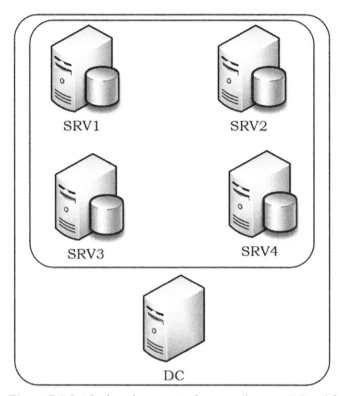

Figure 7.1 Our hadomain setup environment has one DC and four SQL member servers.

The environment does not have any shared disks between them. To know about the quorum majority refer back to Chapter 4.

Now that we understand the environment, the next operation will be to follow the six steps that this chapter outlines.

Step 1: Add the Failover Clustering feature in Windows

Before we begin, we will need to create a Windows Failover Cluster. As we know this can be done without having the Windows Cluster and special hardware. To join a Windows Failover Cluster each server will need this feature enabled. One of the steps in our deployment will be to add the Failover Clustering feature in windows. This is not SQL Server Clustering on top of Windows Clustering with shared disks. The chapter does outline six major steps but the last two are optional so the deployment of a SQL Server AlwaysOn Availability Group can be divided into four required logical steps:

1. Add the Failover Clustering feature in windows to each server.

2. Create a Windows Failover Cluster.
3. Enable the AlwaysOn Availability Group feature for each SQL Server.
4. Create the Availability Group.

We might want to make changes to our group after it has been created. For example we might want to add or remove a replica from our group. In this case there could be a 5th step for that. If we want to add replicas later we will have five required steps:

1. Add the Failover Clustering feature in windows to each server.
2. Create a Windows Failover Cluster.
3. Enable the AlwaysOn Availability Group feature to each SQL Server.
4. Create the Availability Group.
5. Add a secondary replica to an existing group.

The main requirement to create an AlwaysOn Availability Group is to have the intended SQL Server instances be part of the same Windows Server Failover Cluster in the same domain. To clarify, this just means the Failover Clustering service needs to be enabled. Again, this is not SQL Server Clustering on top of Windows Clustering with shared disks. This can be done by opening Server Manager on the server. The steps to open the Server Manager are as follows:

Select **Start** > **All Programs** > **Administrative Tools** > **Server Manager** and expand the **Features** Tab.

Upon doing these steps we will land on the screen as seen in Figure 7.2.

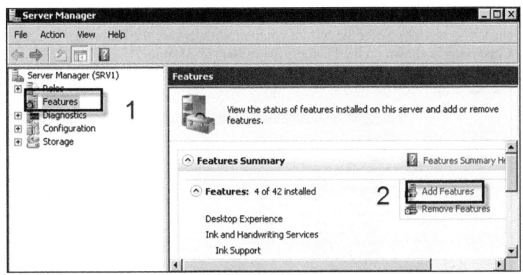

Figure 7.2 Include "Failover Clustering" feature using the "Add Features" option in Server Manager.

In this window we see a "Features Summary" in the middle of the screen. We are going to add another feature called "Failover Clustering". Like all features this can't be added twice so make sure the Failover Clustering (under the Features Summary tab) is not currently on the features list. If this is already enabled then we can skip this step. If the feature is missing we need to continue. To do this click on **Add Features** (seen on the right side of Figure 7.2). This will show us the Add Features Wizard screen where we need to select the **Failover Clustering** checkbox from the Add Features Wizard (Figure 7.3).

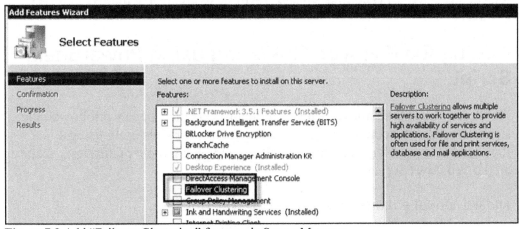

Figure 7.3 Add "Failover Clustering" feature via Server Manager.

Go through the wizard confirmation all the way to the final results page to finish the wizard. This will install the software needed for Windows Server Failover

Clustering. To reiterate, we have not created a cluster so far (we just enabled the clustering service). After the wizard completes make sure the **Failover Clustering** is shown on the Features list of **Server Manager**.

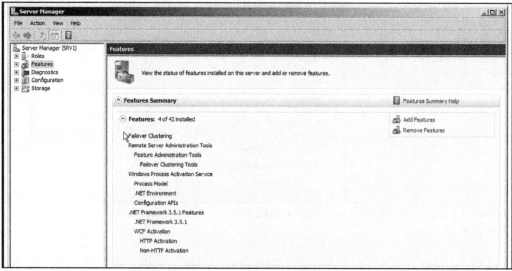

Figure 7.4 The "Failover Clustering" feature is shown in Server Manager.

Repeat this step on all the SQL Servers that will participate in the AlwaysOn Availability Group. In our setup this would be the SRV1, SRV2, SRV3 and SRV4 servers. We have finished enabling this for SRV1 so make sure to log into each of the other machines to complete this same step for all the servers. Once done these servers are capable of joining a Windows Server Failover Cluster. The next logical step (Step 2) is coming up and it will be to create a Windows Failover Cluster.

Adding the Failover Clustering using PowerShell Script

We already have the Failover Clustering feature enabled since we followed the steps in the UI. We could have also deployed Failover Clustering using a PowerShell script. Here is the command for adding a Failover Clustering feature on the Windows Server:

```
Add-WindowsFeature Failover-Clustering
```

This command does not run from PowerShell, by default. You will need to have users 1st type the following:

```
Import-Module ServerManager
```

Step 2: Create a Windows Failover Cluster

Once we have the Failover Clustering feature enabled in Windows for all four servers, we can set up a Windows Failover Cluster for them. We are going to have our four SQL Servers (SRV1, SRV2, SRV3, and SRV4) be part of this cluster. All four servers will be part of this cluster but we do not need to log into each of them to set up this one cluster. A domain administrator can create the cluster and join the servers from one machine. This means we can set this up entirely from any of the servers while logged in as a domain administrator. We will use the Failover Cluster Manager while logged into SRV1 for our example.

The next step starts with opening the Failover Cluster Manager. This can be done with the following steps:

Start > **All Programs** > **Administrative Tools** > Select **Failover Cluster Manager**.

 *READER NOTE: If we love shortcuts then **Start** > **Run** > **Cluadmin.msc** will also launch the same Failover Cluster Manager.*

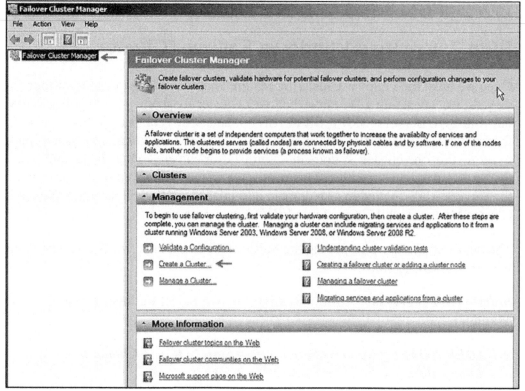

Figure 7.5 The Failover Cluster Manager.

In the Failover Cluster Manager, choose the option called **Create a Cluster...** which appears as a link in the management section of the window (Figure 7.5). This initializes the Create Cluster Wizard and we will add our four SQL Servers (SRV1, SRV2, SRV3 and SRV4) as shown in Figure 7.6. To add a server type in the fully qualified server name as seen in Figure 7.6. The first one will be srv1.hadomain.com. Once the name is correct click the **Add** button. Do this for SRV2, SRV3, and SRV4.

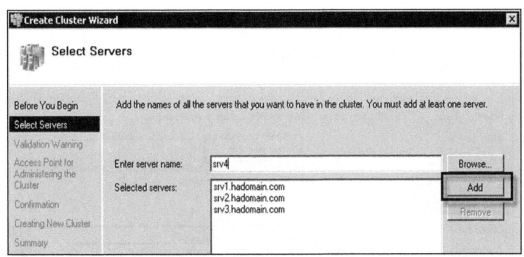

Figure 7.6 Adding Nodes in Create new Windows Cluster Wizard.

Once we have added all the needed servers, just follow the wizard and run the validation tests. This is really simplified if we have done all the previous steps correctly.

While moving forward in the wizard we will see the **Access Point for Administering the Cluster** screen. In this screen we need to provide a Windows Cluster name and a new IP address which will to be used by the cluster. A Failover Cluster must have its own IP address. In our current configuration the SQL Servers (Srv1 to Srv4) have the IP address ranging from 192.168.1.11 to 192.168.1.14. Those addresses are in use so we must choose another IP address that is free so the cluster can use its own address. In this example we will give the cluster the address of 192.168.1.10.

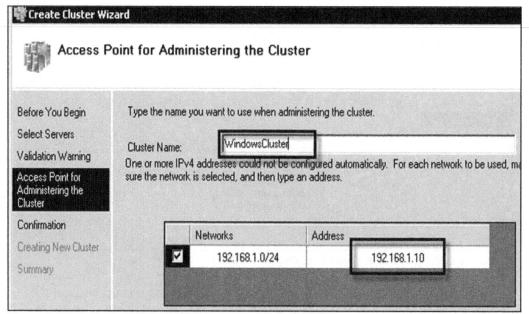

Figure 7.7 Specify the Windows Cluster name and an IP address

Click **Next** on the **Access Point for Administering the Cluster** screen. After providing all the details we will be prompted for confirmation to complete this step. Simply click **Next**.

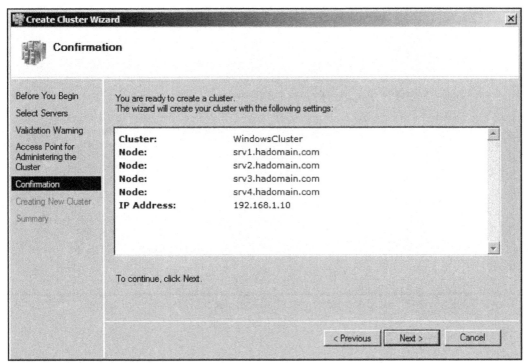

Figure 7.8 Confirmation Screen.

Now we should be able to see the cluster (defined as WindowsCluster.hadomain.com) in the Failover Cluster Manager. In this configuration notice there is no shared storage available at this moment. Shared Storage is not a requirement for an AlwaysOn Availability Group. If our Summary page shows a warning (about this quorum disk) we can ignore it and click **Next**.

Back in our Failover Cluster Manager we can now see the nodes listed in the Windows Cluster with SRV1 to SRV4.

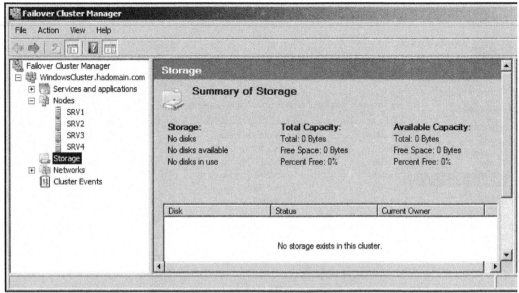

Figure 7.9 Failover Cluster Manager showing all four nodes with no shared storage.

PowerShell Script

The command to create the same Windows Cluster step via PowerShell is as follows:

```
new-cluster -Name WindowsCluster -Node SRV1, Srv2, Srv3,
Srv4 -StaticAddress 192.168.1.10 -NoStorage
```

When does PowerShell get new cmdlets for us to use? Since we installed the cluster feature in an earlier step, some needed cmdlets would not be imported until the new PowerShell command prompt is opened. If we are using the same command prompt (which was used to enable Windows Clustering feature from the last step) then we will need to run the following command before attempting to create a new cluster:

```
import-module FailoverClusters
```

Step 3: Enabling AlwaysOn in each SQL Service

To summarize this step we can say that we need to enable the AlwaysOn Availability Group feature for each SQL Server before we can use it. The AlwaysOn Availability Group is a feature of the SQL Server service that is not enabled by default. This step needs to be done to the SQL Server service before we can use any AlwaysOn feature. If we go directly to Management Studio and attempt to expand the AlwaysOn High Availability folder in Figure 7.10 we will get an error.

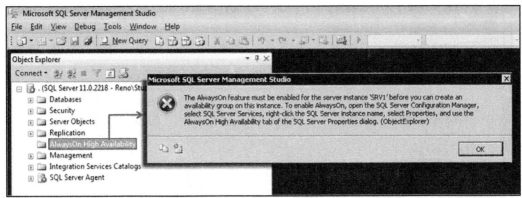

Figure 7.10 The error message if we try to access the Availability Group folder without enabling the AlwaysOn High Availability feature.

READER NOTE: *If we read the message carefully, it has enough information to tell us what is needed. The message outlines the following steps:*

- On the Start menu, point to **All Programs > Microsoft SQL Server 2012 > Configuration Tools**, and click **SQL Server Configuration Manager** (a.k.a. SSCM).

- In the SQL Server Configuration Manager, click the **SQL Server Services** on the left side of the screen, right-click **SQL Server** (<instance name>), and click **Properties**.

- Select the **AlwaysOn High Availability** tab as shown in Figure 7.11.

- Enable this by selecting the **Enable AlwaysOn Availability Groups** check box and click **OK**.

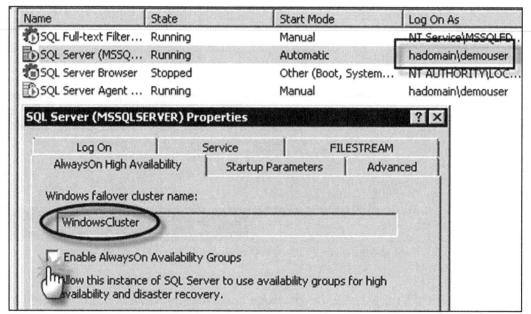

Name	State	Start Mode	Log On As
SQL Full-text Filter...	Running	Manual	NT Service\MSSQLFD...
SQL Server (MSSQ...	Running	Automatic	hadomain\demouser
SQL Server Browser	Stopped	Other (Boot, System...	NT AUTHORITY\LOC...
SQL Server Agent ...	Running	Manual	hadomain\demouser

SQL Server (MSSQLSERVER) Properties   ? X

| Log On | Service | FILESTREAM |
| AlwaysOn High Availability | Startup Parameters | Advanced |

Windows failover cluster name:

WindowsCluster

☐ Enable AlwaysOn Availability Groups
Allow this instance of SQL Server to use availability groups for high availability and disaster recovery.

Figure 7.11 Enable the AlwaysOn Availability Group Feature using SQL Server Configuration Manager.

Also in the Properties page, we see the Windows Failover Cluster name (WindowsCluster) that we created in step 2 (Figure 7.11). This smart UI has detected the existing Windows Cluster name and prepopulated it for our reference. We have highlighted the checkbox that will enable this service to use AlwaysOn Availability Groups.

It would be a good idea for all four of our nodes in this cluster to agree on using the same security credentials. This means the account being used for the SQL Server service for all members would ideally use the same Windows Domain Account. Otherwise we can have a spaghetti configuration of permissions needed for all servers to recognize all the other servers.

As DBAs we normally do not change the service account credentials of SQL Server. This is because SQL Server has been mostly running in a standalone mode and not interacting with other SQL Servers. For configuring a SQL Server AlwaysOn Availability Group we will keep things simple by having all SQL Servers use the same Windows Domain account.

To change the credentials used by the SQL Server (MSSQLSERVER) service click the **Log On** tab in the properties window. The **This account** section needs to be a domain account as shown in Figure 7.12.

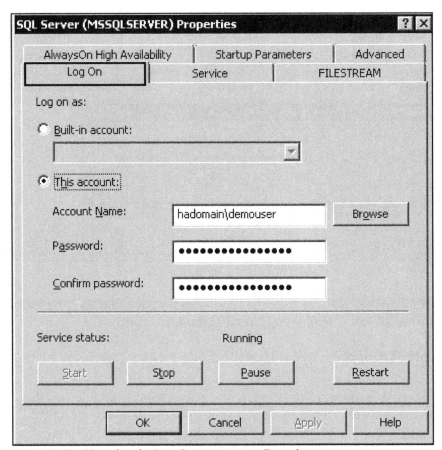

Figure 7.12: Changing the Log On account to a Domain user.

This process needs to be repeated for the SQL Service on all the nodes in the cluster that will be part of the Availability Group. In our case we have finished SRV1 and need to do this for SRV2, SRV3, and SRV4.

If the screen on the availability tab doesn't show the Windows Failover Cluster name automatically, then we have missed something in step 2 (discussed in the *Create a Windows Failover Cluster* section). If that is the case then a typical screen would look like Figure 7.13 and the Enable AlwaysOn Availability Groups checkbox will be disabled.

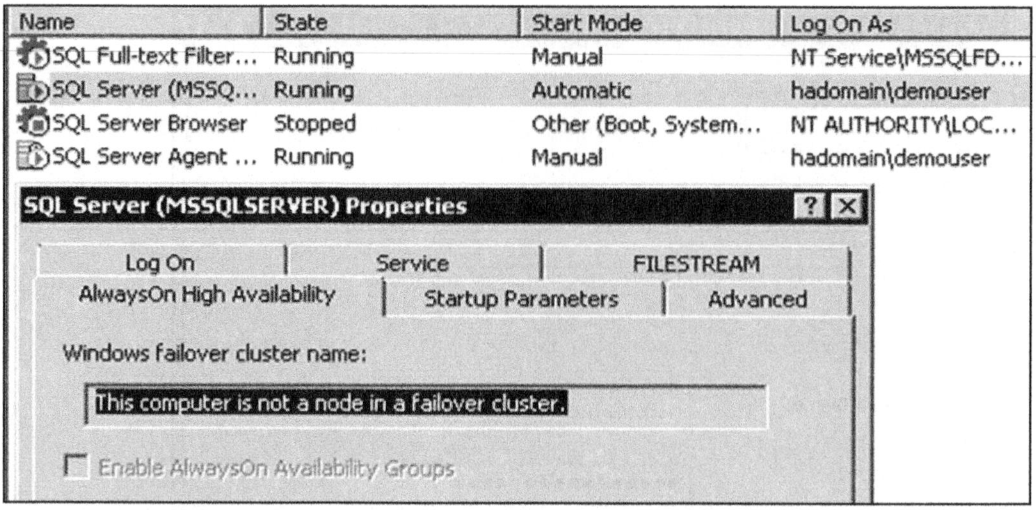

Name	State	Start Mode	Log On As
SQL Full-text Filter...	Running	Manual	NT Service\MSSQLFD...
SQL Server (MSSQ...	Running	Automatic	hadomain\demouser
SQL Server Browser	Stopped	Other (Boot, System...	NT AUTHORITY\LOC...
SQL Server Agent ...	Running	Manual	hadomain\demouser

SQL Server (MSSQLSERVER) Properties ? X

| Log On | | Service | | FILESTREAM |
| AlwaysOn High Availability | | Startup Parameters | | Advanced |

Windows failover cluster name:

This computer is not a node in a failover cluster.

☐ Enable AlwaysOn Availability Groups

Figure 7.13 Trying to enable option without Windows Cluster creation.

READER NOTE: *To initialize the SQL Server Configuration Manager, we can also use the shortcut:* **Start** > **Run** > **SQLServerManager11.msc**

PowerShell Script

Since this step is not a Windows Server operation but a property enabled on the SQL Server service, we need to run this command from the SQL Server's PowerShell console. This can be initialized by calling SQLPS from the command prompt as shown in Figure 7.14. Running SQLPS switches the context to "PS SQLSERVER:\>" allowing us to run the PowerShell command seen in Figure 7.14.

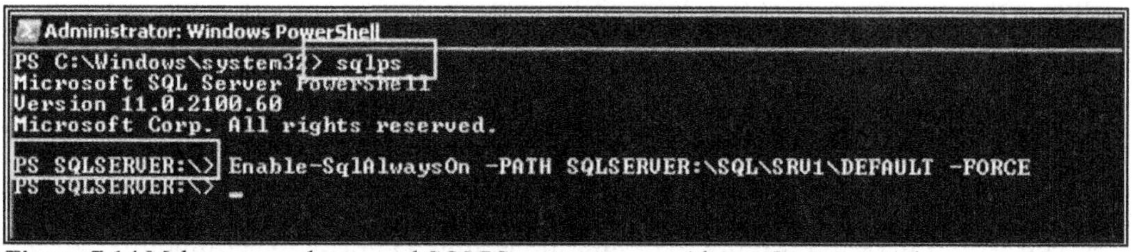

```
Administrator: Windows PowerShell
PS C:\Windows\system32> sqlps
Microsoft SQL Server PowerShell
Version 11.0.2100.60
Microsoft Corp. All rights reserved.

PS SQLSERVER:\> Enable-SqlAlwaysOn -PATH SQLSERVER:\SQL\SRV1\DEFAULT -FORCE
PS SQLSERVER:\>
```

Figure 7.14 Make sure we have used SQLPS prompt to run AlwaysOn command.

```
Enable-SqlAlwaysOn -PATH SQLSERVER:\SQL\SRV1\DEFAULT -FORCE
```

This single command would also take care of restarting the SQL Service after the settings have changed. This step needs to be repeated for the SQL Service on all the nodes in the cluster which will be part of the AlwaysOn Availability Group. The advantage of scripting is the ability to deploy from a single machine. This means we would not need to log in and enable this feature using the Configuration

Manager on each of the nodes. The following command enables the AlwaysOn Availability Group on all the SQL Server nodes from a single location (provided the permissions exist).

```
foreach($Node in "SRV1","SRV2","SRV3","SRV4")
{
"Enabling AlwaysOn Availability Groups for" +
replica.tostring()
Enable-SqlAlwaysOn -PATH SQLSERVER:\SQL\$Node\DEFAULT -FORCE
}
```

READER NOTE: *The DEFAULT keyword at the end refers to default instance of SQL Server.*

Step 4: Create the AlwaysOn Availability Group

For any building to be built, we need to have a proper foundation in place before constructing it. Having a strong foundation is not optional as the building will collapse if the foundation is too weak. Along the same lines our current setup needs a good foundation. This foundation is the SQL Service that has AlwaysOn enabled. Our group will have two databases called MyNorthwind and MyAdventureWorks. Both of these databases will participate in the AlwaysOn Availability Group.

READER NOTE: *The MyAdventureWorks database was the* AdventureWorks2012 database *downloaded from CodePlex as attached a MyAdventureWorks. All the other databases we created them using the UI in Management Studio.*

Figure 7.15 MyNorthwind and MyAdventureWorks databases.

Understanding Prerequisites

There are two prerequisites we need to have in our awareness. In our setup we have made sure these are properly addressed:

- The databases must be in the full recovery model.
- The full recovery model does not fully kick in until we run our first backup. So at a minimum, one full backup must have been done on the databases to initialize the log backup chain.

It is important to know that if a database is in the full recovery model and we have not taken a full backup yet, this database would act as if it were in a simple recovery model. In this case, the AlwaysOn Availability Group UI would block us from selecting the database. The option would be greyed out as shown in Figure 7.16. We can see the database names and what indicates the problem listed in message to the right.

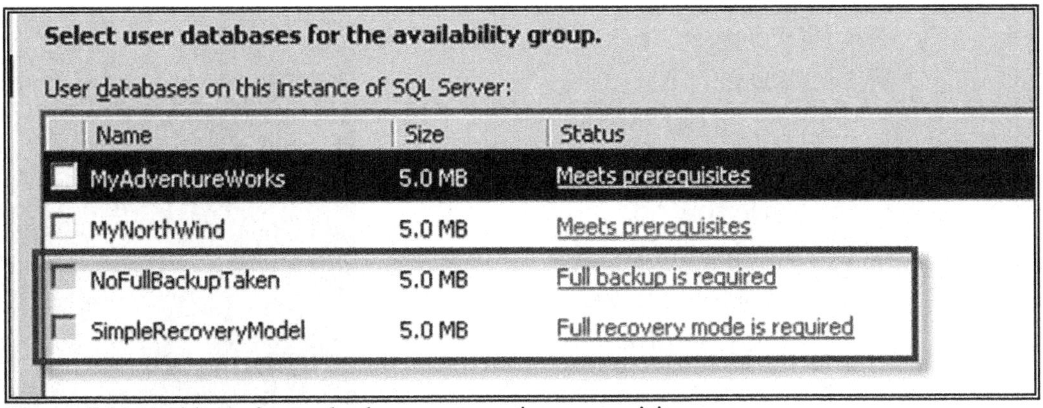

Select user databases for the availability group.

User databases on this instance of SQL Server:

Name	Size	Status
MyAdventureWorks	5.0 MB	Meets prerequisites
MyNorthWind	5.0 MB	Meets prerequisites
NoFullBackupTaken	5.0 MB	Full backup is required
SimpleRecoveryModel	5.0 MB	Full recovery mode is required

Figure 7.16 Unable to choose databases not meeting prerequisites

We will get to see this screen later during the steps of the "Availability Group Wizard" topic which is next.

Initializing the Availability Group Wizard from SSMS

The easiest way to configure an AlwaysOn Availability Group is with SQL Server Management Studio (SSMS). In SSMS, connect to what will become the primary replica (we will use SRV1). On SRV1 we need to make sure the databases exist. In **Object Explorer** get to the **AlwaysOn High Availability** folder. Inside this folder, select the **Availability Groups** folder and right-click it to choose the **New Availability Group Wizard**.

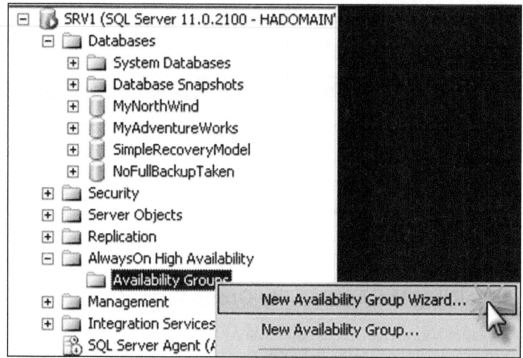

Figure 7.17 Wizard to create new Availability Group.

This step will initialize the New Availability Group Wizard. Click **Next** to get past the Welcome screen and we will see the window shown in Figure 7.18 called Specify Availability Group Name. This name is for manageability purposes only and this will be shown in the Failover Cluster Manager as well. We have chosen the name of **MyAvailabilityGroup** as we are going to select the databases with the prefixes of "My".

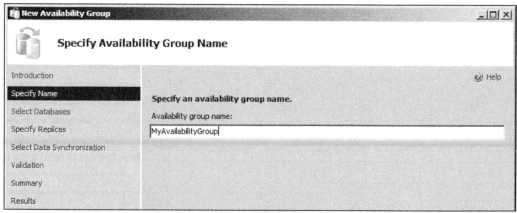

Figure 7.18 Define name of Availability Group.

Moving forward in the wizard by using the **Next** button presents us with a list of databases. For our configuration we have selected databases with the "My" prefix to form what will be part of our group (Figure 7.19).

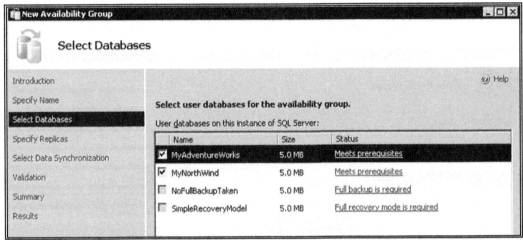

Figure 7.19 Choose database(s) to be a part of Availability Group.

The selection in Figure 7.19 ensures that both the databases (MyAdventureWorks and MyNorthwind) are seen as a single logical unit connected by the Availability Group.

This logical unit means these two databases will stay together in the event of any failure. At this point we want to mention that one database cannot be part of two Availability Groups. In other words if the MyNorthwind database is assigned to the MyAvailabilityGroup then MyNorthwind can't be part of another Availability Group.

Options for Replica

This is an interesting section because all the theory of automatic failover settings and readable secondary replicas are configured here. After we have selected all the databases; we need to specify the various options for the replicas. We can add one or more (up to four) secondary replicas (Figure 7.20). We can add more replicas later if we miss them in this step. Step 5 will do this optional step of adding a replica after the group is already set up. The **Replicas** tab gives us the following option:

- **Automatic failover** (checkbox): Can be configured up to a maximum of two SQL Server machines. This is done by selecting this checkbox.

- **Synchronous Commit** (checkbox): We can have up to a maximum of two synchronous secondary servers. Including the primary, this is three and the option has to be checked.

- **Readable Secondary** (dropdown): This option will be discussed in more detail in Chapter 8.

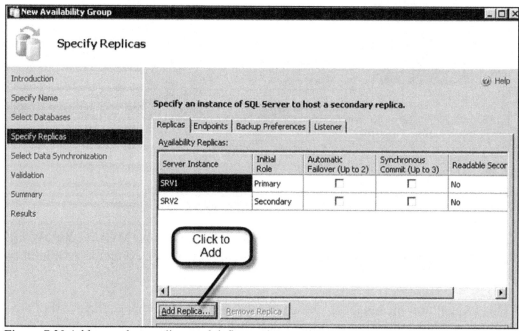

Figure 7.20 Add secondary replicas and define various options.

In our environment, we want two secondary replicas (screenshot shows one, SRV2) and we will add SRV3 using the **Add Replica** button seen at the bottom of Figure 7.20.

Let's say on SRV3 we did not enable the AlwaysOn Availability Group for the SQL Service (Step 3). Now when we try to add it to the Availability Group using the wizard, we will get the error seen in Figure 7.21. This error message says "AlwaysOn feature is not enabled on SQL Server instance 'SRV3.'"

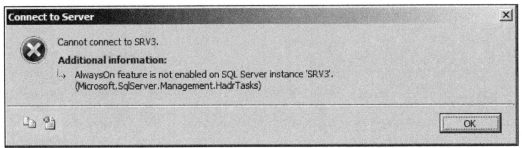

Figure 7.21 Error while adding Availability Group replica when AlwaysOn has not been enabled on the replica.

If we try to add SRV3 using an ALTER AVAILABILITY GROUP ... JOIN command on the secondary replica, we will get the following error:

```
Messages
Msg 35221, Level 16, State 1, Line 3
Could not process the operation. AlwaysOn Availability Groups replica manager
is disabled on this instance of SQL Server. Enable AlwaysOn Availability
Groups, by using the SQL Server Configuration Manager. Then, restart the SQL
Server service, and retry the currently operation. For information about how
to enable and disable AlwaysOn Availability Groups, see SQL Server Books
Online.
```

Configuring Endpoints

The concept of endpoints was introduced with the release of SQL Server 2005. Endpoints can be defined as the point of entry into a SQL Server. Endpoints contain a mode and a port of communication to SQL Server. In the Availability Groups configuration the primary needs to talk to each replica. This is defined in the second tab called **Endpoints**.

In Figure 7.22 we can see the endpoints used by various instances of SQL Server selected in the **Endpoints** tab. The endpoint using port 5022 is available and the wizard will set this up for us. If our team needs to use a different endpoint configuration we can specify that here. Once this is done and the Availability Group is set up we cannot change these endpoint settings for these servers.

Specify an instance of SQL Server to host a secondary replica.

Replicas Endpoints | Backup Preferences | Listener |

Endpoint values:

Server Name	Endpoint URL	Port Number	Endpoint Name	Encrypt Data	SQL Server Service Account
SRV1	TCP://SRV1.hadomain.com:5022	5022	Hadr_endpoint	☑	HADOMAIN\demouser
SRV2	TCP://SRV2.hadomain.com:5022	5022	Hadr_endpoint	☑	hadomain\demouser
SRV3	TCP://SRV3.hadomain.com:5022	5022	Hadr_endpoint	☑	hadomain\demouser

Figure 7.22 View/create new endpoint definition.

Please note that SQL Server AlwaysOn and Database Mirroring use the same endpoint. Therefore if we have Database Mirroring configured already on a server, AlwaysOn will reuse that same endpoint.

We are going to skip the explanation for the Backup Preferences tab in Figure 7.23 since it was discussed earlier in Chapter 6.

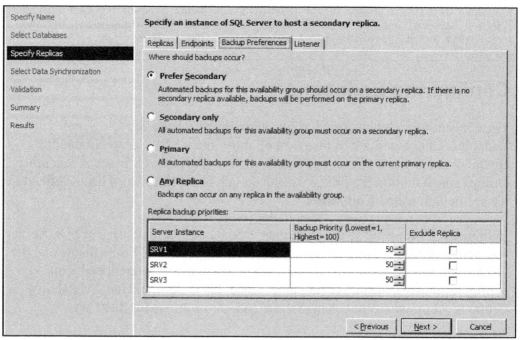

Figure 7.23 Backup Preferences.

Configuring the Listener

The last tab is called Listener which allows us to create a new virtual network name (VNN). The clients will connect to the Listener name on the network. The Listener will connect the clients to the working primary replica flawlessly. This means the clients will not need to worry about who is the current owner (or current primary server) of the Availability Group.

Think of this Listener as a SQL Server virtual name in a SQL Server Clustering scenario. In this the client always connects to a Virtual Server Name regardless of who has the primary role. In the Windows Clustering world this virtual name is called the Client Access Point. In AlwaysOn Availability Group context, it is called the Listener.

As we can see in Figure 7.24, the first option is called **Do not create an Availability Group Listener now**. If that is chosen as a step in the wizard then the Listener can be added later (see step 6 at the end of this chapter "Adding a Listener"). We want to create the Listener now. The Listener must have its own address and name. To do this we have prepopulated this screen with some reasonable values (Figure 7.24).

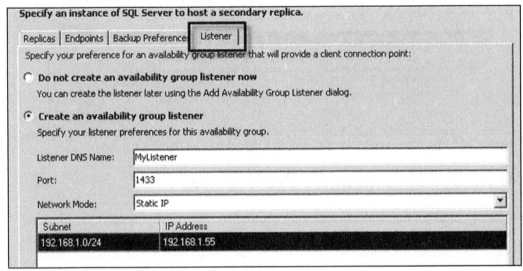

Figure 7.24 Define virtual network name (Listener).

Let's assume a scenario where were we selected to not create the Listener. In this case the wizard would provide us a warning once we move to the Validation page (Figure 7.25).

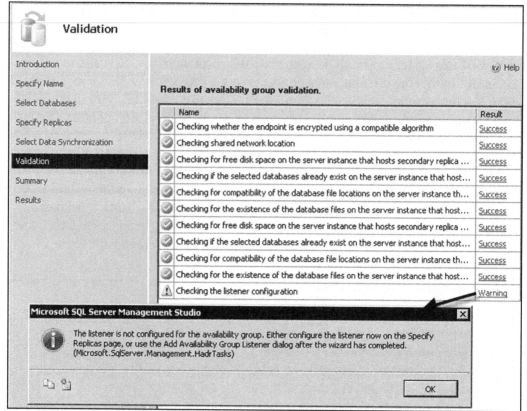

Figure 7.25 The Wizard gives a warning if the Listener configuration is not used.

Data Synchronization Preference

After we add all the replicas and the required options in that screen, by clicking **Next** we are presented with the Select Initial Data Synchronization page. In this page we can choose between various data synchronization methods available. What does this mean?

Currently the databases in our group are up to date on SRV1 and they don't even exist yet on SRV2 or SRV3. Somehow we need to get these two databases over to them. We can send these databases over the network or (if they are too big) do an actual backup and restore from physical media. We get to choose how this propagation will be done.

Here is a refresher from other HA options that apply to what we are doing now. In a Database Mirroring configuration there is no option to perform backups of a database during the configuration. The only option for Mirroring is to perform a manual backup on the principal server and restore with NORECVOERY on a mirror server before configuring. This means we need to do this before we start the configuration wizard to set up Database Mirroring. Only after we did this can we start the wizard for setting up a Mirroring configuration.

The Log Shipping wizard was a bit better since it allowed us to perform a backup and restore operation during the setup. SRV1 is going to back up to a shared location and the other servers will retrieve this backup and perform a restore.

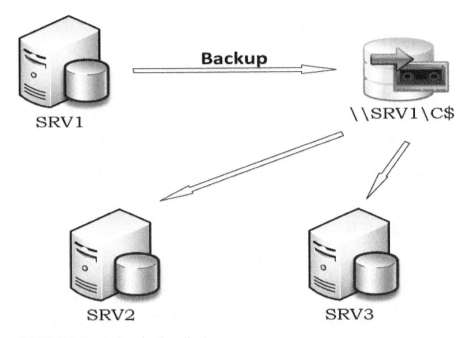

Figure 7.26 Full data synchronization diagram.

In the AlwaysOn configuration wizard we do have the flexibility to do the same convenient backup and restore over the network. As shown in Figure 7.27, we have three options to choose from. Let's talk about each of these options.

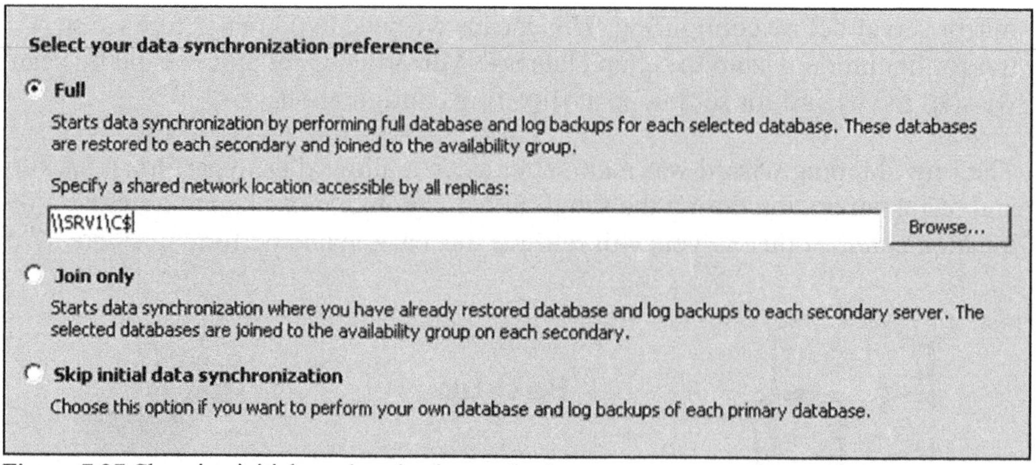

Select your data synchronization preference.

⊙ **Full**

Starts data synchronization by performing full database and log backups for each selected database. These databases are restored to each secondary and joined to the availability group.

Specify a shared network location accessible by all replicas:

| \\SRV1\C$ | Browse... |

○ **Join only**

Starts data synchronization where you have already restored database and log backups to each secondary server. The selected databases are joined to the availability group on each secondary.

○ **Skip initial data synchronization**

Choose this option if you want to perform your own database and log backups of each primary database.

Figure 7.27 Choosing initial synchronization method.

Synchronization method - Full

Full is basically allowing the wizard to do all the work and will get SRV2 and SRV3 to have all the databases in the Availability Group from SRV1.

Synchronization method – Join only

This option is used if we have already performed the backup/restore operation on the secondary replicas using physical media. When doing this step, please ensure that the database is restored in the no recovery state. This means it should be in a Restoring state in the Object Explorer of SQL Server Management Studio.

Synchronization method – Skip Initial Data Synchronization

The last option is used if we want to do a backup and restore operation later. In this case the wizard would enable the endpoint, provide the connect permission on the endpoint to the service account, start the XEvent Health Session, and create the Availability Group. We will discuss the AlwaysOn Health Session more in Chapter 11.

Synchronization method facts

While we are getting ready to select the synchronization methods, here are a few important points to remember about Data Synchronization:

- The wizard takes the full backup and then the transaction log backup of all the databases in the group.

- If we are dealing with large databases then it might be best to use the Join only option because the wizard would take time to complete and this may not be acceptable by the business to have large loads on the network traffic.

- Remember to secure the backup location because any unauthorized person who may have access to the shared location would have backups of the database. This can become a compliance issue.

- The .mdf, .ndf, and .ldf files for our database must be in the same location for all servers. If we are saving our MyNorthwind to the H:\SQL folder on SRV1 then there must be an H:\SQL folder on SRV2 and SRV3. Make sure the folder structure is in place before we do the synchronization. If the database file directory doesn't exist on the secondary server(s) then the wizard can't be used to perform a full synchronization.

Validation

After clicking **Next**, the Validation screen would perform a few important checks. The wizard checks for free disk space, database file locations, and database existence on all secondary replicas.

These checks are performed so the final screen (Summary screen) does not encounter errors during the backup or restore operations.

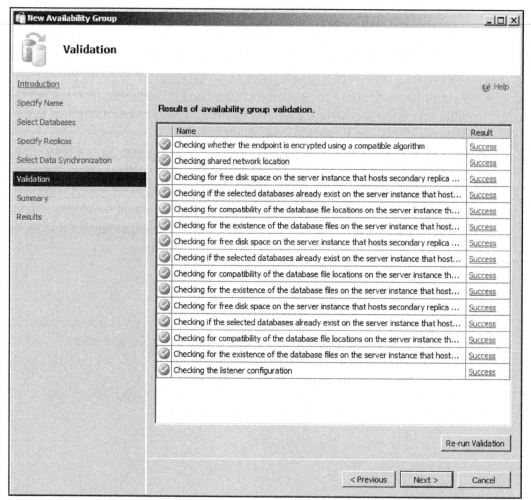

Figure 7.28 validation screen.

This is just a validation screen and there is no input required by us at this time. If everything is ready we can move ahead in the wizard.

The Summary Screen

The last step in this wizard is the summary page. This page gives us an opportunity to review all the details entered so far in the wizard. From here we can finish the setup of the Availability Group or have a script generated. We are going to click **Finish** but also walk through what happens when we generate the script.

SQL Script

There is an interesting button at the bottom of the Validation page called Script. We would highly suggest readers to click on this button and have a look at the SQL script that is generated. Using this script, we can verify the steps that would happen when we click Finish. If we want to automate the deployment steps for a future use, then this script option can be a very useful step.

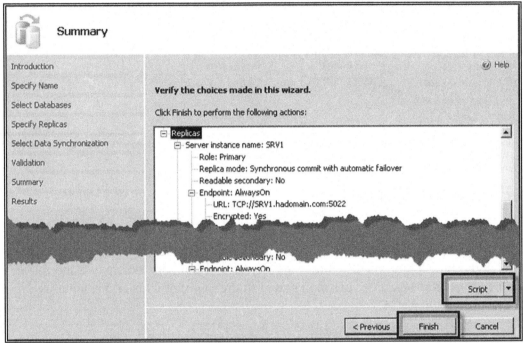

Figure 7.29 Summary screen in wizard to review all settings.

Let's assume the script is generated from our previous step. The script generated from the wizard must be run in SQLCMD mode in SQL Server Management Studio. The SQLCMD mode allows us an easy way to connect to multiple servers using the same query window and is very convenient too. In the script, we will notice the ":connect" keyword as highlighted in Figure 7.30 to connect to different SQL instances. To execute this script in SSMS we must enable SQLCMD mode. Enable this from the **Query** menu > and select **SQLCMD** mode.

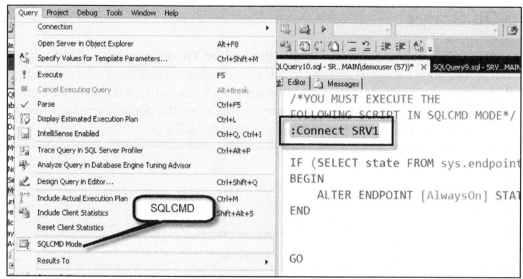

Figure 7.30 SQLCMD mode in Management Studio gives a query window the power to connect to multiple instances.

Finish the Wizard

If we had opted to click the Finish button, the wizard would run the various T-SQL queries on all replicas and would create the Availability Group. We will click the Finish button. Assuming this step ran without any errors, we should be able to see new resources getting created in the Failover Cluster Manager as shown in Figure 7.31.

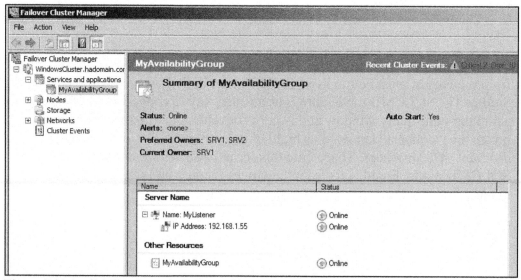

Figure 7.31 Availability Group in Failover Cluster Manager.

If we try to correlate with the various options provided in the wizards interface then it is easy to remember that MyAvailabilityGroup is the name of the resource and the name of the group as well. These were created for us by the wizard and it would make sense to keep the same name. MyListener was created as the network name resource in the cluster with the dependency using the IP address defined earlier in the wizard.

As we mentioned earlier, the cluster is tightly coupled with the Availability Group now. SQL Server does not store the name but stores the resource and group GUID to identify the resource. Figure 7.32 shows the SSMS query result along with the registry editor to show the correlation between them.

For reference the REGEDIT path for the cluster groups is:
HKEY_LOCAL_MACHINE\Cluster\Groups\<GUID>.

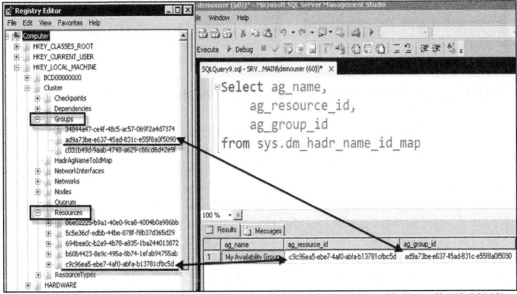

Figure 7.32 Mapping of Availability Group id to cluster resources/group id. (Regedit VS SSMS)

Creating the Group without the Wizard

For advanced users who do not want to use the wizard, we always have an option to directly right-click on the AlwaysOn **Availability Group** node in SQL Server Management Studio and choose the **New Availability Group** option as shown in Figure 7.33. It makes sense to prefer the use of the wizard as it helps us with a number of validation checks and gives us a chance to correct them. It also allows us to choose our initial data synchronization methods.

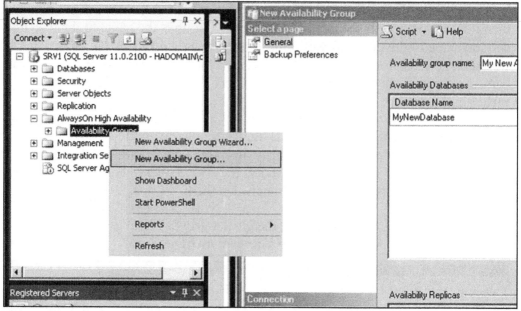

Figure 7.33 Creating AlwaysOn Availability Group without the wizard.

Data Synchronization with Named Instances

Let's assume that we have a named instance on two nodes called Bogota and Tampa. Folder structure of the named SQL instances would be *%Program Files%\ Microsoft SQL Server\MSSQL11.Bogota\MSSQL\DATA* on our first node and *%Program Files%\Microsoft SQL Server\MSSQL11.Tampa\MSSQL\DATA* on the other node. Creating the AG using the wizard would mean that SQL Server we created the group on will look for exactly the same folder structure and drive letters on the other nodes too. If they are not present, this will result in an error stopping us from moving forward in the wizard. To mimic this scenario, we have created a database called "InvalidLocationOnsecondary" on the *C:\FolderOnprimary* location on our primary server. We ran the wizard for this database with the more automated Full data synchronization option between the nodes. Since the database folder location does not exist on the secondary, the error message which we would receive is seen in Figure 7.34.

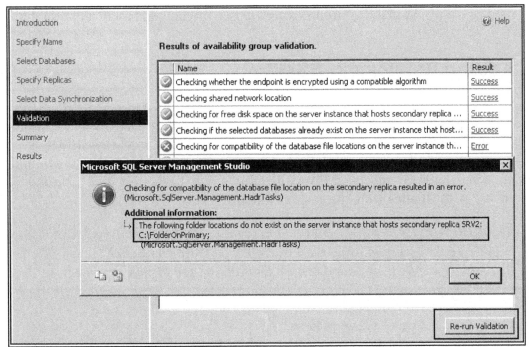

Figure 7.34 Error message if database location of primary replica doesn't exist on secondary replica.

The workaround for the error in Figure 7.34 is to simply perform the backup and restore activities manually. We can fix this by creating the same folder on the same drive letter on secondary.

The best part of this wizard is that if the check fails we can rectify it immediately and there is no need to cancel the wizard. There is a button called "Re-run Validation" which can be used to run the checks again and move forward rather than cancelling and starting the wizard all over again.

Availability Group Changes

Using the wizard, we have added three nodes to the Availability Group along with the Listener configuration. In the next section, we will add one more secondary replica using the wizard.

Step 5: Adding a secondary replica to an Existing Group

We can add more replicas to an Availability Group either using the wizard or entering the details in the properties window of the Availability Group. We will modify the MyAvailabilityGroup created in our previous steps and add SRV4 to it.

Adding Replicas in SSMS

We need to connect to the primary replica in SQL Server Management Studio in order to add a secondary replica. In our example we will connect to SRV1. Inside the Object Explorer of SSMS on the primary node, go to the **AlwaysOn High Availability** folder and expand the **Availability Group** folder. Here we will find our Availability Group called MyAvailabilityGroup. Right-click this node and choose **Add Replica** from the context window.

READER NOTE: The Properties option in the same right-click menu can be used to add a replica without using the wizard. We can also right-click on the **Availability Replicas** *node and choose the same option of* **Add Replica***.*

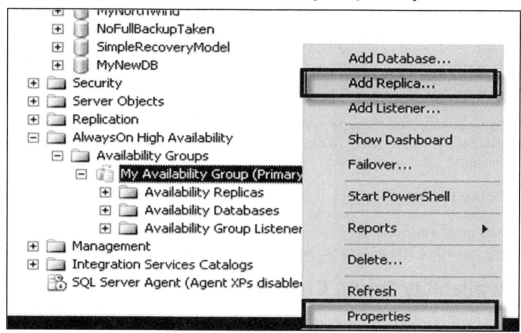

Figure 7.35 Various ways to add secondary replicas.

After the introduction screen, we see the Connect to Replicas dialog. Since we are a domain admin we can choose the **Connect All** button to use the same account to connect to all secondary replicas.

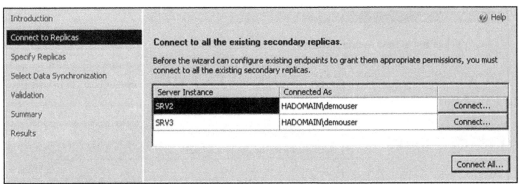

Figure 7.36 We can provide different accounts to connect to secondary replicas.

Once the replicas get connected, the next task is to specify the new replica which we want to add along with its settings. In Figure 7.37, we have added a member server named SRV4 and selected it as a readable secondary. This is exactly the same screen as the one we used during the creation of a new Availability Group.

Specify an instance of SQL Server to host a secondary replica.

Replicas | Endpoints | Backup Preferences

Availability Replicas:

Server Instance	Initial Role	Automatic Failover (Up to 2)	Synchronous Commit (Up to 3)	Readable Secondary	
SRV1	Primary	☑	☑	No	▾
SRV2	Secondary	☑	☑	Yes	▾
SRV3	Secondary	☐	☑	Read-intent only	▾
SRV4	Secondary	☐	☐	Yes	▾

Figure 7.37 Add Replica and choose settings.

The tabs used in this wizard are the same ones we had in the Create Availability Group wizard. The main difference in this wizard is that it allows us to modify or add the settings for a new replica while the old settings (for SRV1, SRV2, and SRV3) are greyed out. Also the Listener tab is not available in this wizard. Click **Next**.

READER NOTE: *To change the setting of existing replicas get the Availability Group properties, don't use this wizard.*

The next screen is the Select Initial Data Synchronization (Figure 7.38). Again we will choose the **Full** option.

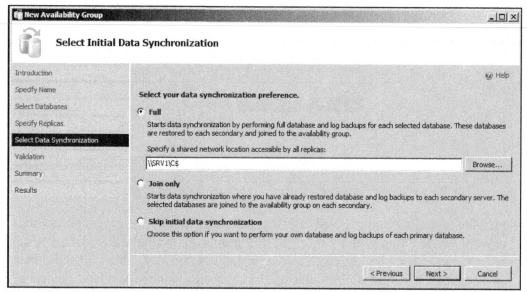

Figure 7.38 Use the same Data Synchronization as the original group.

The Validation screen is the same as before. Once the wizard finishes, we can verify that we have successfully created an Availability Group with four replicas (one primary replica and three secondary replicas) by using Management Studio.

Figure 7.39 and Figure 7.40 shows the various states on the primary and secondary servers. On the primary server the databases will be in a synchronized state. The synchronized status will be seen on all Synchronous secondary replicas. In our setup, SRV2 and SRV3 will show Synchronized next to their database name in Object Explorer.

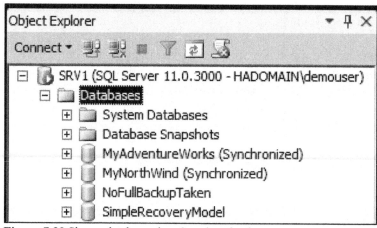

Figure 7.39 Shows databases in a Synchronized state.

For the asynchronous replicas the status for the database will show as Synchronizing. In our setup, this represents SRV4 in Figure 7.40.

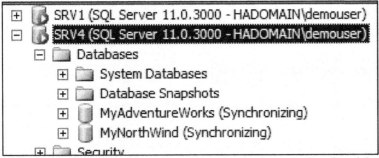

Figure 7.40 Asynchronous replicas show the databases as Synchronizing.

Connecting to Secondary Replicas

We set SRV4 to be a readable secondary replica. This means we can run reports from this server. In case we try to connect to a secondary where the readable flag is set to No, we would get the following error when trying to connect to the MyNorthwind database:

```
Messages
Msg 976, Level 14, State 1, Line 1
The target database, 'MyNorthwind', is participating in an Availability Group
and is currently not accessible for queries. Either data movement is
suspended or the availability replica is not enabled for read access. To
allow readonly access to this and other databases in the Availability Group,
enable read access to one or more secondary availability replicas in the
group. For more information, see the ALTER AVAILABILITY GROUP statement in
SQL Server Books Online.
```

Step 6: Adding a Listener (Only if not done in Step 4)

An Availability Group can have only one Listener. The last step only needs to be done if we did not configured the Listener using the wizard. To add a Listener using SQL Server Management Studio, we can right-click on the Availability Group and choose **Add Listener** as shown in Figure 7.41.

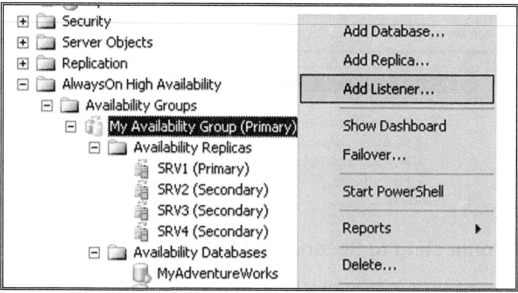

Figure 7.41 Add Listener for Availability Group.

Please note that this can only be done from the primary replica. Attempting this on a secondary replica would cause the following error message:

```
Messages
Msg 41140, Level 16, State 48, Line 1
Availability Group 'MyAvailabilityGroup' cannot process the ALTER
AVAILABILITY GROUP command, because the local availability replica is not the
primary replica. Connect to the server instance that is currently hosting the
primary replica of this Availability Group, and rerun the command.
```

Once the screen opens up we need to provide a Listener name, port number, and IP address as shown in Figure 7.42.

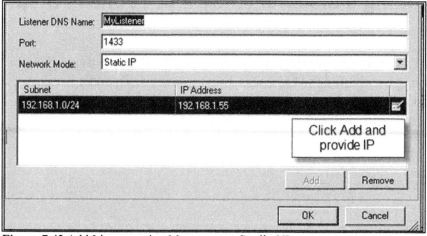

Figure 7.42 Add Listener using Management Studio UI.

We can add a Listener using the T-SQL equivalent code with the name, port, and IP address for the Listener. The following example shows the T-SQL code to add this Listener:

```
USE [master]
GO
ALTER AVAILABILITY GROUP [MyAvailabilityGroup]
ADD LISTENER N'MyListener' (
WITH IP
((N'192.168.1.55', N'255.255.255.0'))
, PORT=1433);
GO
```

Once the Listener is created with T-SQL code or the SSMS wizard, we should be able to see it in the Windows Server Failover Cluster Manager.

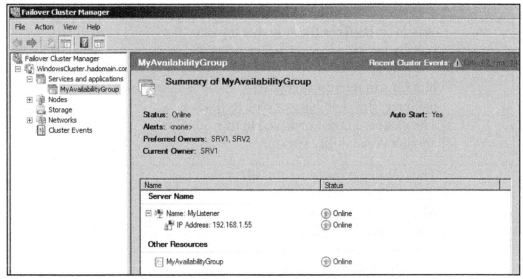

Figure 7.43 See the Listener using Windows Server Failover Cluster Manager.

Summary

In this chapter we created an Availability Group in four logical steps. In two more steps as we wrap up the chapter with adding a secondary replica and adding a listener. Once done it might be handy to have a checklist. Here is a quick checklist which we can follow to make sure we would not face any error while setting up the AlwaysOn Availability Group.

Step #	Item to verify	Status
1.	Minimum Service Pack level for the Windows 2008 Operating System is SP2, for Windows 2008 R2 it is SP1 and for Windows Server 2012 RTM (and above) no service pack is needed.	☐
2.	All nodes have Windows clustering feature installed and Windows Cluster is configured	☐
3.	All SQL instances should be SQL 2012 Enterprise Edition and have the same collation.	☐
4.	All SQL instances have 32 bit SQL on 32 bit operating system or 64 bit SQL on 64 bit system.	☐
5.	All nodes are part of the same domain and none of them is a domain controller.	☐
6.	Windows hotfixes listed in this link are installed. http://msdn.microsoft.com/en-us/library/ff878487.aspx#WinHotfixes	☐
7.	The database is not involved in mirroring or another Availability Group.	☐
8.	The following query returns all zeros: **SELECT is_read_only 'ReadOnly_0_1',** **user_access 'MultiUser_0_1',** **is_auto_close_on 'Auto_Close_0_1',** **CASE recovery_model** **WHEN 1 THEN 0** **ELSE 1** **END AS 'Recovery_model_0_1'** **FROM sys.databases** **WHERE name = '***Availability Database Name Here***'**	☐
9.	At least one full backup has been taken.	☐

Step #	Item to verify	Status
10.	Make sure that ports are accessible. The best test would be to try to use telnet command in all directions.	☐
11.	Make sure that the AlwaysOn feature is enabled in the SQL Server Configuration Manager.	☐

Table 7.1 AlwaysOn setup checklist.

Points to Ponder – Deploying AlwaysOn Availability Groups

1. The deployment and modification of a SQL Server AlwaysOn Availability Group can be divided into logical steps:
   1. Add the Failover Clustering feature in Windows to each server.
   2. Create a Windows Failover Cluster.
   3. Enable the AlwaysOn Availability Group feature to each SQL Server.
   4. Create the Availability Group.

2. The primary requirement to create an Availability Group is to have the servers that are hosting the SQL Server instances be a part of the same Windows Server Failover Cluster and in the same domain.

3. The AlwaysOn Availability Group feature can be enabled in the SQL Server service properties dialog from the SQL Server Configuration Manager or from PowerShell.

4. The databases should be in the full recovery model to participate in an Availability Group.

5. In order to select a database for an Availability Group there must be a minimum of one full backup already done on that database.

6. Automatic failover can be configured for up to a maximum of two SQL Server instances.

7. We can have up to a maximum of two synchronous secondary replicas plus one primary. This means we can have three synchronous replicas including the primary.

8. The Listener allows us to create a new virtual network name (VNN). This is the name which can be used by the clients to connect to the current primary replica automatically.

9. The full synchronization method takes a full backup and then the transaction log backup of the databases from the primary replica and it restores them on all of the secondary replicas.

10. If a backup has already been restored on a secondary replica, then we need to use the Join only option in the AlwaysOn Availability Group Wizard.

11. There can be only one port used for an AlwaysOn Availability Group and Database Mirroring. This is known as an endpoint.

12. We can define only one Listener per Availability Group.

13. Settings for the secondary replica, the Listener, and others can be changed later using PowerShell, Management Studio UI, or T-SQL.

Review Quiz - Chapter Seven

1.) Which one below doesn't require a shared storage in an HA and a DR Solution?

O a. Availability Group
O b. Multi-site Failover Cluster Instance
O c. Failover Cluster Instance for Local HA and Availability Group for DR

2.) What quorum mode is recommended if there are an even number of nodes in a cluster across data centers (multi-site clustering)?

O a. Node majority
O b. Node and file share majority
O c. Disk only

3.) How many total availability replicas can we have in an Availability Group?

O a. 2
O b. 3
O c. 4
O d. 5

4.) We use the Availability Group Listener to connect to the primary replica in an AlwaysOn Availability Group?

O a. True
O b. False

5.) Which of the following descriptions of an Availability Group in an HA and a DR solution is NOT true?

O a. Can use contained database to failover login info.
O b. Can combine multiple databases in one Availability Group.
O c. Can do read workloads from DR site.
O d. Can provide Instance Level protection.

6.) Which of the following answers are not prerequisites for an availability database?

- ☐ a. Must be in full Recovery Model.
- ☐ b. Must be a contained database.
- ☐ c. Must be a part of Database Mirroring.
- ☐ d. Must be a part of AlwaysOn FCI.

Answer Key

1.) Only AlwaysOn Availability Group doesn't require a shared storage. This makes (b) Multi-site Failover Cluster Instance and (c) Failover Cluster Instance for Local HA and Availability Group for DR wrong. Option (a) Availability Group is the correct answer.

2.) The options (a) Node majority and (c) Disk Only are both wrong. Since (b) is not one of them, it is the correct answer.

3.) We can have up to 5 replicas in an Availability Group, with 1 primary replica and up to 4 secondary replicas. Hence the correct answer is (d) 5. While answers (a) 2, (b) 3, (c) 4 are wrong answers.

4.) The virtual network name (VNN) configured via Listener screen can be used by clients to connect to proper server. The correct answer is (a) True. Option (b) False is wrong.

5.) SQL Server AlwaysOn Availability Group cannot give Instance Level protection. Answer (d) is NOT true for AlwaysOn Availability Group which makes it the correct answer. All other options (a), (b), and (c) are wrong.

6.) Full recovery model is a prerequisite and therefore option (a) Must be in full recovery model, is the wrong answer. All other options are not a prerequisite and therefore options (b) Must be a contained database, (c) Must be a part of Database Mirroring and (d) Must be a part of AlwaysOn FCI are the correct answers.

[NOTES]

Chapter 8. Features of AlwaysOn Availability Groups

At the end of the year, there is always a shopping spree because of the holiday season. The time is very compressed with Thanksgiving, Christmas, and the New Year all in a span of less than two months. This is also the season when manufactures give huge discounts to entice us into buying their products. We have a tendency to wait for a sale before we buy something big (like a vehicle).

When the investment is big, we look over our choices more carefully. Before we even started our buying process we know the basic requirements needed from the vehicle we are going to buy. These requirements are a high priority like the gas mileage of the vehicle, or the number of seats needed to carry the family. These major requirements narrow our choices down to a few models. From these few models we need to narrow our search even more. At this stage we will look over some cool features that each of the models has to offer before we make the final choice. Hence our final decision is made based on a combination of all the high priority requirements and a few nice-to-have features.

In the previous chapter, we discussed the basic features while deploying an AlwaysOn Availability Group. In this chapter, we will discuss a few additional features and their implementation.

Client Connectivity to the Group

Have you ever had a chance to drive through the Pacific Coast Highway from San Francisco to Los Angeles? It is a breathtaking drive along the coast with a number of paradise vista points. To reach our destination from point-A to point-B we need directions or assistance. Most highways have road signs giving us the location as we travel along. If we did our homework we would ideally use Google or Bing maps for general directions. Even though we have the general directions in hand a GPS can double check our progress. In the SQL Server AlwaysOn Availability Group world with multiple secondary replicas available, connections also need assistance to reach the correct server. In other words this Listener (which is like Google Maps) needs to route the SQL activity to the correct node.

If database traffic will be making updates to one or more of the databases then that traffic needs to be done on the primary replica. At the same time a company report needs read access to some of the data from a database in the group. That readonly report might be directed to a readable secondary instead of the primary.

When connecting to the group we will often specify the Listener name for the server and allow the Listener to direct traffic to the correct node in the group (Figure 8.1). But simply connecting to the Listener might not tell us what type of traffic this will be. The connectivity of the client needs to be routed correctly. We will cover the configuration of Readonly Routing (RoR) for the servers and the clients.

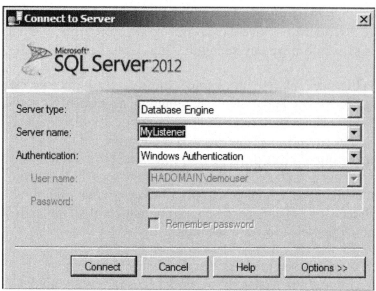

Figure 8.1 The Connect to Server will connect using the Listener VNN.

Configuring Readonly Routing

Just who is the primary replica of our group and which secondary replicas are readable? As explained earlier in this chapter, the client connection behavior depends on the settings defined under the Availability Group replica options for the servers in the group. This value determines if connections can read from the replicas in the secondary role. There are three options for the readable secondary property (Figure 8.2). These properties and their descriptions are listed below for how this server will operate while in the secondary:

- **No**: No connections allowed.

- **Yes**: All connections are allowed and readonly operations work while any writes operations are rejected.

- **Read-intent Only:** Connections which are specifying the *ApplicationIntent=ReadOnly* in the connection string are allowed to connect.

In our example we will make it so all the servers in our group can have a readable copy. To do this we will need to change SRV4 from No to Yes (Figure 8.2).

Server Instance	Role	Availability Mode		Failover Mode		Connections in Primary Role		Readable Secondary	
SRV1	Primary	Synchronous commit	▼	Automatic	▼	Allow all connections	▼	No	▼
SRV2	Secondary	Synchronous commit	▼	Automatic	▼	Allow all connections	▼	Yes	▼
SRV3	Secondary	Synchronous commit	▼	Manual	▼	Allow all connections	▼	Read-intent only	▼
SRV4	Secondary	Asynchronous commit	▼	Manual	▼	Allow all connections	▼	No Yes →	▼

Figure 8.2 Three choices exist for readable secondary.

Since SRV1 is the primary replica it should handle all the write traffic. If an application is connecting to the Listener by name (by using the virtual network name of MyListener) and providing its intent to connect with readonly, then the Listener would reroute the connection to an available secondary replica (like SRV1, SRV2 or SRV3). But which secondary replica should it use as its first choice? Another way to ask this is what does our Routing List look like for the group? This will be based on the Readonly Routing (RoR) list defined for our Availability Group. This is a three-step process summarized in the following list:

- Define the Listener by making the needed secondary replicas readable (which we did after Figure 8.2).
- Configure the RoR connection URL for each server.
- Configure the RoR routing list.

One of the common mistakes made by DBAs is to configure just the first step of making the secondary replicas readable (Figure 8.2). Why do people stop there, thinking they are done? This is because the next steps have no user interface in SQL Server Management Studio. To define the RoR connections and the RoR list we must use code.

Configure Routing URL with T-SQL

In the last chapter we configured the Listener and its IP address (192.168.1.55). Now we will look at configuring the routing URL and the routing list.

We now have three readable secondary replicas but four replicas are readable (the primary is always readable). The current primary (SRV1) could failover which would make SRV2 the primary replica. If this happens then SRV1 would become a secondary replica. How would we connect to SRV1 as a secondary? SRV1 needs to have a secondary role connection ready. For this reason, all nodes will need a Routing URL defined. We will define the secondary role URL for all four servers in our group.

The routing URL of any node is a fully-qualified-domain-name (FQDN) followed by a port number on which the SQL Engine is listening. Since it is in the same format as a Database Mirroring endpoint, the common mistake people make is they give that same port for Database Mirroring. Mirroring is read/write traffic and we want to specify how to connect using readonly traffic.

We will now define the TCP URL for each instance. This will use a tcp:fqdn,port format for connecting to each node. The code to setup the connection for the Readonly Routing URL to SRV1 and SRV2 is shown as follows:

```
ALTER AVAILABILITY GROUP [MyAvailabilityGroup]
MODIFY REPLICA ON 'SRV1'
WITH
(
SECONDARY_ROLE
(
READ_ONLY_ROUTING_URL='TCP://SRV1.hadomain.com:1433'
));

ALTER AVAILABILITY GROUP [MyAvailabilityGroup]
MODIFY REPLICA ON 'SRV2'
WITH
(
SECONDARY_ROLE
(
READ_ONLY_ROUTING_URL='TCP://SRV2.hadomain.com:1433'
));
```

If SRV1 is the primary why did we set up a secondary role connection? So if it does become a secondary it has a secondary connection ready. To make sure that the defined routing URL command was set up properly, we can use Management Studio and connect to it using the "tcp:fqdn,port" format (Figure 8.3).

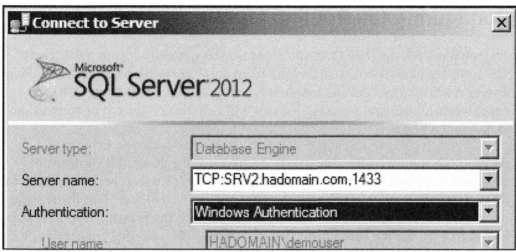

Figure 8.3 Use Management Studio and connect to it using the tcp:fqdn,port format.

Configure Routing URL with PowerShell

In the previous example, we have demonstrated the T-SQL setup code for RoR (Readonly Routing) for SRV1 and SRV2. We need to do this for the remaining replicas (SRV3, and SRV4). If we want to use PowerShell then the "set" cmdlet can be used with the "readonly routing" option.

```
Set-SqlAvailabilityReplica cmdlet
```

```
ReadOnlyRoutingConnectionUrl
```

The following example is the PowerShell equivalent of the T-SQL command:

```
Set-SqlAvailabilityReplica -PATH
"SQLSERVER:\SQL\SRV1\DEFAULT\AvailabilityGroups\MyAvailabili
tyGroup\AvailabilityReplicas\SRV3" -
ReadOnlyRoutingConnectionUrl "TCP://SRV3.hadomain.com:1433"
```

```
Set-SqlAvailabilityReplica -PATH
"SQLSERVER:\SQL\SRV1\DEFAULT\AvailabilityGroups\MyAvailabili
tyGroup\AvailabilityReplicas\SRV4" -
ReadOnlyRoutingConnectionUrl "TCP://SRV4.hadomain.com:1433"
```

In this example, SRV3 and SRV4 are the SQL Server names while DEFAULT specifies the default instance of the SQL Server.

Configuring the Routing List

The routing URLs are like direction signs we see while driving on the freeway. The signs are of no use if we never put them up. A correctly placed sign can help drivers reach the right destination. In the same way when the routing URL is done, we need to create a routing list that will help the movement of connections to the right replica.

SRV1 is the current owner (the primary replica) of the group. SRV1 does not want to be bothered with readonly traffic and must pick the secondary replicas to offload that traffic to. Now that all the TCP URLs are set for each of the replicas we want the make sure readonly traffic does not go to the primary. The next step is to define the list the current primary will redirect the readonly connections to. Let's say SRV1 likes to hand the readonly traffic to SRV3 and SRV4. In our example we will say that SRV3 should get the readonly traffic for the group unless it is not available. In that case then SRV4 should take the traffic. The T-SQL command for defining that routing list is seen in the following code:

```
ALTER AVAILABILITY GROUP [MyAvailabilityGroup]
MODIFY REPLICA ON 'SRV1'
WITH
(
 PRIMARY_ROLE
  (
   READ_ONLY_ROUTING_LIST= ('SRV3','SRV4')
  )
);
```

If a readonly request is coming to SRV1 while in the primary role then that request really needs to be sent to SRV3. In case SRV3 is not available then SRV4 would be the next logical server to receive the connection. We need to understand that this not a SQL Server load balancing solution of sharing read traffic with SRV3 and SRV4. If the first server in the routing list is available (SRV3) then the request would only go to SRV3. In other words it is likely that SRV3 will handle 100% of the readonly traffic and SRV4 will get none.

PowerShell Script

In the following code we are using the same example using a typical PowerShell script to configuring the routing list:

```
Set-SqlAvailabilityReplica -PATH
"SQLSERVER:\SQL\SRV1\DEFAULT\AvailabilityGroups\MyAvailabili
tyGroup\AvailabilityReplicas\SRV1" -ReadOnlyRoutingList
"SRV3", "SRV4"
```

Testing Client Connectivity to an Availability Group

Validation and verification (as a process) is something we do in many of our daily activities. Take the examples of locking our house, writing a check, or adding a new battery into a toy. We check to see that this activity worked by trying the door without a key to see that it is really locked or turning on the toy with the new batteries to make sure we did it right. There are various ways a client can connect to the Listener with its intent to get readonly data from the group. We will show a couple of ways to achieve this readonly intended connection to the Listener. In doing this we will see how it routes a readonly connection to SRV3.

To route readonly connections to a secondary in the routing list, we need to specify that the application intends this connection as readonly. The application needs to do this while making the initial connection to the Listener.

There are often many databases in our Availability Group. In addition to connecting with readonly we also need to provide the default database. This must be a database which is part of the Availability Group. If we miss specifying a database then our readonly connection would end up at the primary replica.

Connecting to the Listener with SSMS

The easiest way to check if we are getting redirected to the appropriate secondary is via the SSMS interface. The login screen of the SQL Server 2012 Management Studio has a "Server name" text box. Instead of specifying one of the server names we will connect to the VNN name of the Listener (named MyListener as seen in Figure 8.4).

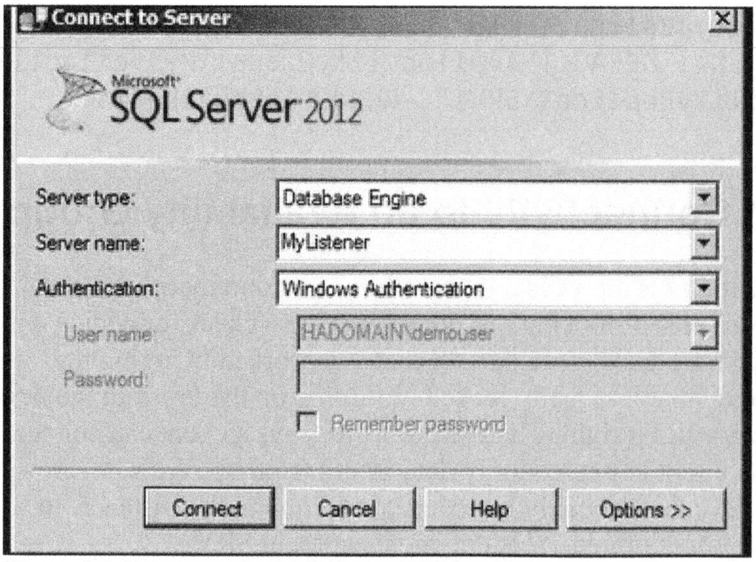

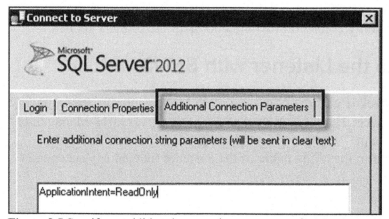

Figure 8.4 Connect to the MyListener VNN and not a server name.

We have more to do before we can connect to the secondary replica. We have not specified this as a readonly intended connection. From here click the **Options>>** button and then the **Additional Connection Parameters** tab. In Figure 8.5, we have specified **ApplicationIntent=ReadOnly** in the **Additional Connection Parameters** panel (Figure 8.5).

Figure 8.5 Specify an additional connection parameter via SQL Server 2012 Management Studio.

Remember that in addition to the readonly connection parameter we need to provide the default database (Figure 8.5). This is done in the Connection Properties tab. If we don't specify ApplicationIntent=ReadOnly then our readonly connection will be made to the primary replica.

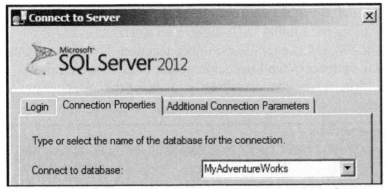

Figure 8.6 Specify the database to connect to for the readonly data.

Once the connection happens we might be curious as to which of the servers the Listener has routed the traffic to. From a query window we can query the function @@SERVERNAME to find which server accepted our connection.

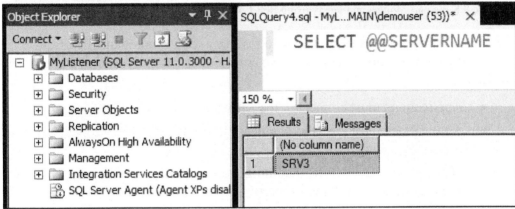

Figure 8.7 Selecting from the @@SERVERNAME global variable will show which server has the connection.

Connecting to the Listener with SQLCMD

There is a new parameter, -K (upper case), that was introduced for the SQLCMD command which can be used to specify a readonly intent connection. The following code is a sample command to specify readonly intent with SQLCMD:

sqlcmd -E -S MyListener –d MyAdventureWorks -K ReadOnly

In this example we are using Windows authentication (-E) connecting to our Listener name (-S MyListener) and giving the additional intent option (-K ReadOnly).

Simple routing logic through the SQLCMD command shows us how we can connect to a secondary using the routing URL logic. You can connect to SRV3 directly but the goal is to let the Listener handle the connection. To effectively use this, applications need to connect to the Listener endpoint or else this routing logic is never utilized. If the server connects directly to any of the instances the redirection is not enforced.

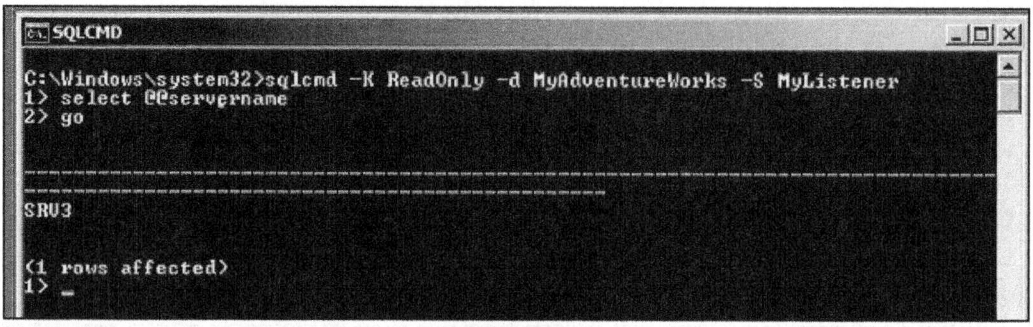

Figure 8.8 We can connect and verify using SQLCMD.

In order for applications to connect to a readonly replica automatically, SQL Server uses a few routing checks before connections reach a readonly node. These include:

- Applications must connect to the Listener endpoint.
- Applications must pass the ApplicationIntent=ReadOnly property in the connection string.
- SQL Server checks if the incoming request is using the Listener endpoint and the connection string property. If this is missing the ApplicationIntent=ReadOnly property then Readonly Routing is not initiated.
- SQL Server identifies if the Data Source (the Database) is part of an Availability Group. If not, Readonly Routing is not initiated.
- If a database is part of an Availability Group, then the Readonly Routing list is checked on the primary node. If the routing list is not set then routing is disabled.
- If the routing list has been set, SQL Server enumerates to check each replica of its URL and availability.
- The first replica which is in the synchronizing or synchronized state and the allow_connections state is set as Read Intent will get the traffic for readonly queries.

- If none of the secondary replicas in the routing list are synchronized or synchronizing then they are not available for readonly queries. In this case the traffic is sent to the primary replica.

- Now the application redirects the queries to the readable secondary replica.

Connection String Parameters related to AlwaysOn (AG and FCI)

While we have seen various parameters available in connection strings, it would be good to discuss some of the specific parameters to understand the implication of them in an AlwaysOn deployment.

MultiSubnetFailover

The possible values for this parameter are true or false. In the case of multi-site clustering, there would be multiple IPs bound to a VNN (virtual network name). Only one IP would be online. Once the client connects to a Virtual Server Name, it would contact the DNS (Domain Name Service) and get back multiple IPs. In case of a legacy client library, the request would be sent to one of the IPs. If the response times out, the request would be sent to the next IP address. The new version of client connection libraries supports a new parameter. If we specify MultiSubnetFailover=True, the connection request would be sent to all IP addresses in parallel, and whichever returns the connection first would be established connection.

Applications can use a typical connection string (like the following) in their .NET code:

```
Server=tcp:MyListener,1433;Database=MyAdventureWorks;Integra
tedSecurity=SSPI;MultiSubnetFailover=True
```

This parameter is supported and recommended while connecting to an Availability Group Listener or an AlwaysOn FCI only. From the name of this parameter (MultiSubnetFailover), it looks like it is used for only multiple subnet scenarios, but in reality it can work for multiple IP addresses on a single subnet.

Failover_Partner

This parameter is not new to AlwaysOn. It was introduced to support Database Mirroring. Back in Database Mirroring one limitation was the secondary was not readable. This means all traffic went to the primary since topology is an active\passive node. For backward compatibility for the applications, we may want to use AlwaysOn with the same behavior as Database Mirroring.

While using this with Database Mirroring, the principal and the mirror server names are provided. This parameter works for the AlwaysOn Availability Group as well. Since the connection request might go to any of the servers during the initial connection, it would be recommended to configure the secondary to not allow the connections.

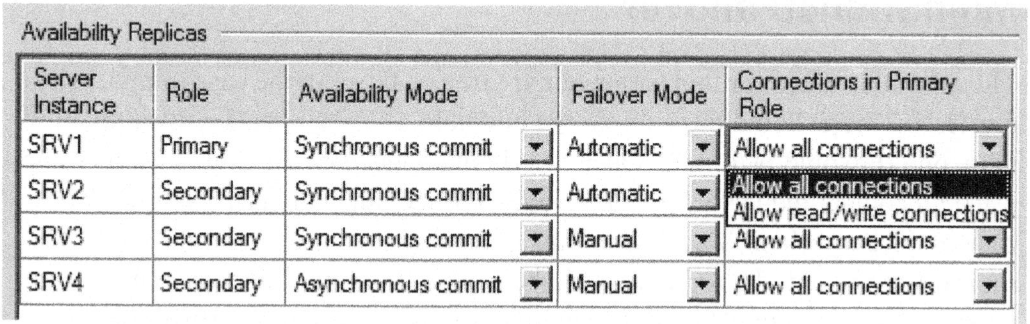

Figure 8.9 The option to allow or not allow read\write connections while acting as the primary.

ApplicationIntent

The main purpose of this keyword is to enable Readonly Routing (RoR). This is a new keyword/property which can be set in the connection string and can have two values of either ReadWrite or ReadOnly. The default value of this parameter is ReadWrite.

If we connect to the Availability Group Listener and provide this parameter in the connection string, the connection would be routed to the secondary replica. This is what we showed earlier in this chapter. To use this property with .NET (or other applications) a typical connection string would look like the following example:

```
Data Source=MyListener; Initial Catalog =MyAdventureWorks;
ApplicationIntent=ReadOnly
```

In an Availability Group, we can set the property "Connections in Primary Role" to "Allow read/write connections" (Figure 8.9). The primary can handle all types of traffic but we might want all readonly queries to be sent to the secondary replicas to keep the primary focus on write operations. This parameter, Allow read/write connections (on the primary), can be used to stop readonly traffic from using the resources of connecting to the primary replica. If set, and we attempt to connect to the primary with ApplicationIntent=ReadOnly, then the following error would be raised:

```
Messages
Msg 979, Level 14, State 1, Line 1
The target database ('MyAdventureWorks') is in an Availability Group and
currently does not allow readonly connections. For more information about
application intent, see SQL Server Books Online.
```

Let's summarize the connectivity behavior for easy access:

- For a read/write workload here are the following two choices:
  o Connect using the Availability Group Listener.
  o Connect using the FAILOVER_PARTNER. This is if the connection string of the existing applications cannot be changed.

- For a readonly workload here are the following three choices:
  o Configure (ROR) Readonly Routing.
  o Connect using the VNN and the property set to ApplicationIntent=ReadOnly.
  o Try connecting to the secondary instance directly.

- For a Multi-subnet failover scenario the following is what needs to be done:
  o Use new client libraries and use the connection string property of MultiSubnetFailover=True.

SQL Statistics on Secondary Replicas

We are not surprised to see warm ski jackets appearing on display shelves starting in September. It's not cold yet, but we know that winter time is a few months away based on our own recollection of the weather, which we've observed in previous seasons and prior years. Our own memory of temperature and weather patterns is a knowledge store we informally draw upon when planning for steps we will take before the cold weather arrives. By sampling existing data, we can make reasonable decisions about things which have not yet happened.

This is precisely what SQL Server does when it comes to statistics. Similar to how we might look or step outdoors to sample the temperature; SQL Server observes our data to understand how certain selective values are within a field. With these statistics collected, SQL Server's query optimizer can make good "seek and scan" decisions on fields with covering indexes.

SQL Server uses a cost based optimizer which relies highly on object statistics. When we run queries on a database, it would always be useful to have the latest statistics ready for the optimizer for running a query. The SQL Server engine can generate auto statistics on columns to have it handy.

Readonly reports are often queries run on the secondary replica in an AlwaysOn Availability Group. Let's assume a read query was executed on the secondary replica and this query was never executed on the primary replica. This new query might need some new statistics. Even if the optimizer feels that statistics are needed on a column, it cannot create statistics from there because the secondary replica is a readonly copy.

To solve this issue in an Availability Group, auto-statistics are created in the tempdb database of the secondary. This feature allows the optimizer to generate optimal query plans on that secondary replica. To use this feature the "Auto Update Statistics" and "Auto Create Statistics" property should be ON for the database.

To understand it better, we will create a sample table on the primary replica and execute a read query on a secondary replica. Most of the existing tables in the MyNorthwind database already have many statistics on them. We want a table with no statistics so we can see how they get created. For this reason we need a new table with no statistics and many rows to demonstrate this effectively. We will follow these steps:

1. Create table on the primary replica of MyNorthwind database and insert 10,000 random rows that will also get replicated to the secondary replicas.

```
CREATE TABLE MyTestTable
( iID INT,
  cFName CHAR(100),
  cLName CHAR(100),
  iAge INT);
```

```
SET NOCOUNT ON
DECLARE @iCounter INT = 1,
 @nRand NUMERIC(10,2),
 @iRand1 INT,
 @iRand2 INT,
 @cFName CHAR(100),
 @cLName CHAR(100)

WHILE (@iCounter <= 10000)
BEGIN
 SET @nRand =RAND()
 SET @iRand1 = CONVERT(INT, @nRand*RAND()*100)
 SET @iRand2 = CONVERT(INT, @nRand*RAND()*100)
 SET @cFName =
 SUBSTRING('ABCDEFGHIJKLMONPQRSTUVWXYZ', @iRand1, 10)
  SET @cLName =
 SUBSTRING('ABCDEFGHIJKLMONPQRSTUVWXYZ', @iRand2, 10)
 INSERT INTO MyTestTable VALUES (@iCounter, @cFName,
@cLName,
  convert(int, rand()*100) )
 SET @iCounter = @iCounter + 1
END
```

2. Query the sys.stats catalog view to see there are no statistics as of yet on this new table.

```
SELECT *
FROM  sys.stats
WHERE OBJECT_ID = OBJECT_ID('MyTestTable')
```

3. To generate some statistics, execute a read query on the secondary replica with the following query:

```
SELECT COUNT(*)
FROM  MyTestTable
WHERE iAge = 55
```

4. Again query the sys.stats catalog view from step 2 and it will show us the temporary statistics were created on the iAge column.

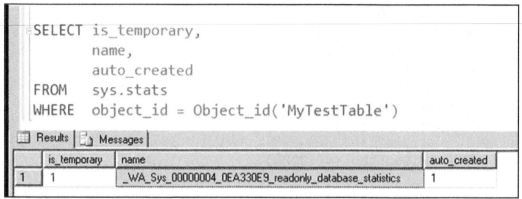

Figure 8.10 Temporary statistics created on iAge column.

Figure 8.10 shows us that the new temporary statistics were created with the name of *_WA_Sys_00000004_0EA330E9_readonly_database_statistics*. Also notice the 'is_temporary' flag is set to 1. This indicates that it is a temporary statistic. As explained earlier, the statistics were automatically created because the optimizer saw the need for it. The suffix "_readonly_database_statistics" was added to identify that this is created from the secondary replica. The statistics name contains the Object_ID and the Column_ID in hexadecimal (i.e. numeric 245575913 = hex 0EA330E9 and column 00000004 in the table is iAge column).

5. Query another column (cFName for example) so the optimizer will create new auto statistics on that column.

```
SELECT COUNT(*)
FROM  MyTestTable
WHERE cFName = 'ABC'
```

Run the sys.stats query again (Figure 8.11) and as expected the new statistics are created on the cFName column (column id=2).

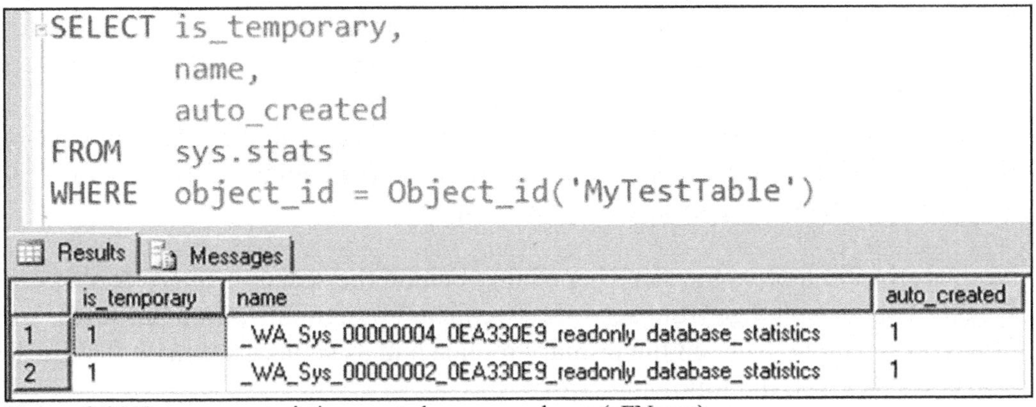

```
SELECT  is_temporary,
        name,
        auto_created
FROM    sys.stats
WHERE   object_id = Object_id('MyTestTable')
```

	is_temporary	name	auto_created
1	1	_WA_Sys_00000004_0EA330E9_readonly_database_statistics	1
2	1	_WA_Sys_00000002_0EA330E9_readonly_database_statistics	1

Figure 8.11 Temporary statistics created on new column (cFName).

One of the important concepts to understand is that these statistics are created in the tempdb database of the secondary replica. The tempdb is recreated every time the SQL service is restarted. This means that the statistics would be lost once the SQL Server service on that secondary replica restarts. This will not cause any data loss because statistics can be recreated easily by querying the underlying objects again.

In the case that any auto statistics are created on the primary replica, it would automatically be sent to the secondary replica.

One of the most common question asked is, what if the statistics on the column are also created on the primary replica (and these are the latest statistics), which one will the optimizer use? In this case, the optimizer is smart enough to use the latest up-to-date statistics.

In the event of a failover from the primary to a secondary replica, all the temporary statistics of all the secondary nodes will be lost. If we want the statistics to persist in a database these have to be created on the primary replica.

Automatic Page Repair

Mechanical parts can fail and data loss is a big concern for organizations. Let's take a scenario where one of the hard disk sectors gets corrupted. SQL Server will not be able to read from that sector. SQL Server 2008 had a feature where it would catch this page IO error and it would automatically restore it from the mirrored database (. This feature has been carried forward to SQL Server 2012 AlwaysOn Availability Groups. Personally, we call this a Band-Aid feature to fix corruption caused on the primary replica.

To simplify, this feature would replace a corrupted page with a good copy taken from the secondary replica. SQL Server cannot repair system level pages (i.e. PFS, GAM and SGAM pages). This feature should not be considered as a complete replacement of the DBCC repair options. We could hit a corrupt page on the primary replica or secondary replica and the action behind the scene would vary based on which server is asking for the page.

Next, we would look at the steps happening behind the scene. A query could be accessing a corrupt page from secondary replica. For demonstration purposes, we have corrupted one page on the primary replica and as soon as we ran a SELECT query, we received the following error:

```
Messages
Msg 824, Level 24, State 2, Line 1
SQL Server detected a logical consistency-based I/O error: incorrect checksum
(expected: 0xadd24e48; actual: 0xac43ffd8). It occurred during a read of page
(1:276) in database ID 6 at offset 0x00000000228000 in file 'C:\Program
Files\Microsoft SQL
Server\MSSQL11.MSSQLSERVER\MSSQL\DATA\MyAdventureWorks.mdf'. Additional
messages in the SQL Server error log or system event log may provide more
detail. This is a severe error condition that threatens database integrity
and must be corrected immediately. Complete a full database consistency check
(DBCC CHECKDB). This error can be caused by many factors; for more
information, see SQL Server Books Online.
```

Upon receiving this error, a message is broadcasted to all secondary replicas asking for the page along with the LSN. Once the secondary catches up with the primary replica to undo all changes on the page, it would send the page to the primary replica. Further responses from other replicas would be ignored. The output from DMV is seen in Figure 8.12.

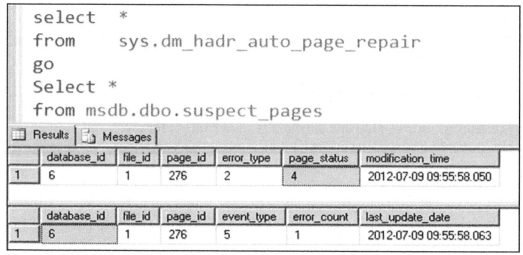

Figure 8.12 Entries in DMV about page repair.

A corrupt page could be encountered doing either a read from a query or a read performed from the redo thread.

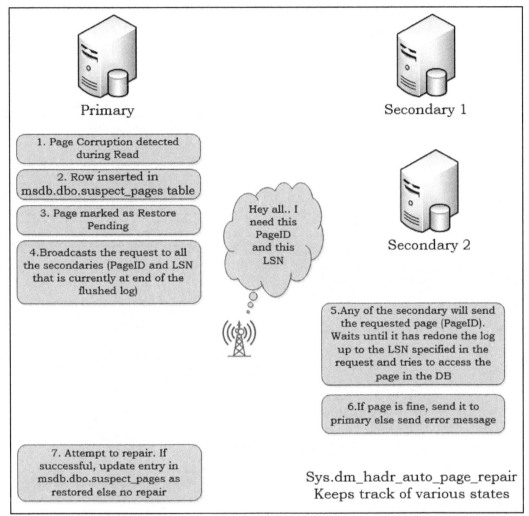

Figure 8.13 Typical flow when page corruption is detected on the primary.

The restore mechanism is the same with a minor difference in that a redo failure would bring a synchronizing state into a suspended state. User intervention is needed to execute a resume command for the Availability Group. A slight extension to this concept is when the secondary has a corrupt page. In this case, the process is reversed with a little modification as seen in Figure 8.14.

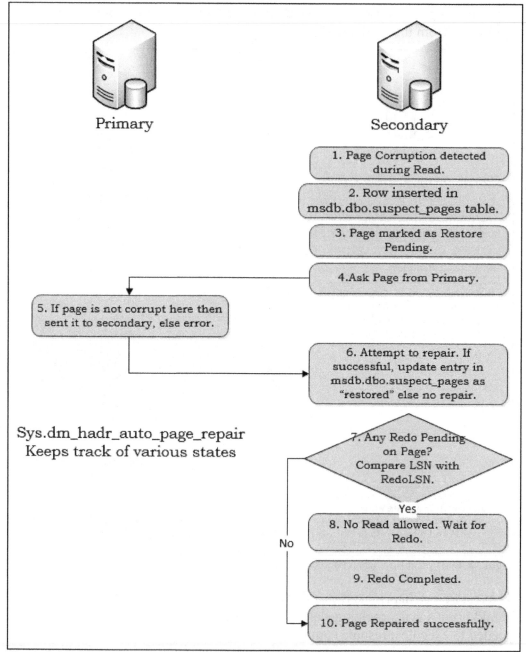

Figure 8.14 Flow when there is page corruption on the secondary and how the repair happens.

DBCC Checks on Secondary

A SQL Server runs on hardware and mechanical devices can fail once in a while. One of the important components in that piece is the hard disk. SQL Server DBAs are known to run the DBCC CHECKDB on the database occasionally as part of their maintenance plans. These are run during a maintenance window as they are resource intensive. Therefore one of the biggest advantages that an Availability Group introduces is the ability to run the DBCC CHECKDB command on the secondary replica.

Any secondary database that is configured to allow connections can execute the DBCC CHECKDB. This command can be executed in two modes, conventional ONLINE mode or with TABLOCK. The only difference between them is that the CHECKDB in ONLINE mode executes by creating internal snapshots while TABLOCK does not create the snapshot. A typical command would look like the following example:

```
-- DBCC CHECKDB in ONLINE mode
DBCC CHECKDB(MyAdventureWorks)
GO
```

Running the DBCC command on the secondary means that the secondary can be lagging behind the primary replica. It will lag behind until the DBCC finally finishes on the secondary. If we run CHECKDB with TABLOCK on the secondary we will get the following error:

```
Messages
Msg 7934, Level 16, State 1, Line 1
DBCC CHECK cannot proceed on database MyAdventureWorks because it is a
secondary replica and either Snapshot creation failed or the WITH TABLOCK
option was specified. secondary replica databases cannot be exclusively
locked for DBCC CHECK. Reason may have been given in previous error.
```

The best part about the AlwaysOn Availability Group is the "shared nothing architecture". Even the storage is separate for each of the replicas, giving us great resilience from failures involving the disk storage. This means that the disk used on the primary is different as compared to disks used in each of the secondary replicas. Therefore it is likely that disks can get corrupt in any replica and it is important for us to perform DBCC CHECKDB on each of the replicas from time-to-time.

We might want to test our High Availability solution by failing over to the secondary to switch roles. Here is a typical flow of how we can keep rotating our hardware utilization and still make sure they are clean when the need for a failover happens:

1. Run the DBCC CHECKDB on the primary replica every week to check for any possible hardware errors.

2. Do a failover during non-peak times. For example test every Sunday when the number of users accessing the application is low. Switch the role of primary and secondary by performing a manual failover.

3. Perform the DBCC CHECKDB on the new secondary and repeat Step 1.

There are advantages to rotating the hardware and having one of the secondary replicas take over the role as the primary. One advantage of rotating our hardware is this makes sure our CHECKDB is run on our hardware from time-to-time which mitigates any possible storage failures.

Though these can be additional manual steps for a DBA, we are sure this can be scripted and automated. Besides, doing this also perfects the failover scenario performed by the team. If a team is not prepared for the round-robin style of hardware utilization, we highly recommend performing a DBCC CHECKDB on all replicas occasionally to make sure we don't get into any hardware failure at the time of a failover.

Connectivity Flowchart

As we define various routing policies it is important to know the effective landing point for connections for applications. This is seen in Figure 8.15.

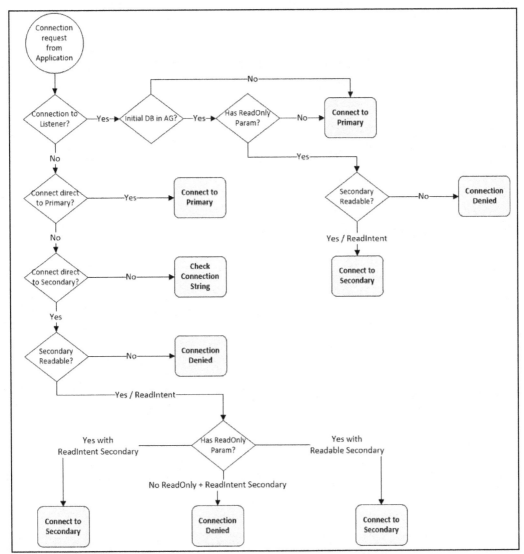

Figure 8.15 Effective connectivity flowchart for application connections.

Summary

In this chapter we have discussed various features of SQL Server AlwaysOn Availability Groups. These features are more about using the secondary in a better way to get a better return on investment from a server procured for High Availability. While the readable secondary feature allows us to take backups, run readonly queries, and perform DBCC checks on the secondary replica, we can also get better performance by building auto statistics on the tempdb of the secondary for reporting needs. On the other hand, automatic page repair allows us to get a good copy of the database page from the secondary replica. This eliminates the manual restore of pages.

Points to Ponder – Features of AlwaysOn Availability Groups

1. The secondary role has three read choices:
    *   **No** – This allows no connection.
    *   **Yes** – This allows all read traffic.
    *   **Read-Intent** – This allows only connections which specify ApplicationIntent=ReadOnly in the connection string.

2. The routing URL of the instance is its fully-qualified-domain-name (FQDN) followed by a port number.

3. Use the ALTER AVAILABILITY GROUP statement to add a Routing List.

4. The verification of Readonly Routing can be done easily with SSMS and SQLCMD.

5. A secondary that is in readonly mode cannot create statistics on the secondary database(s) directly.

6. Statistics on the secondary are achieved by storing auto-statistics in the tempdb database.

7. The DMV sys.stats can be used to check on the statistics of tables.

8. Automatic page repair is a feature that replaces a corrupted page with a good copy taken from a secondary replica.

9. DBCC Checks can also be performed on a secondary.

10. The MultiSubnetFailover parameter can be used for a single subnet or many subnets using multiple IP addresses.

11. The ApplicationIntent parameter (along with the Listener name) can be used to seamlessly redirect reporting applications to connection to the secondary replica.

Review Quiz - Chapter Eight

1.) The Readonly Routing (RoR) option requires the Read-Intent of a connection parameter by using which one of the following?

O a. ApplicationIntent=ReadOnly
O b. ApplicationIntent=Read Only
O c. ApplicationIntent=ReadOnly

2.) A routing URL consists of which of the following two components?

□ a. Name of all replicas
□ b. Full qualified Domain name
□ c. Port number

3.) Which DMV can we use to find out which automatic page repairs have happened inside an AlwaysOn configuration? Choose all that apply.

□ a. msdn.dbo.suspect_pages
□ b. sys_dm_hadr_auto_page_repair
□ c. msdb.dbo.suspect_pages
□ d. sys.dm_hadr_auto_page_repair

4.) Under which circumstances will statistics on the tempdb of a secondary be lost? Choose all that apply.

□ a. When no query is executed.
□ b. Restart of secondary.
□ c. When failover happens to the secondary.

5.) For Readonly Routing to work, the secondary must be a synchronous replica?

O a. True
O b. False

Answer Key

1.) Option (c) ApplicationIntent=ReadOnly is the correct answer. There is no space in the keywords, therefore (a) and (b) are all wrong answers.

2.) (a) Name of all replicas is a wrong answer. The routing URL needs to be created on the secondary, but nor defined in a single URL. Hence, (b) Full qualified Domain name and (c) Port number - are correct answers.

3.) (a) msdn.dbo.suspect_pages and (b) sys_dm_hadr_auto_page_repair are wrong answers because there is no DMVs that exists with that name. The correct answers are (c) msdb.dbo.suspect_pages and (d) sys.dm_hadr_auto_page_repair are correct options.

4.) If no query is executed on the secondary, statistics are not created or deleted. Hence option (a) When no query is executed is wrong. The correct answer is (b) Restart of secondary and (c) When failover happens to the secondary.

5.) The correct option is (b) False. To implement Readonly Routing the secondary does not need to be in synchronous mode.

[NOTES]

Chapter 9. AlwaysOn Monitoring and Troubleshooting

What will you do when your car suddenly refuses to start when it is parked at home and you need to get to work as soon as possible? Our imaginations run wild around what happened to our car making it not start today. Did we drive in a rough patch and hit a sudden hard bump recently? Maybe when our friend borrowed the car something happened then. As we focus on a solution we automatically try to look at the engine to see if something is visible and obvious. Even though we may know nothing about cars, it is in our DNA to do a visual check for disconnected wires to troubleshoot. We might try to get back inside the car to start it again and look at the Dashboard to see if there are any obvious clues. If all these techniques don't help then we think about calling the service station to get an expert to solve the problem.

Monitoring and troubleshooting SQL Server is also generally along the same lines. If we understand SQL Server better, the chances for solving a problem ourselves, increases. SQL Server AlwaysOn provides various ways to monitor the health of the Availability Group. One of the visual ways to monitor the health is to use the AlwaysOn Dashboard. This Dashboard is part of SQL Server Management Studio. First, we will look at the various distinctions of what the Dashboard gives us and then move on to the non-visual methods (like DMVs, catalogs views, extended events and performance counters) later in this chapter.

AlwaysOn Dashboard

Have you ever had a chance to watch the movie "The Taking of Pelham 123"? This can be either the 1974 classic or the remake done in 2009. In the recent version Denzel Washington sits in the command center for the New York subway system as a dispatcher. For the majority of the movie the team has its eye glued to the large screen which gives them insight into where each train is and how they are moving. They can even see if a train is stopped at a location. This is a bird's eye view of the complete network and the command center uses this Dashboard to get information quickly and act accordingly. In the case of an AlwaysOn Availability Group, the Dashboard shows us all the key indicators and policies of the servers participating in our deployment.

The Dashboard helps administrators check the overall health of an Availability Group along with the individual replicas and the databases. It does this in a visual way with green, yellow, and red icons. This also helps the administrator troubleshoot Availability Groups in their environments.

To launch the AlwaysOn Dashboard, connect to a replica in the group (like SRV1) using SQL Server Management Studio, then expand the **AlwaysOn High Availability** folder and right-click the **Availability Groups** folder and then choose the **Show Dashboard** option (you can also right-click the name of the group). Based on the context of the right-click, the Dashboard will show us either all Availability Groups (Figure 9.1: left) or the selected Availability Group (Figure 9.1: right).

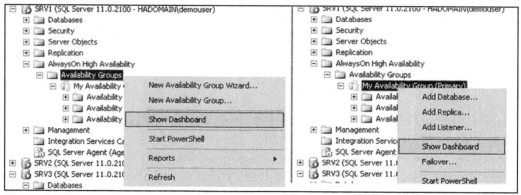

Figure 9.1 Ways to launch Dashboard in SSMS.

Notice in Figure 9.1 we launched this from SRV1 (the primary replica). The Dashboard can be launched from any replica but the information of all of the availability replicas can only be monitored from primary replica.

There are three major sections in the Dashboard as shown in Figure 9.2.

- **Section 1:** This allows us to perform a failover to any available replica. We can also get quorum voting information and look at extended event (XEvents) traces which are running behind the scene. These extended event sessions were created as soon as we created the AlwaysOn Availability Group via the Create Availability Group Wizard. XEvent traces can be used to view recent Availability Group activity, state changes, and other interesting events.

- **Section 2:** This shows the availability replicas (SRV1, SRV2, SRV3, and SRV4) and their current state. An important point to note is that the Synchronization State column always shows Synchronizing for replicas which are configured in an asynchronous mode. Even if there is no activity on the primary replica (nothing left to synchronize), we would see the state as Synchronizing.

- **Section 3**: This shows the state for each database involved in the Availability Group and their state on each replica. In case of any errors and/or warnings the Dashboard will show us the error message and provides us with guidance to fix the error.

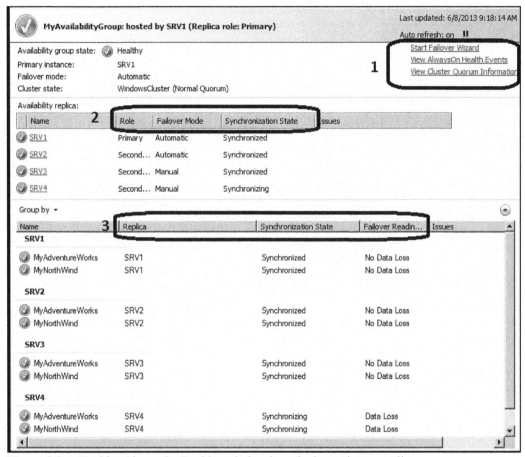

Figure 9.2 A Healthy AlwaysOn Dashboard view launched on primary replica.

Dashboard Metadata

For the Dashboard to work it needs to know how we have set it up and if the current state of its operation is working. Much of our group setup metadata is can be seen in DVMs and the current operation is set up in SQL Server's Policy based management.

The information shown under section 2 and 3 are gathered from various DMVs and visually displayed in the Dashboard. There is much more information available in the Dashboard which is not shown by default. We can customize the Dashboard and add more columns by right-clicking on the column headers under the replica scope (section 2 - Figure 9.2) or the database scope (section 3 - Figure 9.2) and choose from the list of columns available (Figure 9.3). The DMVs of sys.dm_hadr_availability_replica_states and sys.dm_hadr_database_replica_states are used to gather replica level and database level information respectively.

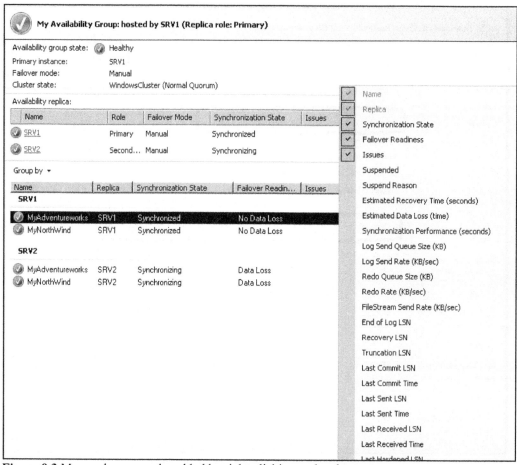

Figure 9.3 More columns can be added by right-clicking on header.

In the case of any warnings or errors shown in the Dashboard, it allows us to drill down further to find the cause. The Dashboard uses Policy Based Management rules behind the scenes to show the health of the Availability Group, the replicas, and the databases. The definitions of these policies are stored in the MSDB database. To see the policy definitions, click on an error or warning in the Dashboard to see the resulting values or even run them one at a time to evaluate them. We will show a typical error and evaluation in the next section. In Figure 9.4 we can see the various system policies available and used by the Dashboard.

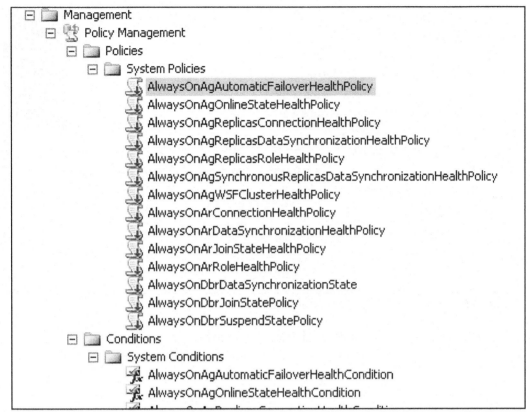

Figure 9.4 List of system policies and conditions related to AlwaysOn in Management Studio.

Looking at the policies' names, they can be logically divided into three categories.

- Availability Group (AlwaysOn**Ag...**)
- Availability Replica (AlwaysOn**Ar...**)
- Database Replica (AlwaysOn**Dbr...**)

We will discuss these policies in the next section.

Troubleshooting using the Dashboard

For illustration purposes, we have suspended the data movement to one of the databases (MyNorthwind) in the Availability Group. We did this on SRV1 by right-clicking the **MyNorthwind** database under **Availability Databases** and selecting **Suspend Data Movement**.

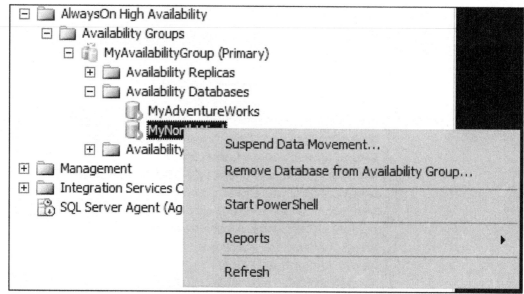

Figure 9.5 Suspending the data movement for MyNorthwind.

After doing this, we have launched the Dashboard as shown in Figure 9.6.

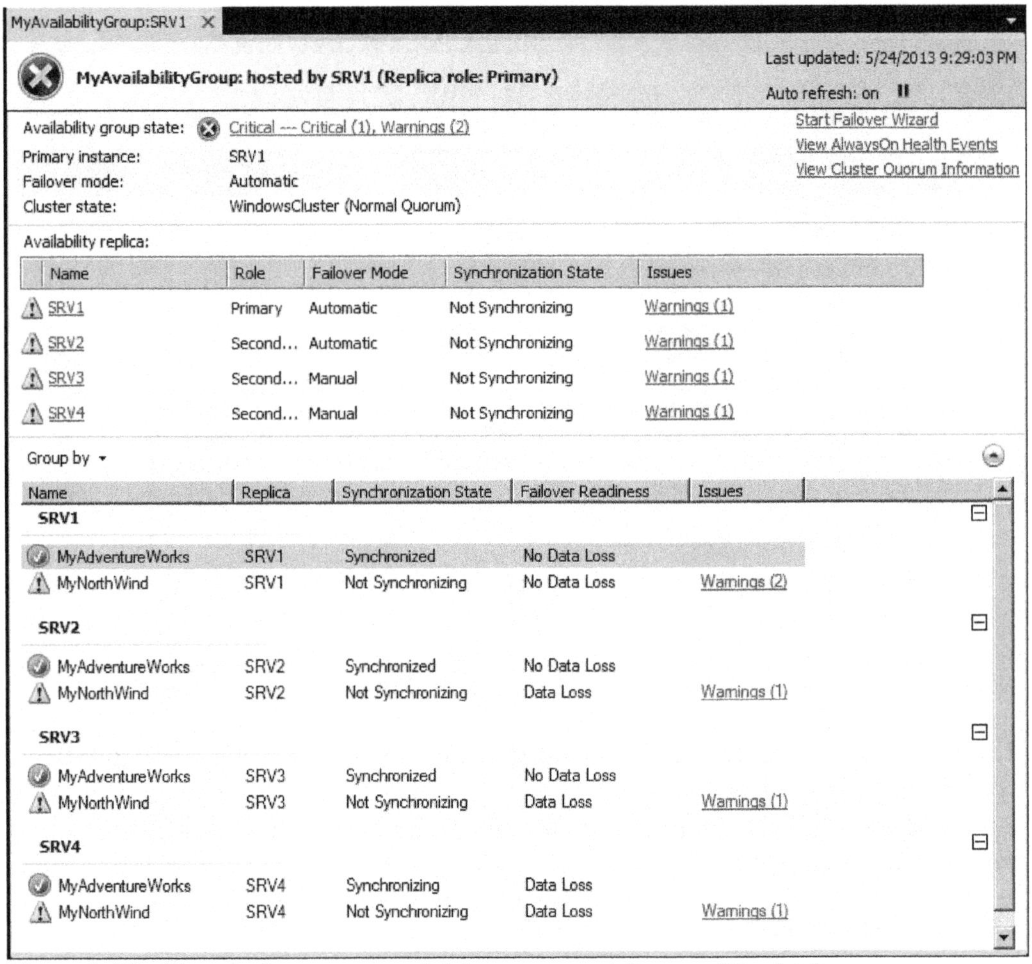

Figure 9.6 Dashboard when we suspended data movement for one of the databases.

At the top of the Dashboard we see a critical state and several warnings. We can drilldown further by clicking on the **Critical/Warnings** hyperlink. As soon as the link is clicked the policy evaluation runs and shows the results. We have clicked on the first hyperlink in Figure 9.6 and the Dashboard runs the policies and shows one error and two warnings as shown in the main page of Figure 9.7.

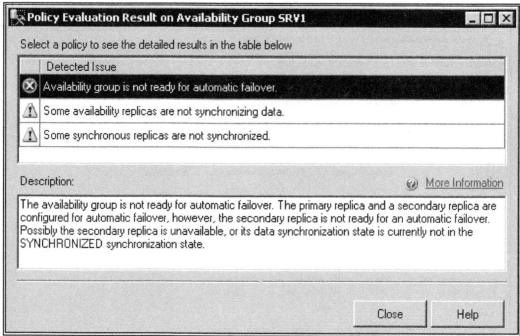

Figure 9.7 Policy Evaluation Results after clicking on Critical or Warnings on Dashboard.

The Dashboard is a great visual indicator and it helps us take quick action based on a given AlwaysOn server setup. If we check the Availability Databases Node for the MyAvailabilityGroup group we can see the MyNorthwind database is in a paused state as shown in Figure 9.8.

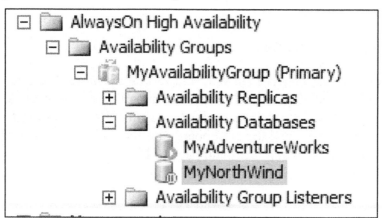

Figure 9.8 MyNorthwind is showing as paused.

To resume the data movement for the MyNorthwind database, right-click it and choose the **Resume Data Movement ...** option. This pops up a dialog box, click **OK**.

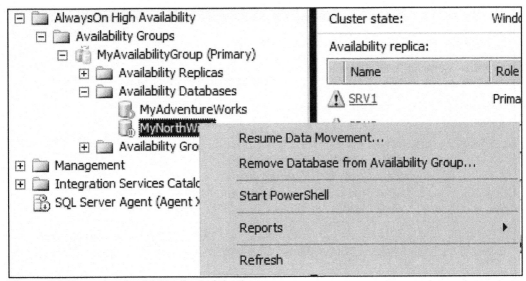

Figure 9.9 Resuming the MyNorthwind database.

If we need to know which policy is fired off by various sections in the Dashboard then we can read about it in the PowerShell section discussed next.

PowerShell

In the real world a typical DBA handles multiple SQL Servers with potentially hundreds of Availability Groups. It would be humanly impossible to open SSMS for all those servers and look at the health of each Availability Group. Dashboards are great for a quick view but cannot be used for 24x7 monitoring techniques. If a critical error occurs in the middle of the night, the Dashboard cannot send us alerts. This is the scenario where SQL PowerShell comes to our rescue. SQL PowerShell cmdlets are one of the powerful ways to administer and manage AlwaysOn Availability Groups.

Let's first understand the mapping between the Dashboard and some PowerShell cmdlets. As explained earlier, there are three major sections in the Dashboard and each section gets mapped to one of the following cmdlets:

- Test-SqlAvailabilityGroup
- Test-SqlAvailabilityReplica
- Test-SqlDatabaseReplicaState

Figure 9.10 provides a mapping of the cmdlets to the section in Dashboard.

MyAvailabilityGroup:SRV1 ✕

MyAvailabilityGroup: hosted by SRV1 (Replica role: Primary) Last updated: 5/24/2013 9:29:03 PM
Auto refresh: on ▌▌

Availability group state:	✖	Critical --- Critical (1), Warnings (2)			Start Failover Wizard
Primary instance:		SRV1		**Test-SQLAvailabilityGroup**	View AlwaysOn Health Events
Failover mode:		Automatic			View Cluster Quorum Information
Cluster state:		WindowsCluster (Normal Quorum)			

Availability replica: **Test-SQLAvailabilityReplica**

Name	Role	Failover Mode	Synchronization State	Issues
⚠ SRV1	Primary	Automatic	Not Synchronizing	Warnings (1)
⚠ SRV2	Second...	Automatic	Not Synchronizing	Warnings (1)
⚠ SRV3	Second...	Manual	Not Synchronizing	Warnings (1)
⚠ SRV4	Second...	Manual	Not Synchronizing	Warnings (1)

Group by ▾ **Test-SQLDatabaseReplicaState**

Name	Replica	Synchronization State	Failover Readiness	Issues
SRV1				
✓ MyAdventureWorks	SRV1	Synchronized	No Data Loss	
⚠ MyNorthWind	SRV1	Not Synchronizing	No Data Loss	Warnings (2)
SRV2				
✓ MyAdventureWorks	SRV2	Synchronized	No Data Loss	
⚠ MyNorthWind	SRV2	Not Synchronizing	Data Loss	Warnings (1)
SRV3				
✓ MyAdventureWorks	SRV3	Synchronized	No Data Loss	
⚠ MyNorthWind	SRV3	Not Synchronizing	Data Loss	Warnings (1)
SRV4				
✓ MyAdventureWorks	SRV4	Synchronizing	Data Loss	
⚠ MyNorthWind	SRV4	Not Synchronizing	Data Loss	Warnings (1)

Figure 9.10 Mapping between AlwaysOn Dashboard and cmdlets.

Again, to reiterate, we get information about all replicas from only viewing it from the primary replica. To understand this option, let's run the cmdlets and see the output. To achieve this, we need to first open the sqlps command prompt. This can be done by typing sqlps in the PowerShell command prompt.

Test-SqlAvailabilityGroup

In the following command, SRV1 is the node name and DEFAULT stands for default instance of SQL Server:

```
PS SQLSERVER:\> cd
SQLSERVER:\SQL\SRV1\DEFAULT\AvailabilityGroups

PS SQLSERVER:\SQL\SRV1\DEFAULT\AvailabilityGroups> DIR
```

Name	PrimaryReplicaServerName
MyAvailabilityGroup	SRV1

PS SQLSERVER:\SQL\SRV1\DEFAULT\AvailabilityGroups> **Test-SqlAvailabilityGroup "MyAvailabilityGroup"**

HealthState	Name
Error	MyAvailabilityGroup

The previous code is precisely what we have in the first section of the Dashboard. We get an error on our Availability Group health as seen in Figure 9.10. Next let's use the second cmdlet to get the health of the replicas.

Test-SqlAvailabilityReplica

The name of the Availability Group in our environment is MyAvailabilityGroup. The following code shows how to use the Test-SqlAvailabilityReplica cmdlet to show the replica state:

PS SQLSERVER:\SQL\SRV1\DEFAULT\AvailabilityGroups> **cd '.\MyAvailabilityGroup'**

PS SQLSERVER:\SQL\SRV1\DEFAULT\AvailabilityGroups\MyAvailabilityGroup> **cd .\AvailabilityReplicas**

PS SQLSERVER:\SQL\SRV1\DEFAULT\AvailabilityGroups\MyAvailabilityGroup\AvailabilityReplicas> **dir**

Name	Role	ConnectionState	RollupSynchronizationState
SRV1	primary	Connected	NotSynchronizing
SRV2	secondary	Connected	NotSynchronizing
SRV3	secondary	Connected	NotSynchronizing
SRV4	secondary	Connected	NotSynchronizing

PS SQLSERVER:\SQL\SRV1\DEFAULT\AvailabilityGroups\MyAvailabilityGroup\AvailabilityReplicas> dir | Test-SqlAvailabilityReplica

HealthState	AvailabilityGroup	Name
Warning	MyAvailabilityGroup	SRV2
Warning	MyAvailabilityGroup	SRV2
Warning	MyAvailabilityGroup	SRV2
Warning	MyAvailabilityGroup	SRV2

As expected, and seen in the Dashboard, the Test-SqlAvailabilityReplica shows the HealthState as "Warning".

Test-SqlDatabaseReplicaState

Now let's drill further and get the details for the third section in the Dashboard and use the Test-SqlDatabaseReplicaState cmdlet. This section shows us the databases which are not healthy:

```
PS
SQLSERVER:\SQL\SRV1\DEFAULT\AvailabilityGroups\MyAvailabilit
yGroup> cd .\DatabaseReplicaStates
```

```
PS
SQLSERVER:\SQL\SRV1\DEFAULT\AvailabilityGroups\MyAvailabilit
yGroup\DatabaseReplicaStates> dir
```

```
<< We have removed/modified some columns for clarity >>
```

Availability Replica	AvailabilityDatabaseName	SynchronizationState
SRV1	MyAdventureWorks	Synchronized
SRV1	MyNorthwind	NotSynchronizing
SRV2	MyAdventureWorks	Synchronized
SRV2	MyNorthwind	NotSynchronizing
SRV3	MyAdventureWorks	Synchronized
SRV3	MyNorthwind	NotSynchronizing
SRV4	MyAdventureWorks	Synchronized
SRV4	MyNorthwind	NotSynchronizing

```
PS
SQLSERVER:\SQL\SRV1\DEFAULT\AvailabilityGroups\MyAvailabilit
yGroup\DatabaseReplicaStates> dir | Test-
SqlDatabaseReplicaState
```

HealthState	AvailabilityGroup	AvailabilityReplica	Name
Healthy	MyAvailabilityGroup	SRV1	MyAdventureWorks
Warning	MyAvailabilityGroup	SRV1	MyNorthwind
Healthy	MyAvailabilityGroup	SRV2	MyAdventureWorks
Warning	MyAvailabilityGroup	SRV2	MyNorthwind
Healthy	MyAvailabilityGroup	SRV3	MyAdventureWorks
Warning	MyAvailabilityGroup	SRV3	MyNorthwind
Healthy	MyAvailabilityGroup	SRV4	MyAdventureWorks
Warning	MyAvailabilityGroup	SRV4	MyNorthwind

As seen in the Dashboard, there is a warning for the MyNorthwind database on all servers (SRV1 – SRV4).

For all three cmdlets, there is a parameter called ShowPolicyDetails which can provide additional information about the policy being executed by each test. For better formatting, we have not shown them in the output but here is the list of policies associated with each of the test cmdlets.

cmdlet Name	Policy used
Test-SqlAvailabilityGroup	1. AlwaysOnAgOnlineStateHealthPolicy 2. AlwaysOnAgWSFClusterHealthPolicy 3. AlwaysOnAgAutomaticFailoverHealthPolicy 4. AlwaysOnAgReplicasConnectionHealthPolicy 5. AlwaysOnAgReplicasDataSynchronizationHealthPolicy 6. AlwaysOnAgReplicasRoleHealthPolicy 7. AlwaysOnAgSynchronousReplicasDataSynchronizationHealthPolicy
Test-SqlDatabaseReplicaState	1. AlwaysOnDbrDataSynchronizationState 2. AlwaysOnDbrJoinStatePolicy 3. AlwaysOnDbrSuspendStatePolicy
Test-SqlAvailabilityReplica	1. AlwaysOnArConnectionHealthPolicy 2. AlwaysOnArRoleHealthPolicy 3. AlwaysOnArDataSynchronizationHealthPolicy 4. AlwaysOnArJoinStateHealthPolicy

Table 9.1 Mapping of PowerShell cmdlets to the policies defined.

These are the basic tests which can be done as a part of our automation. Feel free to refer to the SQL AlwaysOn product team blog (http://blogs.msdn.com/sqlalwayson). We can even get this to write complex scripts which can send an email if things go wrong.

AlwaysOn Policy Evaluation

If you work in large organizations, there are policies that govern the workplace. These policies are guidelines and can be used for subjective and objective decisions. A typical policy example for a call center company would be that employees must get to work by 8 AM to take calls from customers. Policies are not laws or rules but guidelines. From time-to-time the policies are used to check if they are adhered to by the employees. In the same way, AlwaysOn policies are used to check if the states of the Availability Group, the Availability Replicas, and the Availability Databases are in order.

In Table 9.1 we defined each cmdlet to a series of SQL Server Policies predefined for AlwaysOn. Let's double-click into each policy listed to understand when they could possibly fail.

Availability Group Level Policy Failures

Policy Name: AlwaysOnAgWSFClusterHealthPolicy

WSFC Cluster State Policy Failure: The WSFC cluster is offline and the Availability Group is not available. This issue can be caused by a cluster service issue or by the loss of quorum in the cluster.

Possible Causes:

- Quorum Loss
- Cluster service is offline
- Cluster service is in the forced quorum.

Policy Name: AlwaysOnAgOnlineStateHealthPolicy

Availability Group Online State Policy Failure: The Availability Group is offline. This issue can be caused by a failure in the server instance that hosts the primary replica or the WSFC Availability Group resource itself is offline.

Possible Causes:

- The primary instance is not available.

- The Availability Group Listener cluster resource is offline, which causes the Availability Group to be offline.
- The automatic failover operation has failed.
- The cluster or the Availability Group has a connectivity issue.
- A failover is in process.
- The cluster hit the max failover threshold.

Policy Name: AlwaysOnAgAutomaticFailoverHealthPolicy

Availability Group automatic failover State Policy Failure: The secondary replica that is configured for automatic failover is currently NOT SYNCHRONIZED. This means the Availability Group is not ready for automatic failover. This is evaluated as false when the secondary replica is not ready for automatic failover.

Possible Causes:

- The secondary replica for the automatic failover is down.
- The secondary replica for automatic failover is not synchronized (not failover ready).

Policy Name: AlwaysOnAgReplicasDataSynchronizationHealthPolicy

Availability Replicas Data Synchronization State Policy Failure: In this Availability Group, at least one secondary replica in the Dashboard has a NOT SYNCHRONIZING synchronization state and is not receiving data from the primary replica.

Possible Causes:

- A connectivity issue to the primary.
- A secondary replica instance is down.
- Any database in one of the availability replicas is suspended.
- Any database in one of the availability replicas is not synchronizing properly.
- The Availability Group is in a failover transition state.

Policy Name:
AlwaysOnAgsynchronousReplicasDataSynchronizationHealthPolicy

**Availability Group synchronous replicas Data Synchronization State Policy
Failure:** In this Availability Group, at least one synchronous replica is not
currently synchronized. The replica synchronization state possibilities can be
either SYNCHONIZING or NOT SYNCHRONIZING.

Possible Causes:

- One of the synchronous commit replicas is not synchronized.
- One of the asynchronous commit replicas is not synchronizing.

Policy Name: AlwaysOnAgReplicasRoleHealthPolicy

Availability Group Replicas Role State Policy Failure: In this Availability
Group, at least one availability replica does not currently have the primary or
secondary roles.

Possible Causes:

- One of availability replicas is not in a primary or a secondary role state.

Policy Name: AlwaysOnAgReplicasConnectionHealthPolicy

Availability Group Replicas Connection State Policy Failure: In this
Availability Group, at least one secondary replica is not connected to the primary
replica.

Possible Causes:

- One of secondary replica connections is disconnected.

Availability Replica Level Policy Failures

Policy Name: AlwaysOnArRoleHealthPolicy

Availability Group Role State Policy Failure: The role of this availability
replica is unhealthy. The replica is not in any role (primary or secondary).

Possible Causes:

- The replica is not a primary or secondary. Most likely the role is a
  resolving state.
- The availability replica is down or not operational.

Policy Name: AlwaysOnArConnectionHealthPolicy

Availability Replica Connection State Policy Failure: Here the secondary replica is not connected to the primary replica. The connected state in the Dashboard is showing as DISCONNECTED.

Possible Causes:

- Port conflict issues.
- Endpoint encryption handshake issue.
- The endpoint does not exist or has not started.
- An endpoint type mismatch.
- The authentication failed.

Policy Name: AlwaysOnArDataSynchronizationHealthPolicy

Availability Replica Data Synchronization State Policy Failure: At least one database replica on this availability replica has an unhealthy data synchronization state. If this is an asynchronous commit availability replica, all databases' replicas should be in the SYNCHRONIZING state. If this is a synchronous commit availability replica, all databases replicas should be in the SYNCHRONIZED state.

Possible Causes:

- The replica is disconnected.
- One of the databases is suspended.
- One of the databases is not joined.
- One of the databases is having a data synchronization issue.

Policy Name: AlwaysOnArJoinStateHealthPolicy

Availability Replica Join State Policy Failure: This happens when the secondary replica is not joined to the Availability Group.

Possible Causes:

- The replica join configuration has failed or has not completed.

Database Replica Level Policy Failures

Policy Name: AlwaysOnDbrSuspendStatePolicy

Availability Database Suspension State Policy Failure: The DBA has suspended data synchronization on this availability database.

Possible Causes:

- The system has suspended the data movement because of some error.
- The user has explicitly suspended the database.

Policy Name: AlwaysOnDbrJoinStatePolicy

Availability Database Join State Policy Failure: The secondary database is not joined to the Availability Group. The configuration of this secondary database is incomplete.

Possible Causes:

- The database is not properly joined.

Policy Name: AlwaysOnDbrDataSynchronizationState

Availability Database Synchronization State Policy Failure: The data synchronization state of the availability database is unhealthy. On an asynchronous commit availability replica, every availability database should be in the SYNCHRONIZING state. On a synchronous commit replica, every availability database should be in the SYNCHRONIZED state.

Possible Causes:

- Connectivity issue stopped the data movement.
- Suspended database.
- Redo is blocked and it is causing the synchronization issue.

Catalogs Views and DMVs

If you have been working in the computer field for a while, then you might remember the era of programs like FoxPro. They were developments in environments that were command-line based. Even in today's modern programming, the UI based operations are easy and they get our work done faster. Sometimes this ease of use comes at a cost. Visual programming can fail to teach administrators the actual workings behind the scenes. Even though such UIs exist, the nuts and bolts of understanding the system can't always be learned by using UI tools. The learning takes place by writing scripts built on top of the system. The biggest advantage of any script is its ability to automate and replicate easily across systems. In this section we will demonstrate some important catalog views and DMVs which were specifically added for the AlwaysOn Availability Group.

Almost all the metadata properties of AlwaysOn are exposed via catalog views. For example the name of the group, MyAvailabilityGroup, was chosen by us and is a property of the group. Properties set by the administrator are often stored in SQL Server catalog views.

Some metadata does not involve properties set by the administrator. For example the healthy state of the group could go to critical as we encounter some runtime failure. The runtime metadata is shown in dynamic management views (DMVs). In this section we will discuss the available catalog views and the DMVs for AlwaysOn Availability Groups.

Catalog Views

Catalog views are the views defined on system tables that contain the configuration of the system. The catalog views relating to AlwaysOn are seen in Table 9.2.

What do we want to check?	Catalog View
Availability Group	sys.availability_groups
Availability Replica	sys.availability_replicas
Availability Group Listener	sys.availability_group_Listeners sys.availability_group_Listener_ip_addresses
Database Replica	sys.databases sys.availability_databases_cluster
Routing	sys.availability_read_only_routing_lists
AlwaysOn Endpoints	sys.database_mirroring_endpoints

Table 9.2 AlwaysOn related catalog views.

Dynamic Management Views

Table 9.3 provides the high level information about AlwaysOn DMVs and their usage.

What do we want to check?	Dynamic Management View
Availability Replica Health	sys.dm_hadr_availability_replica_states
Availability Group Health	sys.dm_hadr_availability_group_states
Availability Replica Information	sys.dm_hadr_availability_replica_cluster_nodes
Availability Group Database Health	sys.dm_hadr_database_replica_states
Availability Group Failover Readiness	sys.dm_hadr_database_replica_cluster_states
Cluster Quorum Information	sys.dm_hadr_cluster
Information about cluster resource and SQL Server name	sys.dm_hadr_instance_node_map
Cluster Node Information	sys.dm_hadr_cluster_members
Cluster Network Information	sys.dm_hadr_cluster_networks
Repaired Page Information	sys.dm_hadr_auto_page_repair
Listener State and Information	sys.dm_tcp_Listener_states

Table 9.3 DMVs and their usage explained.

A visual representation of the DMVs and their levels seen in Figure 9.11 makes an easy understanding.

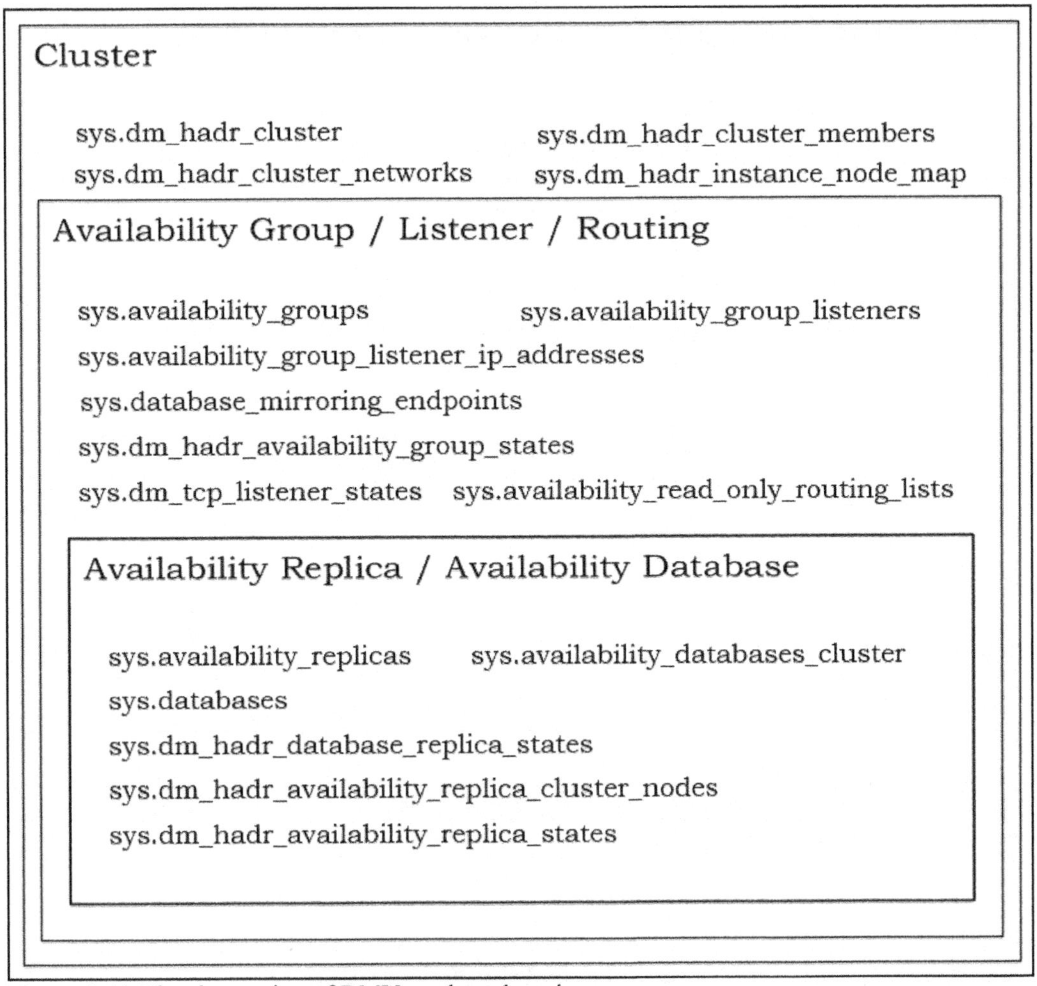

Cluster

sys.dm_hadr_cluster   sys.dm_hadr_cluster_members
sys.dm_hadr_cluster_networks   sys.dm_hadr_instance_node_map

Availability Group / Listener / Routing

sys.availability_groups   sys.availability_group_listeners
sys.availability_group_listener_ip_addresses
sys.database_mirroring_endpoints
sys.dm_hadr_availability_group_states
sys.dm_tcp_listener_states   sys.availability_read_only_routing_lists

Availability Replica / Availability Database

sys.availability_replicas   sys.availability_databases_cluster
sys.databases
sys.dm_hadr_database_replica_states
sys.dm_hadr_availability_replica_cluster_nodes
sys.dm_hadr_availability_replica_states

Figure 9.11 Visual grouping of DMVs and catalog views.

Checking Quorum Configurations via DMV

To check the information about quorum configuration and votes by each member, we can use catalog views as shown in Figure 9.12.

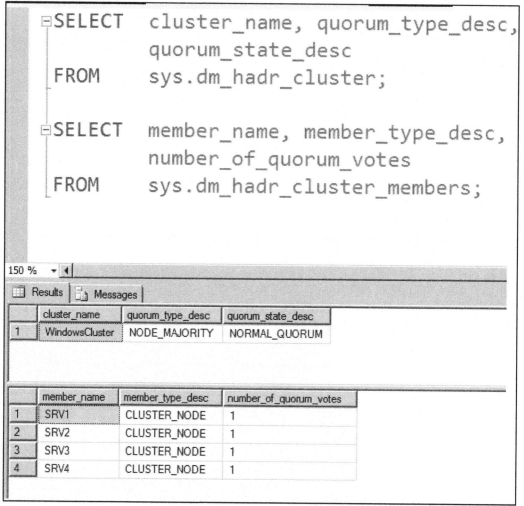

Figure 9.12 DMVs show quorum and voting information.

The same information contained in the DMVs is also available via the Dashboard. If we click on the link that says **View Cluster Quorum Information**, we can see the cluster name, the type of quorum, and the various members along with their votes (Figure 9.13).

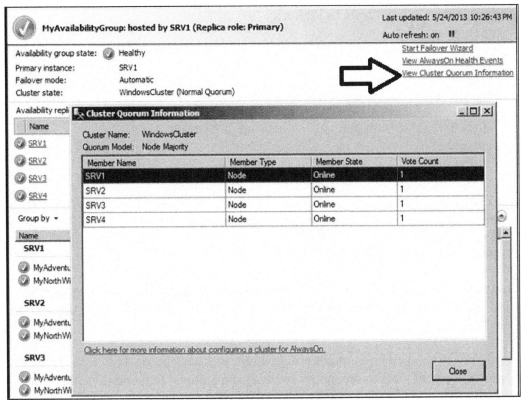

Figure 9.13 Quorum and node voting information via Dashboard.

In Chapter 4, we covered various ways to view/modify the quorum model and the NodeWeight using windows tools. In SQL Server there are dynamic management views which allow us to view the same information. Please note that to modify the setting, there is no T-SQL command and it must be done from one of the Windows Cluster tools (cluster.exe, PowerShell, or the UI)

View Endpoint Information

In an AlwaysOn Availability Group the communication between two replicas is done through endpoints. Each replica has one endpoint and all the sessions for each of the Availability Groups goes over this common endpoint. All the information about the endpoints is exposed through DMVs seen in Table 9.4.

What do we want to check?	Views to look at
Endpoints configured	sys.endpoints
Endpoint status	sys.tcp_endpoints
Endpoint Configuration information	sys.database_mirroring_endpoints
Endpoint runtime information	sys.dm_db_mirroring_connections
Connection state information	sys.dm_hadr_availability_replica_states

Table 9.4 Endpoint related DMVs.

To troubleshoot an endpoint failure, we can refer to the last_connect_error field from the sys.dm_hadr_availability_replica_states DMV to understand the resolution.

To demonstrate the endpoint communication, we used the ALTER ENDPOINT command on SRV2 (the secondary replica) and stopped that endpoint. In our example the endpoint name is HADR_Endpoint:

```
ALTER ENDPOINT HADR_Endpoint STATE = STOPPED
```

As soon as the statement was executed we observed the following error messages in SQL Server Error Log on SRV2:

Message	Explanation
The Database Mirroring endpoint has stopped listening for connections. The Database Mirroring endpoint is in disabled or stopped state.	This is the AlwaysOn Availability Group endpoint name.
The connection between server instances 'SRV2' with id [778951FB-726B-41FB-8E7E-F7E512B9F20E] and 'SRV1' with id [CAEFEABB-4228-490B-8538-AE8A4962542A] has been disabled because the Database Mirroring endpoint was either disabled or stopped. Restart the endpoint by using the ALTER ENDPOINT Transact-SQL statement with STATE = STARTED.	SRV2 (secondary) is unable to communicate to SRV1 (Primary). Message has given solution as well.
AlwaysOn Availability Groups connection with primary database terminated for secondary database 'MyAdventureWorks' on the availability replica with Replica ID: {caefeabb-4228-490b-8538-ae8a4962542a}. This is an informational message only. No user action is required.	We had two availability databases and connection to both have been terminated. This caused database to go to Not Synchronizing state
AlwaysOn Availability Groups connection with primary database terminated for secondary database 'MyNorthwind' on the availability replica with Replica ID: {caefeabb-4228-490b-8538-ae8a4962542a}. This is an informational message only. No user action is required.	

Table 9.5 Error messages in the SQL Server Error Log of the secondary when stopping the endpoint.

On the primary replica the following messages would appear:

Message	Explanation
A connection timeout has occurred on a previously established connection to availability replica 'SRV2' with id [778951FB-726B-41FB-8E7E-F7E512B9F20E]. Either a networking or a firewall issue exists or the availability replica has transitioned to the resolving role.	Unable to communicate to SRV2.
AlwaysOn Availability Groups connection with secondary database terminated for primary database 'MyAdventureWorks' on the availability replica with Replica ID: {778951fb-726b-41fb-8e7e-f7e512b9f20e}. This is an informational message only. No user action is required.	Both availability databases are not synchronizing with replica (ID is for SRV2, previous message, also highlighted)
AlwaysOn Availability Groups connection with secondary database terminated for primary database 'MyNorthwind' on the availability replica with Replica ID: {778951fb-726b-41fb-8e7e-f7e512b9f20e}. This is an informational message only. No user action is required.	

Table 9.6 Error messages in the SQL Server Error Log of the primary when stopping the endpoint.

Performance Counters

Have you ever had a chance to see how athletes train? The coach is constantly watching the stopwatch while the athletes make multiple runs. The stopwatch is used to check the performance of students as they perform the run. In a similar way, SQL Server AlwaysOn performance can be monitored using Performance Monitor (PerfMon). This section calls out some of the performance counters we can use to monitor AlwaysOn Availability Groups.

There is constant data movement and communication between the servers in our group that can be measured. In addition we might want to check how much data each database has flowing through the system. Performance Monitor (PerfMon) is one of the most common tools we use for troubleshooting SQL Server.

The performance counters we are interested in are divided into three major object categories: Availability Replica, Database Replica and Databases Object. Databases Object is not specific to AlwaysOn but there are a few counters it has that can be useful in monitoring and troubleshooting data synchronization issues. To view these counters we need to use Windows Performance Monitor. To start

PerfMon go to **Start** Menu > **Programs** > **Administrative Tools** > **Performance Monitor**. For fans of shortcuts use **Start** > **Run** > **perfmon**. After the tool gets launched, we can use the **Add Counters** button (looks like a green plus sign) to add counters and view their output values.

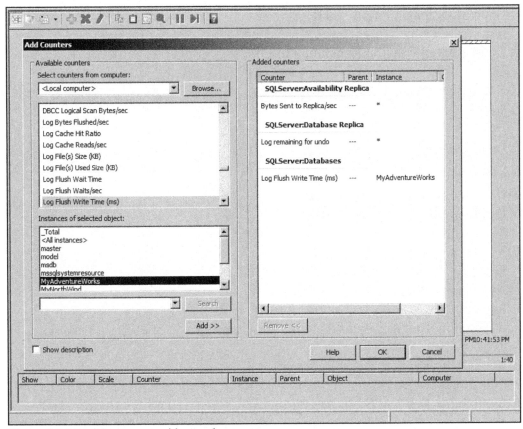

Figure 9.14 PerfMon screen with sample counters.

Table 9.7 shows the counters list and when they are available on the primary replica, the secondary replica or both.

Counter Name	Primary	secondary
Database Replica: Redo Bytes Remaining		✓
Database Replica: Log Bytes Received / sec		✓
Database Replica: File Bytes Received / sec		✓
Database Replica: Log Remaining to Undo		✓
Database Replica: Total Log Requiring Undo		✓
Database Replica: Redone Bytes / sec		✓
Database Replica: Recovery Queue		✓
Database Replica: Log Send Queue		✓
Database Replica: Transaction Delay	✓	
Database Replica: Mirrored Write Transactions / sec	✓	
Availability Replica: Sends to Replica / Sec	✓	✓
Availability Replica: Receives from Replica / Sec	✓	✓
Availability Replica: Bytes Sent to Replica / Sec	✓	✓
Availability Replica: Bytes Received from Replica / sec	✓	✓
Availability Replica: Sends to Transport / sec	✓	✓
Availability Replica: Bytes Sent to Transport / sec	✓	✓
Availability Replica: Resent Messages / sec	✓	✓
Availability Replica: Flow Control Time	✓	
Availability Replica: Flow Control / sec	✓	

Table 9.7 Availability of performance counters on primary and secondary replicas.

Counter Name
Database: Delayed Transactions\sec
Database: Transaction Delay (ms)
Database: Log Pool Requests\sec
Database: Log Pool Cache Misses\sec
Database: Log Pool Disk Reads\sec
Database: Log Bytes Flushed\sec
Database: Log Flush Wait Time

Table 9.8 Availability Group Performance counters that are common from general database counters.

PerfMon is one of the most common tools we use for troubleshooting SQL Server. Availability Groups can also benefit from this tool. Below is a simple flowchart that shows the various operations that happen behind the scenes as the availability replicas communicate. We have taken a few counters and mapped them for reference in Figure 9.15. The Table 9.7 has many more counters that can give us detailed information.

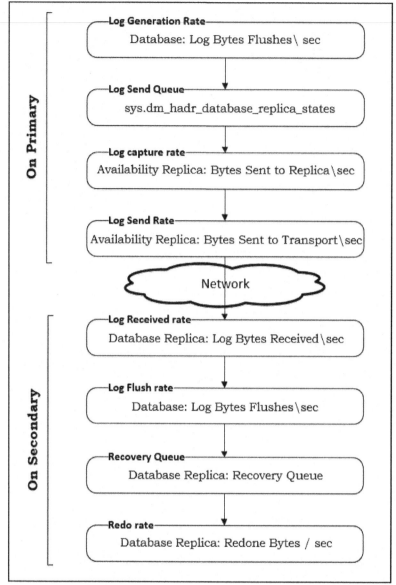

Figure 9.15 Maps PerfMon counters to tasks in primary and secondary.

Summary

Monitoring and troubleshooting is part of all availability scenarios. SQL Server is trying to keep businesses up and running and it is important for us to know all the tricks to troubleshoot in case of problems. In this chapter we saw the options of using the AlwaysOn Dashboard, PowerShell automation scripts, DMVs, AlwaysOn Policies, and high level Performance Counters.

Points to Ponder – AlwaysOn Monitoring and Troubleshooting

1. The AlwaysOn Dashboard is intended to help administrators check the overall health in a visual way inside SSMS. This includes the health of the Availability Group , the individual replicas, and the databases.

2. There are three major sections in the Dashboard:
   - Section 1 allows us to perform failover to any available replica (with or without data loss based on synchronization mode).
   - Section 2 shows the availability replicas and their current state.
   - Section 3 shows the state for each database involved in an Availability Group and their state on each replica.

3. The DMVs of sys.dm_hadr_availability_replica_states and sys.dm_hadr_database_replica_states are used to gather replica level and database level information respectively.

4. The PowerShell cmdlets mapped to the Dashboard sections are:
   - Section 1: Test-SqlAvailabilityGroup
   - Section 2: Test-SqlAvailabilityReplica
   - Section 3: Test-SqlDatabaseReplicaState

5. Performance counters used to monitor the Availability Group are divided into three major categories: Availability Replica, Database Replica, and Database.

6. The Dashboard allows us to view Windows Cluster quorum configurations as well as node voting weights.

7. Most of the DMVs that need to be available for the AlwaysOn Availability Group information has "hadr" in the DMV name.

Review Quiz - Chapter Nine

1.) Which of the following performance counters were added just for AlwaysOn Availability?

  □ a. Availability Replica
  □ b. Database Replica
  □ c. Database Objects
  □ d. Instance Replica

2.) Which PowerShell cmdlet can be used to view the health state of an Availability Group database?

  O a. Test-SqlAvailabilityGroup
  O b. Test-SqlAvailabilityReplica
  O c. Test-SqlDatabaseReplicaState
  O d. Test-SqlAvailabilityGroupState

3.) The Dashboard can be used to perform a failover of the Availability Group?

  O a. TRUE
  O b. FALSE

4.) The Dashboard can be used modify the windows quorum settings and adjust node votes?

  O a. TRUE
  O b. FALSE

Answer Key

1.) There were two performance counter groups added for an AlwaysOn Availability Group, they are (a) Availability Replica and (b) Database Replica. Options (c) Database Objects and (d) Instance Replica are wrong answers.

2.) Since we are looking for the replica Database state, the cmdlet (c) Test-SqlDatabaseReplicaState is correct. All the other options (a) Test-SqlAvailabilityGroup, (b) Test-SqlAvailabilityReplica and (d) Test-SqlAvailabilityGroupState are not correct. In fact (d) cmdlet does not exist.

3.) Using the Dashboard UI in SQL Server Management Studio we can perform the failover of Availability Group. This makes option (a) TRUE the correct option.

4.) Quorum votes cannot be changed or adjusted using the Dashboard UI. Option (b) FALSE is the correct option.

[NOTES]

Chapter 10. AlwaysOn Diagnostics

What do we do when we are not feeling well? In most cases if it is a mild fever or fatigue, we try to get plenty of rest for a couple of days to see if it subsides. If the situation gets worse we might see a doctor for some initial diagnostics. The doctor might make an initial assessment and prescribe a possible remedy. If they find something out of the ordinary they might suggest more tests. Once the test results are in, they might direct us to specialists for more analysis.

The same idea applies to the AlwaysOn world. In this chapter we will look at some interesting diagnostics introduced with SQL Server 2012. The same diagnostics setup can be of great help in AlwaysOn deployments too.

sp_server_diagnostics

For running diagnostics we often need special equipment to find the problem. Most of the equipment we use has great visual indicators that we can easily learn from. Take the example of day-to-day activities like filling up you gas tank when the fuel indicator is nearly empty. Sometimes the indicator is very simple, for example when we forget to wear our seatbelt we hear a beeping sound. These are typical examples of how we can diagnose a problem in our vehicle. In some ways diagnostics is an indicator of what is potentially wrong in our SQL Server environment. In this section we will discuss a system stored procedure called sp_server_diagnostics.

The stored procedure sp_server_diagnostics is used by SQL Server AlwaysOn technology (both the Failover Cluster Instance and the Availability Groups). This is used for failover detection. This procedure is also available for use in any SQL Server instance (even a standalone instance) to assist us in detecting and troubleshooting problems. To prove this theory, in Figure 10.1 we have executed the procedure with a parameter value of 10 (the parameter is the @repeat_interval) on a standalone instance with no Availability Group defined. We can observe that every 10 seconds the results are automatically displayed. Notice the create_time column of the second result set is 10 seconds later. This process will send out results every 10 seconds until it is cancelled.

```
☐sp_server_diagnostics 10
```

150 %

Results | Messages

	create_time	component_type	component_name	state	state_desc	data
1	2013-05-24 22:59:02.600	instance	system	1	clean	<system spinlock
2	2013-05-24 22:59:02.600	instance	resource	1	clean	<resource last No
3	2013-05-24 22:59:02.600	instance	query_processing	1	clean	<queryProcessing
4	2013-05-24 22:59:02.600	instance	io_subsystem	1	clean	<ioSubsystem io L
5	2013-05-24 22:59:02.600	instance	events	0	unknown	<events><sessio

	create_time	component_type	component_name	state	state_desc	data
1	2013-05-24 22:59:12.613	instance	system	1	clean	<system spinlock
2	2013-05-24 22:59:12.613	instance	resource	1	clean	<resource last No
3	2013-05-24 22:59:12.613	instance	query_processing	1	clean	<queryProcessing
4	2013-05-24 22:59:12.613	instance	io_subsystem	1	clean	<ioSubsystem io L
5	2013-05-24 22:59:12.613	instance	events	0	unknown	<events><sessio

Figure 10.1 Executing sp_server_diagnostics with the duration parameter as 10, sends results every 10 seconds automatically.

If we execute the same query on a server that is a primary replica of an Availability Group, we would get more data. We will get one more row per Availability Group as shown in Figure 10.2. We ran this on SRV1 which has one Availability Group called MyAvailabilityGroup. MyAvailabilityGroup is shown as the component_name in the last row. We can also see the component_type of alwaysOn:AvailabilityGroup is listed.

Figure 10.2 Executing sp_server_diagnostics with duration parameter as 10, on server which has AlwaysOn Availability Group configured.

The possible values in the state_desc column are "clean", "warning", "error" or "unknown" (depending upon component name). Let's have a look at the meaning of the various component_name values.

System

This output is helpful and we can get more information about the data of what makes a system "clean", "warning" or even "error". The data field can give us great insight into what is happening.

Figure 10.3 The data field for "system" has information for us to look at.

If we look at the data column for the records listed as the system component, the following information is available and presented in readable format:

```
spinlockBackoffs="0"
sickSpinlockType="none"
sickSpinlockTypeAfterAv="none"
latchWarnings="0"
isAccessViolationOccurred="0"
writeAccessViolationCount="0"
totalDumpRequests="0"
intervalDumpRequests="0"
nonYieldingTasksReported="0"
pageFaults="0"
systemCpuUtilization="0"
sqlCpuUtilization="0"
BadPagesDetected="0"
BadPagesFixed="0"
LastBadPageAddress="0x0"
```

This system component collects data from a system perspective about spinlocks, severe processing conditions, dump generation, non-yielding tasks, page faults, OS, and SQL CPU usage.

Is there anything in our data that is bad? Based on the certain values those attributes, the value of the state_desc column could change to "warning" or even to "error". To demonstrate this, the easiest change in this list to test would be the totalDumpRequests. We have used an undocumented command DBCC DUMPTRIGGER and enabled dump generation for error number 208 (Error 208 is for an invalid object name). We are using the following T-SQL to create this scenario:

```
DBCC DUMPTRIGGER ('SET', 208)
-- 208 is Error for "Invalid Object Name"
GO
SELECT * FROM MissingTable
GO

-- CREATE excessive dump.
SELECT * FROM MissingTable
GO 1000
```

READER NOTE: *Use DUMPTRIGGER cautiously as this is an undocumented statement. Do not use it in a production environment.*

Executing a SELECT command for a table which is not present would cause a 208 error. Normally this is no big deal and the query gets an error. Since we have enabled the DUMPTRIGGER for that error, a dump would get generated. In our example, as soon as the dump gets generated and the totalDumpRequests becomes 1, the state of "system" changes to "warning" (see the middle of Figure 10.4). To stress this further, we have run a SELECT statement in a loop and started getting many dumps.

When dumps get generated continuously and the totalDumpRequests reaches 100, the state changes to error as shown in the bottom of Figure 10.4.

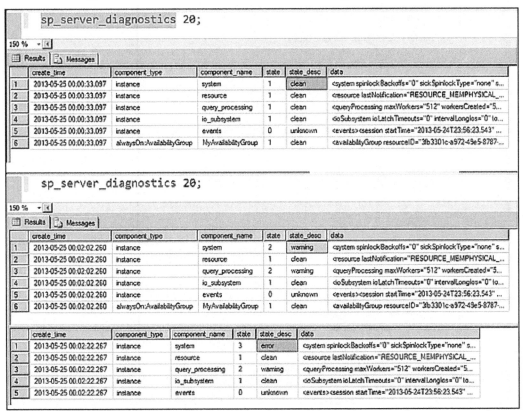

Figure 10.4 Change in system state: Results of sp_server_diagnostics when dumps were getting generated at high rate.

If we cancel the query running in the loop, the dump generation stops and we notice that the state goes back to warning. The problem is not happening anymore but state goes down to warning (not clean).

This means that excessive dump generation at a fast rate was an error condition and not desirable in production servers. The default setting of FailoverConditionLevel = 3 would cause the Availability Group to failover (if auto failover is specified). Note that this is not the only condition that can create an error state for system. There could be many things severe enough to send a system component into a failed state.

Figure 10.5 shows how our server roles have changed. SRV1 is now a secondary while SRV2 is the new primary because the excessive dumps caused a failover.

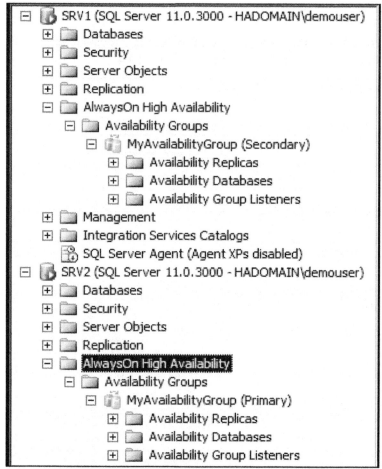

Figure 10.5 After the failover SRV2 is now the primary replica.

Resource

The resource component reports data from a resource perspective. This would include physical and virtual memory, buffer pools, pages, the cache, and other SQL Server memory objects.

To reproduce a warning state in this resource component, we have brought down the max server memory on the instance to 128 MB (minimum possible value) by using the sp_configure system procedure.

```
EXEC sp_configure N'Show advanced options', 1
EXEC sp_configure N'max server memory (MB)', N'128'
GO

RECONFIGURE WITH OVERRIDE
```

As soon as the memory was reduced we started seeing a warning status for resource component. In the data field we see a change in that lastNotification was set to RESOURCE_MEMPHYSICAL_LOW.

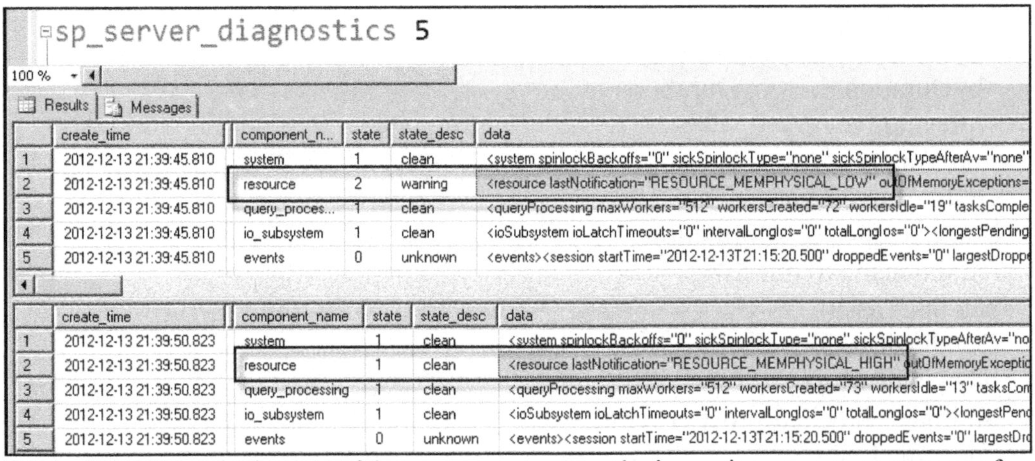

```
sp_server_diagnostics 5
```

100 %

Results | Messages

	create_time	component_n...	state	state_desc	data
1	2012-12-13 21:39:45.810	system	1	clean	<system spinlockBackoffs="0" sickSpinlockType="none" sickSpinlockTypeAfterAv="none"
2	2012-12-13 21:39:45.810	resource	2	warning	<resource lastNotification="RESOURCE_MEMPHYSICAL_LOW" outOfMemoryExceptions=
3	2012-12-13 21:39:45.810	query_proces...	1	clean	<queryProcessing maxWorkers="512" workersCreated="72" workersIdle="19" tasksComple
4	2012-12-13 21:39:45.810	io_subsystem	1	clean	<ioSubsystem ioLatchTimeouts="0" intervalLonglos="0" totalLonglos="0"><longestPending
5	2012-12-13 21:39:45.810	events	0	unknown	<events><session startTime="2012-12-13T21:15:20.500" droppedEvents="0" largestDropp

	create_time	component_name	state	state_desc	data
1	2012-12-13 21:39:50.823	system	1	clean	<system spinlockBackoffs="0" sickSpinlockType="none" sickSpinlockTypeAfterAv="no
2	2012-12-13 21:39:50.823	resource	1	clean	<resource lastNotification="RESOURCE_MEMPHYSICAL_HIGH" outOfMemoryExceptic
3	2012-12-13 21:39:50.823	query_processing	1	clean	<queryProcessing maxWorkers="512" workersCreated="73" workersIdle="13" tasksCom
4	2012-12-13 21:39:50.823	io_subsystem	1	clean	<ioSubsystem ioLatchTimeouts="0" intervalLonglos="0" totalLonglos="0"><longestPend
5	2012-12-13 21:39:50.823	events	0	unknown	<events><session startTime="2012-12-13T21:15:20.500" droppedEvents="0" largestDro

Figure 10.6 Change in the state of the resource component by increasing max server memory of SQL Server instance. lastNotification changed from low memory to high memory.

In Figure 10.6 we have changed the value of the max server memory from 128 MB to 4 GB between the first and second output set and we can see the state changed from warning to back to clean. It never went to an error state since this happened for a short time. We need to have an "out of memory" condition for a long time to reach to error state for this component.

Query_Processing

This is one of the most interesting pieces of data captured as part of the diagnostics data collection. As the name suggests, it collects data from a query-processing perspective. The following is a snippet of data shown in the output:

```
maxWorkers="512"
workersCreated="72"
workersIdle="19"
tasksCompletedWithinInterval="40"
pendingTasks="0"
oldestPendingTaskWaitingTime="0" hasUnresolvableDeadlockOccurred="0"
hasDeadlockedSchedulersOccurred="0" trackingNonYieldingScheduler="0x0"
<topWaits>
 <nonPreemptive>
 <byCount>...</byCount>
 <byDuration> ... </byDuration>
 </nonPreemptive>

 <preemptive>
 <byCount>... </byCount>
 <byDuration>... </byDuration>
 </preemptive>
</topWaits>
<cpuIntensiveRequests>
 Multiple queries information
</cpuIntensiveRequests>
<pendingTasks>
</pendingTasks>
<blockingTasks>
 Multiple <blocked-process-report>
</blockingTasks>
```

In this collection we get details about worker threads (both max and current), tasks, wait types, and CPU intensive sessions. It also provides information about blocking tasks if they occur. If there are multiple blocking chains then we can see all of them under the blockingTasks node.

Here is a little background about the blocked process report. This is an event added to SQL Server 2005. This event is raised if there is blocking for a duration equal to or greater than the "blocked process threshold" value specified via the sp_configure command. In short, if we set the value to 5 seconds and a session is blocked for more than 5 seconds, the event would be raised. This event has information about the blocked process and the blocking process. The information is shown in XML Format. With SQL Server 2012 the sp_server_diagnostics stored procedure reports the blocking in the Query_Processing component even if we did not set it.

IO_Subsystem

As the name indicates, this component would report IO related issues faced by the SQL Server engine. The following is the XML which we would see for this component:

```
<ioSubsystem ioLatchTimeouts="0" intervalLongIos="0" totalLongIos="0">
<longestPendingRequests>
<pendingRequest duration="39" filePath="\\?\C:\Program Files\Microsoft SQL
Server\MSSQL11.MSSQLSERVER\MSSQL\DATA\TempDB.mdf"
offset="16711680" handle="0xa40"/>
</longestPendingRequests>
… and more...
</ioSubsystem>
```

It is important to know that the state of this component can be either clean or warning and this output is not considered in failover detection logic. The state would be changed to warning if there is any IO detected as taking more than 15 seconds. This is the same as the warning message we see in the error log (Error # 833).

Messages
SQL Server has encountered %d occurrence(s) of I/O requests taking longer than %d seconds to complete on file [%ls] in database [%ls] (%d). The OS file handle is 0x%p. The offset of the latest long I/O is: %#016I64x

Events

Similar to the IO_Subsystem, this component also doesn't take part in failure detection. The state of this component is always unknown. It does data collection through the stored procedure on the errors and events of interest recorded by the server. This includes details about ring buffer exceptions, ring buffer events, memory broker, out of memory, scheduler monitor, buffer pool, spinlocks, security, and connectivity.

AlwaysOn: AvailabilityGroup

For each Availability Group we would see one row in the output of the sp_server_diagnostics. The possible states for this would be either clean or error. This component does not help in making decisions about failover conditions. This provides very little information about the Availability Group such as lease state and resource id.

```
<availabilityGroup resourceID="09044c14-8aca-4360-a808-6f034c8639e3"
leaseValid="1"/>
```

If we recall from earlier chapters, the value shown in the resourceID field is the GUID of the resource in the Availability Group. This is for related information in the registry at this location HKEY_LOCAL_MACHINE\Cluster\Resources.

With the help of the diagnostics capability of sp_server_diagnostics, database administrators would be able to find the cause of a server hang. As we can see in the output, it can detect SQL Server internal errors like worker thread exhaustion or persistent "out of memory" conditions in the internal resource pool. Similar to the default trace, sp_server_diagnostics is lightweight and designed for running with a minor performance impact, even during heavy workloads.

Health State Components	Description
Query Processing	Collects worker thread exhaustion, unsolvable deadlocks.
Resource	Collects persistent out of memory conditions.
System	Internal errors such as orphaned spinlocks, frequent dumps are collected.
IO Subsystem	Not used for failure detection, informational only.
Events	Not used for failure detection, informational only.
AlwaysOn:AvailabilityGroup	Not used for failure detection, informational only.

Table 10.1 sp_server_diagnostics components summary

To run sp_server_diagnostics we require VIEW SERVER STATE permission on the server.

Improved Diagnostics

For examination purposes, the information provided by sp_server_diagnostics is written to the local extended event logfile (.xel file). The decision by the resource DLL about the failover (also called SQLDIAG output) is also written. This feature is also applicable for both AlwaysOn Availability Group and AlwaysOn FCI.

This is an internal extended event session which writes data captured by events from the sp_server_diagnostics component result to the file. These diagnostics logs are created under the same folder which contains the ERRORLOG file. These diagnostic files are named:
<ServerName_InstanceName_SQLDIAG_Number>.xel.

These logs can be read by SQL Server Management studio directly or by using the T-SQL function sys.fn_xe_file_target_read_file.

Here is the query which we can use to read the XEL file:

```
SELECT xml_data.value('(/event/@name)[1]','varchar(max)') AS
'Name'
, xml_data.value('(/event/@package)[1]', 'varchar(max)')
    AS 'Package'
, xml_data.value('(/event/@timestamp)[1]', 'datetime') AS
'TimeStamp'
, xml_data.value('(/event/@creation_time)[1]', 'datetime')
AS 'CreationTime',
xml_data.value('(/event/data[@name=''component_type'']/value
)[1]','sysname') AS 'ComponentType'
,
xml_data.value('(/event/data[@name=''component'']/value)[1]'
,'sysname') AS 'Component'
,
xml_data.value('(/event/data[@name=''state'']/value)[1]','in
t')    AS 'State',
xml_data.value('(/event/data[@name=''state_desc'']/value)[1]
','sysname') AS 'State_desc',
xml_data.value('(/event/data[@name=''failure_condition_level
'']/value)[1]','sysname') AS 'failure_condition_level',
xml_data.value('(/event/data[@name=''instance_name'']/value)
[1]','sysname') AS 'instance_name',
xml_data.value('(/event/data[@name=''node_name'']/value)[1]'
,'sysname') AS 'node_name'
, xml_data.query('(/event/data[@name="data"]/value/*)') AS
'Data'
FROM
(
 SELECT
  object_name as event
  ,CONVERT(xml, event_data) as xml_data
 FROM
 sys.fn_xe_file_target_read_file('C:\Program Files\Microsoft
SQL
Server\MSSQL11.MSSQLSERVER\MSSQL\Log\SRV1_MSSQLSERVER_SQLDIA
G_0_129998738743100000.xel', NULL, NULL, NULL)
)
AS XEventData
ORDER BY TimeStamp
```

READER NOTE: The topic on how to query for XML data like the one that comes out of the sys.fn_xe_file_target_read_file function is covered in SQL Queries 2012 Joes 2 Pros Volume 5.

To open the file from SSMS, we can use **File** > **Open** > **File** and select the desired file. As soon as we open the .xel file there is a new menu item added called Extended Events and we can change the look and feel of output. We can add filters, perform aggregations, and add and remove columns to the grid to do analysis. Generally, for finding the root cause we need to open multiple .xel files to see the series of events that have happened on all the nodes of AlwaysOn Availability Group or AlwaysOn FCI. This can be done by using **File** > **Open** > **Merge Extended Event Files** option.

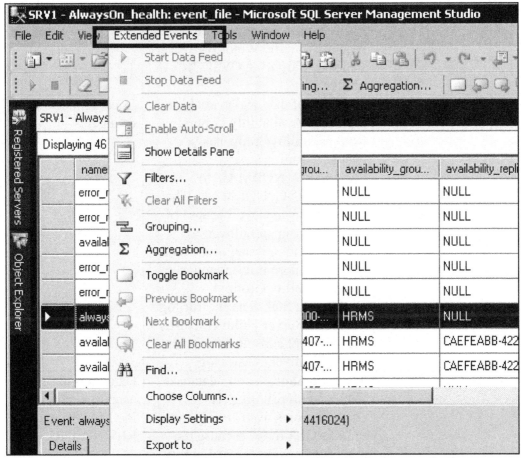

Figure 10.7 Viewing Extended Events files from SQL Server 2012 Management Studio.

To demonstrate the root cause analysis using these files we have simulated a failure due to excessive dump generation and we met the condition of

FailoverConditionLevel = 3 (due to system component error state). Let's look at the various logs captured and see if we can find this information. The very first place to look at is the SQL Server ERRORLOG.

READER NOTE: *For clarity, we have removed the text "This is an informational message only. No user action is required." from all the messages in Table 10.2.*

Time (HH:MM:SS.MS)	Message	Comments
17:24:40.41	AlwaysOn: The local replica of Availability Group 'MyAvailabilityGroup' is preparing to transition to the resolving role in response to a request from the Windows Server Failover Clustering (WSFC) cluster.	Windows Cluster asked AG resource to restart/failover.
17:24:40.41	The state of the local availability replica in Availability Group ' MyAvailabilityGroup' has changed from 'PRIMARY_NORMAL' to 'RESOLVING_NORMAL'. The replica state changed because of either a startup, a failover, a communication issue, or a cluster error. For more information, see the Availability Group Dashboard, SQL Server error log, Windows Server Failover Cluster management console or Windows Server Failover Cluster log.	Local replica state change.
17:24:40.41	The Availability Group database "MyAdventureWorks" is changing roles from "PRIMARY" to "RESOLVING" because the mirroring session or Availability Group failed over due to role synchronization.	Database role changing from PRIMARY to RESOLVING.
17:24:40.41	Stopped listening on virtual network name 'MyListener'.	Connections stopped

Time (HH:MM:SS.MS)	Message	Comments
17:24:51.12	AlwaysOn: The local replica of Availability Group 'MyAvailabilityGroup' is preparing to transition to the primary role in response to a request from the Windows Server Failover Clustering (WSFC) cluster.	Cluster bringing resource online
17:24:51.87	The state of the local availability replica in Availability Group 'MyAvailabilityGroup' has changed from 'RESOLVING_NORMAL' to 'PRIMARY_PENDING'. The replica state changed because of either a startup, a failover, a communication issue, or a cluster error. For more information, see the Availability Group Dashboard, SQL Server error log, Windows Server Failover Cluster management console or Windows Server Failover Cluster log.	Replica State Change of cluster resource state from failed to online pending.
17:24:51.88	Started listening on virtual network name 'MyListener'.	Listener ready

Time (HH:MM:SS.MS)	Message	Comments
17:24:52.08	The state of the local availability replica in Availability Group 'MyAvailabilityGroup' has changed from 'PRIMARY_PENDING' to 'PRIMARY_NORMAL'. The replica state changed because of either a startup, a failover, a communication issue, or a cluster error. For more information, see the Availability Group Dashboard, SQL Server error log, Windows Server Failover Cluster management console or Windows Server Failover Cluster log.	Change of cluster resource state from online pending to online.
17:24:52.18	The Availability Group database "MyAdventureWorks" is changing roles from "RESOLVING" to "PRIMARY" because the mirroring session or Availability Group failed over due to role synchronization.	Database back to normal.

Table 10.2 Information about replica state change is available in ERRORLOG during failover.

From the ERRORLOG file, we know that a resource went to a failed state and then came back online. We are not able to find the cause of this in the ERRORLOG file. Now we will look at the SQLDIAG logfiles to check if there are any insights there. We opened multiple .xel files using SSMS and added a filter for time. Here is the series of events in the .xel files.

Time (HH:MM:SS)	Name	Message
17:23:59	info_message	[hadrag] SQL Server component 'system' health state has been changed from 'clean' to 'warning'
17:24:39	component_health_result	Component - system state_desc – error

Time (HH:MM :SS)	Name	Message
17:24:39	info_message	[hadrag] SQL Server component 'system' health state has been changed from 'warning' to 'error' at 17:24:39.347
17:24:40	info_message	[hadrag] Failure detected, the state of system component is error
17:24:40	info_message	[hadrag] Availability Group is not healthy with given HealthCheckTimeout and FailureConditionLevel
17:24:40	availability_group_is_alive_failure	availability_group_name - MyAvailabilityGroup Reason – NOTHEALTHY
17:24:40	availability_group_state_change	failure_condition_level - SYSTEM_UNHEALTHY target_state – Failed
17:24:40	info_message	[hadrag] Stopping Health Worker Thread
17:24:40	info_message	[hadrag] Health worker was asked to terminate
17:24:40	info_message	[hadrag] SQLMoreResults() returns -1 with following information
17:24:40	info_message	[hadrag] Change diagnostics interval worker is stopped
17:24:40	info_message	[hadrag] ODBC Error: [HY008] [Microsoft][SQL Server Native Client 11.0]Operation canceled (0)
17:24:40	info_message	[hadrag] ODBC Error: [01000] [Microsoft][SQL Server Native Client 11.0][SQL Server] (0)
17:24:40	info_message	[hadrag] No more diagnostics results
17:24:40	info_message	[hadrag] Diagnostics is stopped

Table 10.3 Information available in SQLDIAG log files about component health and failover conditions.

READER NOTE: *In Table 10.3 "hadrag" stands for "High Availability and Disaster Recovery Availability Group".*

We have taken information from the extended event logs. Looking at the shaded portion of Figure 10.3 we see the availability_group_is_alive_failure has a value of NOTHEALTHY. Why did this happen? Notice the info_message shaded portion of the table shows an error in the system component. The IsAlive check was set to FailoverConditionLevel 3 and we encountered a system component error, which caused failover.

Summary

Just like how a doctor can run a battery of tests to identify and diagnose potential health problems, SQL Server can use the output of sp_server_diagnostics to diagnose potential problems on the server. The same diagnostic output can be used for AlwaysOn deployments too. We can use sp_server_diagnostics to identify potential automatic failover conditions also.

Point to Ponder – AlwaysOn Diagnostics

1. The stored procedure sp_server_diagnostic is used by SQL Server AlwaysOn technology (Failover Cluster Instance and Availability Groups both) for failover detection.

2. The sp_server_diagnostics procedure captures the following components:

    *   System
    *   Resource
    *   Query_Processing
    *   IO_Subsystem
    *   Events
    *   AlwaysOn:AvailabilityGroup

3. Query Processing is used to collect worker thread exhaustion and unsolvable deadlocks.

4. Resource is used to collect persistent out of memory conditions.

5. System is used to collect internal errors such as orphaned spinlocks, and frequent dumps.

6. IO Subsystem, Events and AlwaysOn:AvailabilityGroup are used for informational data only. They are not used for failure detection.

7. For postmortem purposes, the information provided by sp_server_diagnostics is written to the local extended event logfile (.xel file) along with the decision taken by the resource DLL about a failover (also called as SQLDIAG output).

Review Quiz - Chapter Ten

1.) Which of the following subsystems don't induce a failover via sp_server_diagnostics? Choose all that apply.

   □ a. System
   □ b. Resource
   □ c. IO_Subsystem
   □ d. Events

2.) The sp_server_diagnostics stored procedure is used by SQL Server automatically for which of the following environments?

   □ a. Failover cluster instance
   □ b. Availability Groups
   □ c. Log Shipping
   □ d. Replication

3.) Which component in sp_server_diagnostics is responsible to find possible unsolvable deadlocks?

   O a. Query Processing
   O b. Resource
   O c. System
   O d. IO Subsystem
   O e. Events

4.) Which component in sp_server_diagnostics is responsible for reporting memory related problems?

   O a. Query Processing
   O b. Resource
   O c. System
   O d. IO Subsystem
   O e. Events

5.) Which component in sp_server_diagnostics is responsible for catching information about frequent dump generation on a SQL Server Instance?

O a. Query Processing
O b. Resource
O c. System
O d. IO Subsystem
O e. Events

6.) Which component in sp_server_diagnostics is responsible for finding possible Disk contention on the server?

O a. Query Processing
O b. Resource
O c. System
O d. IO Subsystem
O e. Events

7.) What happens in a cluster when the sp_server_diagnostics results are not sent by the server?

O a. Value of HealthCheckTimeout is checked
O b. Waits for 60 seconds
O c. Initiates failover
O d. Pings again

8.) What information is dumped into the SQLDIAG output (.xel) file?

O a. DMV of AvailabilityGroups
O b. sp_server_diagnostics
O c. sp_database_diagnostics
O d. sp_server_component_result

Answer Key

1.) sp_server_diagnostics can collect all the components but failover is not considered for errors in (c) IO_Subsystem and (d) Events. This makes (a) System and (b) Resource the wrong answers.

2.) sp_server_diagnostics can be used for both the AlwaysOn configurations of (a) Failover cluster instance and (b) Availability Groups, making them the correct answers. It is not built with (c) Log Shipping and (d) Replication in mind, they are the wrong answers.

3.) Deadlocks are caught by the Query Processing in sp_server_diagnostics so (a) Query Processing is the correct answer. Options (b) Resource, (c) System, (d) IO Subsystem and (e) Events are all wrong answers.

4.) Since memory is related to SQL Server resource, sp_server_diagnostics collects the same under (b) Resource head. So the other options; (a) Query Processing, (c) System, (d) IO Subsystem, and (e) Events are wrong answers.

5.) Information about dumps getting generated is collected by System component in server diagnostics. The correct option is (c) System. All other values of (a) Query Processing, (b) Resource, (d) IO Subsystem and (e) Events are wrong answers.

6.) Option (d) IO Subsystem is the correct answer as Disk is part of the IO subsystem. So options (a) Query Processing, (b) Resource, (c) System and (e) Events are wrong answers.

7.) When server doesn't get a ping response, it initiates a failover. Hence (c) Initiates failover is the correct answer. (a) Value of HealthCheckTimeout is checked, (b) Waits for 60 seconds and (d) Pings again are all wrong.

8.) Options (a) DMV of AvailabilityGroups, (c) sp_database_diagnostics, and (d) sp_server_component_result are all wrong. Since sp_server_diagnostics is not one of them, (b) is the correct answer.

[NOTES]

Chapter 11. AlwaysOn Advanced Monitoring

We use technology in almost every activity that we do. From mobile phones, laptops, cars, to digital television, there is technology everywhere. If you ever get a chance to look at a racecar the technology that goes behind it can be mind-blowing. Even in normal cars these days the amount of technology that gets into it is amazing. With the engine being the heart of vehicle, the Dashboard is the easiest way to find out if there are any problems. Normally we can quickly find out if the seat belts have not been put on or if any of the doors were not closed properly. These are great visual clues when it comes to taking corrective actions for the situation at hand. On the contrary, if we ever watch Formula1 races, the car makes a run and there is a computer attached to get vital data of how the car performed for the previous run. These days' race cars wirelessly transmit vital parameters back to the pit-crew. This information can be critical given that the car gets only a few seconds of its time in the pit. With this information the amount of fuel that is to be injected is controlled and the pit-crew plans accordingly.

In the case of AlwaysOn deployments there is a need to integrate with existing monitoring solutions like System Center or other tools. To keep a close monitor of the AlwaysOn health we might use indicators like Wait Types too. This chapter takes a quick tour of the various advanced options we have in monitoring SQL Server AlwaysOn deployments.

AlwaysOn Health Session

The AlwaysOn health session is an extended event session which captures information about the AlwaysOn Availability Group. This includes DDLs executed to make modifications to the topology. This information is sometimes useful to find the root cause of the failover or the restart of the servers. To view the data captured by this session, we can open **SSMS**, go to the **Management folder > Extended Events > Sessions > AlwaysOn_health** > right-click on the **package0.event** file and choose **View Target Data** as shown in Figure 11.1.

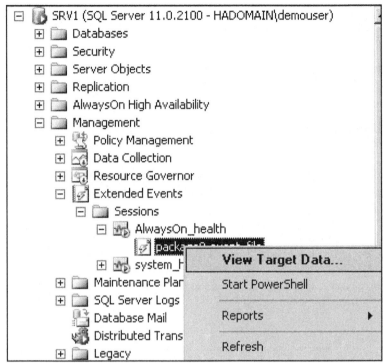

Figure 11.1 How to view data captured by AlwaysOn_health session.

It is important to note that an AlwaysOn extended event session is not started if we are creating the Availability Group using T-SQL or a PowerShell script. When we use the wizard to create the AlwaysOn Availability Group, a session is started on the replicas which are added by the wizard. If initialized by T-SQL or PowerShell, the extended event session can be enabled by using the following T-SQL commands:

```
--This will start a session that is not running.
ALTER EVENT SESSION [AlwaysOn_health] ON SERVER
STATE = START
GO

--This will make sure that the session starts when SQL
Starts.
ALTER EVENT SESSION [AlwaysOn_health] ON SERVER
WITH (STARTUP_STATE = ON)
GO
```

The first T-SQL statement would start the session so it would be running. If we restarted SQL Server service it might not automatically start. We want this to start each time SQL Server service starts. For this to start each time, the second T-SQL Statement will automatically start the session at each SQL startup.

READER NOTE: *The CREATE script can be found under "%ProgramFiles%\Microsoft SQL Server\MSSQL11.<InstanceID>\MSSQL\Install\u_tables.sql"*

We can start an extended event session if it has been created. This code can be used to recreate the session if it gets dropped by mistake. The following is the script of the extended event session taken from SSMS:

```
CREATE EVENT SESSION [AlwaysOn_health] ON SERVER
ADD EVENT sqlserver.alwayson_ddl_executed,
ADD EVENT sqlserver.availability_group_lease_expired,
ADD EVENT
sqlserver.availability_replica_automatic_failover_validation
,
ADD EVENT
sqlserver.availability_replica_manager_state_change,
ADD EVENT sqlserver.availability_replica_state_change,
ADD EVENT sqlserver.error_reported(
WHERE
([error_number]=(9691) OR [error_number]=(35204) OR
[error_number]=(9693) OR [error_number]=(26024) OR
[error_number]=(28047) OR [error_number]=(26023) OR
[error_number]=(9692) OR [error_number]=(28034) OR
[error_number]=(28036) OR [error_number]=(28048) OR
[error_number]=(28080) OR [error_number]=(28091) OR
[error_number]=(26022) OR [error_number]=(9642) OR
[error_number]=(35201) OR [error_number]=(35202) OR
[error_number]=(35206) OR [error_number]=(35207) OR
[error_number]=(26069) OR [error_number]=(26070) OR
[error_number]>(41047) AND [error_number]<(41056) OR
[error_number]=(41142) OR [error_number]=(41144) OR
[error_number]=(1480) OR [error_number]=(823) OR
[error_number]=(824) OR [error_number]=(829) OR
[error_number]=(35264) OR [error_number]=(35265))),
ADD EVENT sqlserver.lock_redo_blocked
ADD TARGET package0.event_file(SET
filename=N'AlwaysOn_health.xel',max_file_size=(5),max_rollov
er_files=(4))
WITH (MAX_MEMORY=4096
KB,EVENT_RETENTION_MODE=ALLOW_SINGLE_EVENT_LOSS,MAX_DISPATCH
_LATENCY=30 SECONDS,MAX_EVENT_SIZE=0
KB,MEMORY_PARTITION_MODE=NONE,TRACK_CAUSALITY=OFF,STARTUP_ST
ATE=ON)
GO
```

There are various error numbers tracked by the event. We have taken this list
from the u_tables.sql file which was mentioned earlier in the reader note.

This list tells the possible areas that get tracked using that specific health session. The error numbers map into these high level types.

- endpoint issue : stopped
- endpoint issue : invalid IP address
- endpoint issue : encryption and handshake issue
- endpoint issue : port conflict
- endpoint issue : authentication failure
- endpoint : listening
- endpoint issue : generic message
- AlwaysOn connection timeout information
- AlwaysOn Listener state
- WSFC cluster issues
- failover validation message
- Availability Group resource failure
- database replica role change
- automatic page repair event
- database replica suspended resumed

Troubleshooting using AlwaysOn_health

While demonstrating the Dashboard, we have created a scenario and showed the results. This is based on captured data in the AlwaysOn_health .xel file when a user has suspended the data movement for one of the databases in the group. Now let's have a look at the AlwaysOn_health session. Figure 11.2 shows the information captured in the extended event logfile.

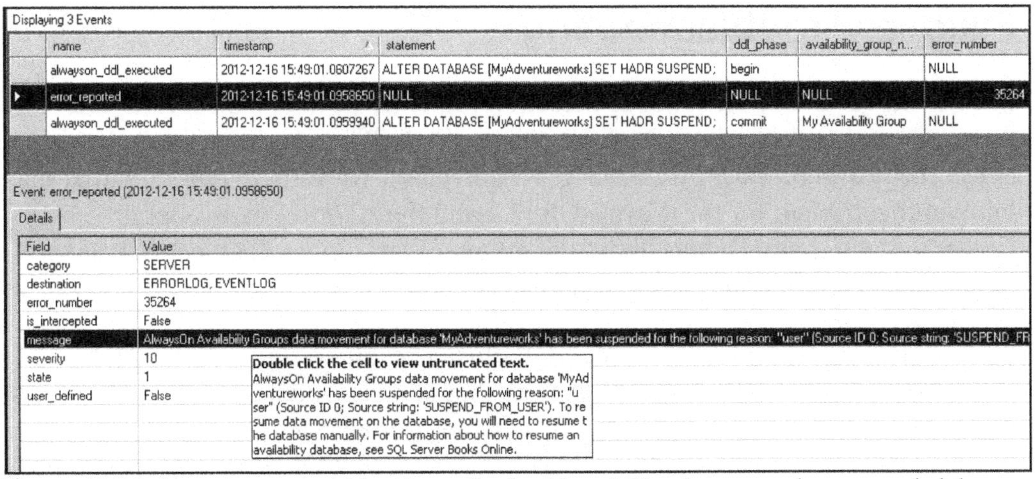

Figure 11.2 Information captured in AlwaysOn_health .xel file when a user has suspended the data movement for one of the databases in the group.

In Figure 11.2 we have displayed only three rows. The first and third rows are for event alwayson_ddl_executed. The first one is the begin/start event and the last one is the commit/complete event. It shows us the command to suspend the event was executed. The following is the T-SQL Statement that did the suspension:

```
ALTER DATABASE [MyAdventureWorks] SET HADR SUSPEND
```

The middle row shows error 35264 which is raised while an availability database was suspended. The following is the complete message from the message field for that event:

AlwaysOn Availability Groups data movement for database 'MyAdventureWorks' has been suspended for the following reason: "user" (Source ID 0; Source string: 'SUSPEND_FROM_USER'). To resume data movement on the database, you will need to resume the database manually. For information about how to resume an availability database, see SQL Server Books Online. The T-SQL code to do this is seen here:

```
ALTER DATABASE [MyAdventureWorks] SET HADR RESUME
```

Extended event sessions will capture the list of errors they are told to track. If we go back and refer to the list of errors captured by the AlwaysOn health session in the T-SQL definition, this is one of the errors, so it appeared in this session. The important information in this message is SUSPEND_FROM_USER which means, it was a user action and this was not done by the system.

Failover Troubleshooting

In SQL Server 2012, the failover detection logic has been enhanced. Instead of the traditional pull mechanism of the cluster, SQL 2012 uses a push mechanism to detect the health of the SQL instance. At this point, we want to point out that the failover mechanism for the AlwaysOn FCI and the AlwaysOn Availability Groups are the same. Details about the output of sp_server_diagnostics was the topic of Chapter 10 - sp_server_diagnostics section.

In SQL Server 2012, as soon as the SQL cluster resource starts, it executes a system stored procedure called sp_server_diagnostics which automatically returns the data at a specified interval. This is different from earlier checks because here the connection is already made and results are sent by SQL Server based on the interval. SQL Server logs this information to the Extended Events Logfile (.xel). Most of the time it will wait for a health check. In fact if the HealthCheckTimeout value is at 30 seconds then the sp_server_diagnostics would run every 10 seconds. The interval parameter to run sp_server_diagnostics would be equal to one third that of the HealthCheckTimeout value.

To determine the health of the SQL instance the cluster would wait for a value defined in the HealthCheckTimeout property (the default is 60 seconds) to get results from sp_server_diagnostics. If no results are received, it is assumed that SQL is unresponsive and a failover is initiated.

On a closer look at the stored procedure results, it collects data from various components of SQL Server and sends the results as output. If everything is fine, then the state value returned for each component is "clean". If something is not right for a component, then the state would be retuned as "warning" or "error". Out of all the available components only system, resource, and query process components are used for failure detection. The IO_Subsystem and events components are designed for diagnostic purposes and not for failover detection.

To decide the failover condition, we can set the FailoverConditionLevel parameter for the Availability Group cluster resource. The value can be found under the Failover Cluster Manager interface. Then choose the **Availability Group** resource, right-click and select **Properties**. The default value of the FailoverConditionLevel is set to 3 (Figure 11.3).

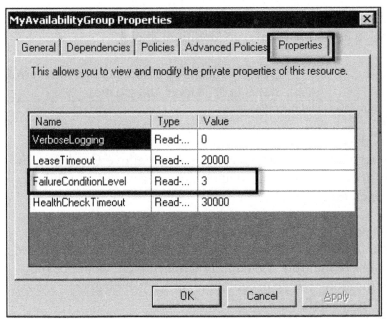

Figure 11.3 Various properties of Availability Group resource using Failover Cluster Manager interface.

Table 11.1 summarizes the various values and their correlation with output of sp_server_diagnostics.

FailoverConditionLevel	Details
0 - No Failover or restart	No failover or restart would be performed by cluster service.
1 - Failover or restart if server down	Restart if SQL Service is down
2 - Failover or restart if server is unresponsive.	FailoverConditionLevel 1 OR If cluster is not getting output of sp_server_diagnostics within HealthCheckTimeout
3 - Failover or restart on critical errors.	FailoverConditionLevel 2 OR System components returns error status in sp_server_diagnostics
4 - Failover or restart on medium errors.	FailoverConditionLevel 3 OR Resource components returns error status in sp_server_diagnostics

FailoverConditionLevel	Details
5 - Failover or restart on any error reported.	FailoverConditionLevel 4 OR Query_Processing components returns error status in sp_server_diagnostics

Table 11.1 Failover condition levels and their details.

Each level includes all the conditions from the previous levels in addition to its own condition. There are more possible events to cause a FailoverConditionLevel of 5 to fail than that of level 4. This means that chances of a restart or a failover increases as the level increases.

We learned earlier that sp_server_diagnostics would be executed to check the health. There are possibilities that we have multiple Availability Groups defined in a cluster. Even if we have multiple Availability Groups, there would be only one execution of the procedure. Single execution of sp_server_diagnostics would cover all Availability Groups defined.

What if we had one server with two groups and one group checking the health more often than the other? If we set a different value of the HealthCheckTimeout for various Availability Groups, the minimum value of all the groups would be used to run sp_server_diagnostics. To explain this better, let us say we have two Availability Groups AG1 and AG2. If the HealthCheckTimeout value is set for 60000 and 90000 for AG1 and AG2 respectively, then 60000/3 =20000 ms =20 (seconds). 20 seconds would be the parameter passed to sp_server_diagnostics.

Monitoring using System Center Operations Manager

This is one of the interesting ways to monitor an AlwaysOn Availability Group. This option is not part of the SQL Server product. We need to purchase a product called System Center Operations Manager (SCOM). System Center is a complete management platform that enables us to easily and efficiently manage our IT environments, including our server infrastructure and client devices. Once SCOM is installed, we need to install the SQL Server 2012 AlwaysOn Management Pack (SQLMP) and then we can monitor all Availability Groups across our enterprise.

Before using the SQL Server 2012 AlwaysOn Management Pack, we needed to import the SQL Server 2012 MP 6.3.0.0 into SCOM. In SQL Server 2012 the AlwaysOn MP includes discovery of AlwaysOn objects, Monitoring of AlwaysOn object's health, and collecting performance data for database replicas and availability replicas. SQL Management Packs have a similar view (like the Dashboard discussed before) because behind the scenes they use the same policies. It supports the raising of alerts on critical health issues. Along with the Availability Group health, it can also monitor performance counters. There are two views of performance counters available in Figure 11.4. This is where we get important counters about the health of the database. This list should have some familiar performance counters and we notice the same counter group names with them.

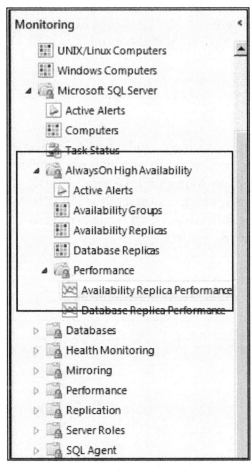

Figure 11.4 A view from SCOM interface shows AlwaysOn High Availability (same as SSMS) and also performance counters.

The beauty of SCOM is that a DBA can define a new user defined policy and SCOM can detect those policies and run them. We highly recommend more reading about this in the SCOM product guide or talk to an SCOM admin within the organization.

Wait Types

While trying to solve any performance issue and monitoring SQL Server health, there could be many approaches. One of the approaches is using wait statistics. In simple terms, whenever we perform any action in SQL Server, it would be either running on the CPU or waiting for some resource. This resource could be a lock on row, a lock on a table or a latch on a page or synchronization activity. In a task's life it would go through a running state, a runnable sate (ready to run, waiting for CPU cycle) and a waiting state. The total task completion time would increase if it had to wait for a longer time. The wait statistics approach can be used as a first step to show us where to move next in troubleshooting a SQL Server performance problem.

READER NOTE: *The topic on wait stats is covered in more depth in SQL Wait Stats Joes 2 Pros.*

In this section, we will focus on the wait types which are available in SQL Server 2012 and specific to AlwaysOn Availability Groups. A list of wait types can be found by running the below query in SQL Server Management Studio. HADR stands for High Availability Disaster Recovery which was part of the HADRON project that was later named AlwaysOn. The following T-SQL code is used to find all the High Availability Disaster Recovery wait stats:

```
SELECT      *
FROM  sys.dm_os_wait_stats
WHERE wait_type LIKE '%hadr%'
```

	wait_type	waiting_tasks_count	wait_time_ms	max_wait_time_ms	signal_wait_time_ms
1	HADR_DB_COMMAND	14	24494	4319	1
2	HADR_TRANSPORT_SESSION	0	0	0	0
3	HADR_CLUSAPI_CALL	695961	172029240	11734	0
4	PWAIT_HADR_CHANGE_NOTIFIER_TERMINATION_SYNC	0	0	0	0
5	PWAIT_HADR_ACTION_COMPLETED	0	0	0	0
6	PWAIT_HADR_OFFLINE_COMPLETED	0	0	0	0
7	PWAIT_HADR_ONLINE_COMPLETED	1	6735	6735	0
8	PWAIT_HADR_FAILOVER_COMPLETED	0	0	0	0
9	PWAIT_HADR_WORKITEM_COMPLETED	5	1049	538	5
10	HADR_WORK_POOL	0	0	0	0

Figure 11.5 Result set for sys.dm_os_wait_stats finding all hadr types.

Once we run the query we would see around 60 rows, they have been documented in Books Online http://msdn.microsoft.com/en-us/library/ms179984(SQL.11).aspx. A few of the important ones and what they do are listed in Table 11.2.

Wait Type	Description
HADR_AR_MANAGER_M UTEX	Used to track internally for a shutdown or startup of availability replica.
HADR_BACKUP_BULK_L OCK	Before a secondary can start a backup it must send a lock message to primary. This wait shows the time taken by background thread to acquire or release this lock.
HADR_CLUSAPI_CALL	Availability Groups do make a lot of Cluster settings and operations to Windows Cluster via T-SQL. This wait type shows time made to Cluster API calls.
HADR_DATABASE_FLO W_CONTROL	High waits here indicated a possible network problem. This can also mean the rate at which log scans are happening is faster than transmission over network.
HADR_FILESTREAM_BL OCK_FLUSH	Waiting for File Stream activities to complete on secondary when a log block has arrived.
HADR_LOGCAPTURE_SY NC	Wait used when attempting to move the next log block, starting a log scan, stopping a scan, routing a file stream message etc. Can also indicate a partner is changing its state.
HADR_PARTNER_SYNC	Used when dealing with partner activities such as when setting the primary availability replica, adding or removing secondary replica.
HADR_SYNC_COMMIT	This represents time to package, send, write and acknowledge log on secondary database in case of synchronized secondary database.
HADR_TRANSPORT_SESS ION	Used in several locations for controlling the transport state. It is used when routing message has been received.
PWAIT_HADR_CHANGE_ NOTIFIER_TERMINATIO N_SYNC	This would loosely equate to number of stop requests and how long it took for the cluster notification and the Availability Group manager handled the Stop.

Table 11.2 Common AlwaysOn Availability Group Wait Types with description.

The complete list of Wait Types is out of scope of this book and we highly recommend checking into it from SQL Server Books Online or the Joes 2 Pros book on Wait Stats.

Application Health AlwaysOn Availability Group

Many business applications need databases to run. Some applications use multiple databases. This is why Availability Group groups make sure one or more databases failover together. This group of databases put inside an Availability Group is done to ensure the health and safety of critical applications that need those databases. Therefore it can be said that an Availability Group's health defines the application's health indirectly.

It is important to understand whether the Availability Group configuration is in a healthy state or not. It is difficult to define the health of an Availability Group from an application perspective, so here is a high level checklist as a starting point. The Availability Group is considered healthy when:

- The read/write application can connect to the primary replica and access all the databases in the Availability Group.

- A readonly application can connect to the secondary replica enabled for read-access and can read from the databases.

- The Availability Group can failover to a replica set for automatic failover in the event of a primary replica failure in order to maintain the availability requirements.

- The Availability Group can manually failover to an asynchronous replica for maintaining availability during a planned maintenance window or during disaster.

- The Availability Group can protect us from any data loss – optional.

Whether the Availability Group is in a state that will support everything in our checklist is based on the underlying states of the following components:

- The Windows Cluster
- The Availability Replicas
- The database replicas
- The databases themselves
- The Listener

The summary of these five components to ensure a healthy application is summarized in these as follows:

Component 1: Windows Cluster

Command: Use the UI of the Failover Cluster Manager and look at the Cluster core resource (Network Name, IP Address of cluster).

Healthy State: Cluster Core resources online

Unhealthy State: Cluster Core resources in failed state or cluster is not accessible.

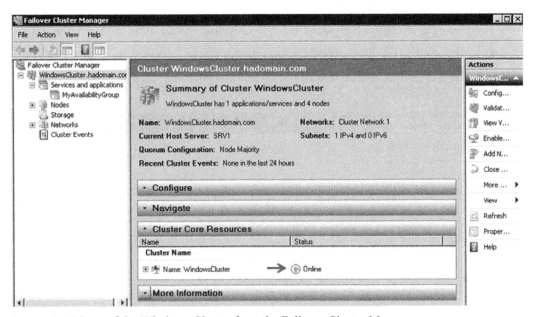

Figure 11.6 State of the Windows Cluster from the Failover Cluster Manager.

Component 2: Availability Replicas

Command:

```
SELECT ar.replica_server_name
 ,role_desc
 ,operational_state_desc
 ,connected_state_desc
 ,synchronization_health_desc
FROM sys.dm_hadr_availability_replica_states ars
INNER JOIN sys.availability_replicas ar
```

```
ON ars.replica_id = ar.replica_id AND ars.group_id =
ar.group_id;
```

Healthy State:

- The role_desc field is primary or secondary.
- The operational_state_desc field is online.
- The connected_state_desc field is connected.
- The synchronization_health_desc is healthy.

Unhealthy State:

- The role_desc field is resolving.
- The operational_state_desc field is any other state than online or NULL.
- The connected_state_desc field is disconnected.
- The synchronization_health_desc field is partially_healthy or not_healthly.

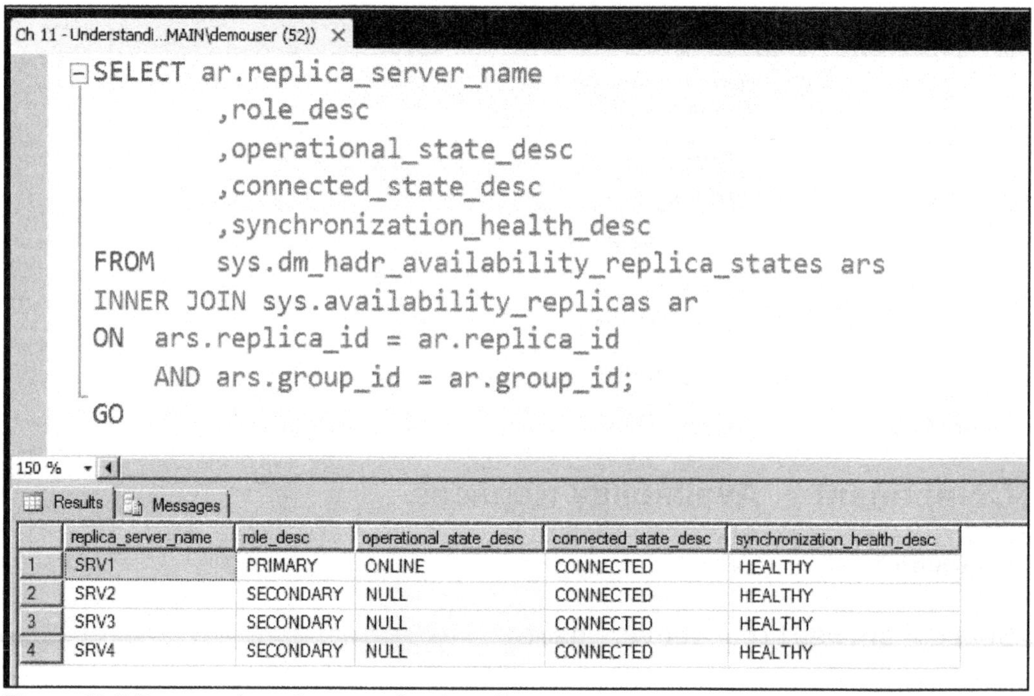

Figure 11.7 Query to show the state of each replica.

Component 3: Database Replicas

Command:

```
-- For Database Replica
SELECT ar.replica_server_name
 ,db_name(database_id) 'Database Name'
 ,synchronization_health_desc
 ,synchronization_state_desc
 ,database_state_desc
 ,is_suspended
FROM sys.dm_hadr_database_replica_states dbrs
INNER JOIN sys.availability_replicas ar
ON dbrs.replica_id = ar.replica_id AND dbrs.group_id = ar.group_id
ORDER BY 1,2;
```

Healthy State:

- The synchronization_health_desc field is healthy.
- The synchronization_state_desc field is synchronized for synchronous replica and synchronizing for asynchronous replica.
- The database_state_desc field is online.
- The is_suspended field is 0.

Unhealthy State:

- The synchronization_health_desc field is partially_healthy or not_healthly.
- The synchronization_state_desc field is INITIALIZING, REVERTING or NOT SYNCHRONIZING.
- The database_state_desc field is having value other than online
- The is_suspended field is 1.

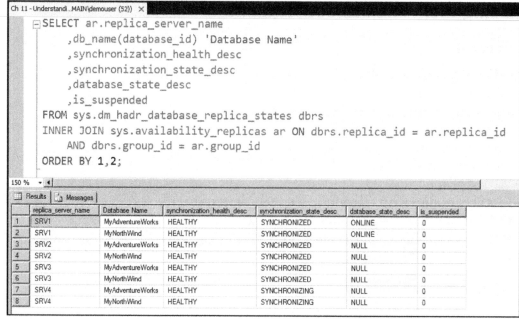

Figure 11.8 Query to show the health state of each database replica in the AG.

Component 4: Databases

Command:

-- For Database States
SELECT replica_server_name
,database_name
,is_failover_ready
FROM sys.dm_hadr_database_replica_cluster_states drcs
INNER JOIN sys.availability_replicas ar
ON drcs.replica_id = ar.replica_id
ORDER BY 1,2

Healthy State:

- The is_failover_ready field is 1.

Unhealthy State:

- The is_failover_ready field is 0.

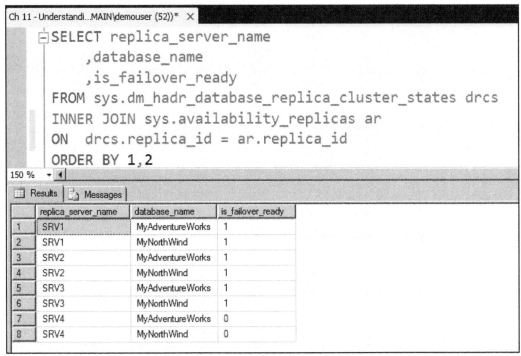

Figure 11.9 Query to show the failover read state of each database in the AG.

Component 5: The Listener

Command: Use the UI of the Failover Cluster Manager and select MyAvailabilityGroup resource and look at MyListener status.

Healthy State: Listener resource is online

Unhealthy State: Listener resource is in offline or failed state.

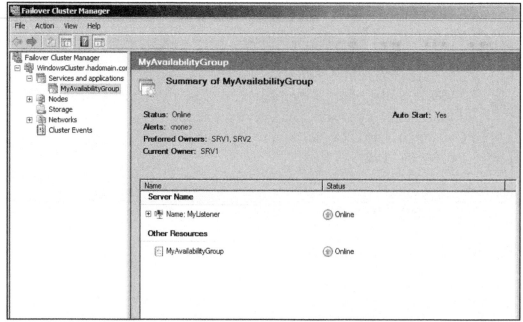

Figure 11.10 The UI of the Failover Cluster Manager shows the health of the listener.

For applications with ApplicationIntent=Readonly, the Availability Group is considered healthy when:

- The primary replica is available and ONLINE to route the connections.
- An ONLINE state of the Listener allows user connections to be directed into the secondary replica.
- At minimum, one availability replica should be in the SECONDARY role and in an ONLINE state.
- All the availability databases on the secondary replica are ONLINE.

The Availability Group is healthy for automatic failover when:

- There is at least one secondary replica available in ONLINE state.
- ALL the availability databases are FAILOVER READY.
- All availability databases (on the secondary replica) must be in SYNCHRONIZED state. This state also indicates that the Availability Group is in a state where it can guarantee zero data loss.

The Availability Group is healthy for manual failover when:

- There is a replica available which is in the SECONDARY ROLE and is ONLINE.

- ALL availability databases are in the SYNCHRONIZED state.
- The fact that databases are SYNCHRONIZED indicates that the Availability Group itself is in a good state and failover will not cause any data loss.

More about failover will be discussed at length in Chapter 14.

Above all this, the fundamental factor that contributes to the health of the Availability Group is the health of the Windows Cluster. Hence the dependency includes:

- For the Availability Group to have a primary replica there has to be a node available in the cluster having a quorum.
- For the Availability Group to have a secondary replica there has to be a primary replica.
- For the Availability Group to allow a read/write application access to the databases there has to be a primary replica. All required databases need to be in an ONLINE state.
- For the Availability Group to allow applications with readonly-intent in a connection string there has to be a secondary replica with the application database in ONLINE.
- For the Availability Group to allow automatic failover there has to be a primary replica and at least one synchronous secondary replica for automatic failover and all the databases need to be SYNCHRONIZED and failover ready.

Summary

The options to troubleshoot and monitor SQL Server AlwaysOn deployments are many. We need to be comfortable in using the right tool to identify the problems at hand. This chapter took a quick tour of advanced monitoring techniques like Health Sessions, System Center monitoring packs, and Wait Types. Using these techniques to our advantage is important while working with AlwaysOn.

Points to Ponder – AlwaysOn Advanced Monitoring

1. The AlwaysOn health session is an extended event session which captures information about the AlwaysOn Availability Group.

2. The AlwaysOn extended event session is not started if we created Availability Group using T-SQL or a PowerShell script.

3. To enable the AlwaysOn extended event session at startup via T-SQL we can use the following statement:
   ```
   ALTER EVENT SESSION [AlwaysOn_health] ON SERVER
   WITH (STARTUP_STATE = ON)
   GO
   ```

4. In order to use a System Center product we need to install the SQL Server 2012 AlwaysOn Management Pack (SQLMP) and that will allow us to monitor all Availability Groups across our enterprise.

5. The AlwaysOn health session is an extended event session which captures information about AlwaysOn Availability Groups including DDL statements executed to make modifications to the topology.

6. The failover detection mechanism for the AlwaysOn FCI and the AlwaysOn Availability Group is the same.

7. Before initiating a failover, the cluster would wait for a value defined in the HealthCheckTimeout property (default 60 seconds) to get results from the sp_server_diagnostics.

8. Using Wait Types is an advanced option to troubleshoot and maintain AlwaysOn deployments.

9. System Center is a product from Microsoft which can be useful in monitoring the AlwaysOn Availability Groups via one interface.

10. The Health of the Availability Group depends on various underlying components like the Windows Cluster, the availability replicas, the database replicas, the database, and the Listener.

Review Quiz - Chapter Eleven

1.) What is the default HealthCheckTimeout property value for which a failover is initiated?

  O a. 30 seconds
  O b. 60 seconds
  O c. 90 seconds
  O d. 120 seconds

2.) Approximately how many wait types are available with SQL Server 2012 that are related to Availability Groups?

  O a. 30
  O b. 60
  O c. 90
  O d. 120

3.) The SQL Server 2012 AlwaysOn Management Pack allows us to monitor for an AlwaysOn Availability Group via System Center Operations Manager for what types of components? Choose all that apply.

  □ a. Database Replicas health.
  □ b. Availability Replicas health.
  □ c. Availability Groups health.
  □ d. Listener's health.

4.) Which files contain important information about the AlwaysOn Availability Group Failover and would be needed a post mortem review? Choose all that apply.

  □ a. ERRORLOGs.
  □ b. SQLDIAG .xel files.
  □ c. Windows Cluster Logs.
  □ d. AlwaysOn Health Session .xel files.
  □ e. Application and System Event logs.

Answer Key

1.) The correct answer is (b) 60 seconds. All other options (a) 30 seconds, (c) 90 seconds and (d) 120 seconds are incorrect.

2.) The number of available wait types can be queried from sys.dm_os_wait_stats DMV's. There are approximately 60+ wait types, therefore option (b) 60 is the correct answer.

3.) Options (a) Database Replicas health, (b) Availability Replicas health and (c) Availability Groups health are the correct options. Option (d) Listener's health is incorrect.

4.) To do post mortem of AlwaysOn Availability Group all the options (a) ERRORLOGs, (b) SQLDIAG XEL files, (c) Windows Cluster Logs (d) AlwaysOn Health Session XEL files and (e) Application and System Event logs can be used.

[NOTES]

Chapter 12. Deployment Variations of AlwaysOn

Being a kid has its own advantages. We spend so much time playing around and those are some fun days. In one of my Christmas gifts, I was given a Lego building blocks set. It was one of the most exciting gifts you can get if you are a creative person. The best part of this gift is that I could build anything in my imagination with the given basic components as part of the kit. Building the colorful homes, machines, helicopters, driveways, parks, and many more was possible with the user's manual inside the kit. New things were possible with my own imagination. Being very experimental is something all of us get into. Along the same lines, SQL Server AlwaysOn technologies give us various ways of doing deployments just like Lego building blocks.

Since an AlwaysOn Availability Group supports multiple secondary replicas (both synchronous and asynchronous) we can be creative in implementing various design patterns to deploy a complete solution based on the requirements. In this chapter, we will discuss the deployment of a High Availability and Disaster Recovery combination using AlwaysOn. Since AlwaysOn is a bigger umbrella which covers AlwaysOn Failover Cluster Instances (FCI) and AlwaysOn Availability Groups, we would combine both of them together in some of the patterns.

On a side note, as a SQL Server database administrator, it would be advisable to gain more knowledge about Windows Clustering or get help from the company Windows team while deploying a complete solution. This is because Microsoft Windows Clustering is the foundation of AlwaysOn.

Just like in the example of building things with Legos, the more Legos we have the more design possibilities. The more secondary replicas we have the more combinations of what topologies we can deploy. For example if we have one secondary replica we must choose between having a synchronous or asynchronous replica. If we have two secondary replicas then we can have one of each type or two of the same type.

The more replicas we have the more combinations that are possible. If we look at various patterns, they can be classified in two major categories:

1. Using AlwaysOn Availability Groups (AG) for a local High Availability and Disaster Recovery solution.

2. Using AlwaysOn FCIs for local High Availability and combining them with Availability Groups (AGs) for Disaster Recovery or reporting.

In the patterns for this chapter we will avoid the need for any special third party solutions like stretch VLANs. Having said that, we have also included a pattern using SAN replication as it is one of the most common deployments across geographies for customers. For the most part, we will look at SQL Server out-of-box configurations in the patterns that can be achieved with AlwaysOn technologies.

Pattern 1: Two Node

We generally call this the "vanilla implementation" because this is the simplest form possible to implement an AlwaysOn Availability Group. In this implementation, we have two nodes in a Windows Cluster which are running one standalone instance each. An AlwaysOn Availability Group is created between the databases on these two instances. Since we have an even number of nodes we need to have a tie-breaker in case one node is down. This can be achieved two ways:

1. Add another node in the Windows Cluster which is used only for voting (it does not need to have SQL Server installed). After having this third server in the Cluster we can use the "Node Majority" quorum model because we now have an odd number of nodes in the Windows Cluster.

2. Use the "Node and File Share Majority" quorum with File Share Witness for voting.

In this pattern, we are going with the second choice of using the File Share Witness to help the cluster in deciding the owner of the Availability Group in case of a tie vote. The following is an overview of this configuration:

Number of Nodes	2
Quorum Model	Nodes and File Share Witness
Nodes are in same data center	Yes. Including File Share
Automatic failover	Yes
Any Clustered SQL Instances	No
Read capability from secondary	No
Sync mode	synchronous

Table 12.1 Overview of the "Two Node" configuration.

Figure 12.1 is the visual representation of this configuration.

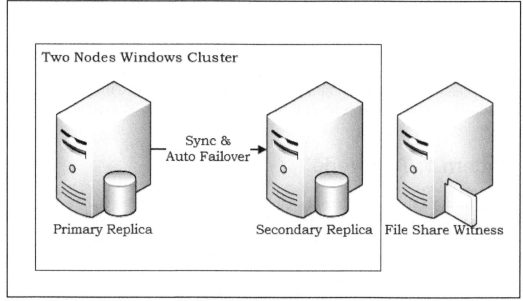

Figure 12.1 Two nodes cluster with File Share Witness in same data center.

Advantage(s):

- Due to standalone instances there is no cost of a special shared storage.
- There is no single point of failure in terms of storage as there are two copies of the database files (one on each node).

Disadvantage(s)

- In case of a data center level disaster, there is no recovery possible in this basic configuration.

If we are looking for more redundancy of secondary replicas, we can add more secondary replicas which could be synchronous and/or asynchronous.

Pattern 2: Two Node with Read Scale-out

This pattern is very similar to the previous configuration that we discussed. In this configuration we have made the secondary to allow reads for reporting needs.

The following is an overview of this configuration:

Number of Nodes	2
Quorum Model	Nodes and File Share Majority

Nodes are in same data center	Yes. Including File Share
Automatic failover	Yes
Any Clustered SQL Instances	No
Read capability from secondary	Yes
Sync mode	synchronous

Table 12.2 Overview of the "Two Node with Read Scale-out" configuration

Figure 12.2 is the visual representation of this configuration.

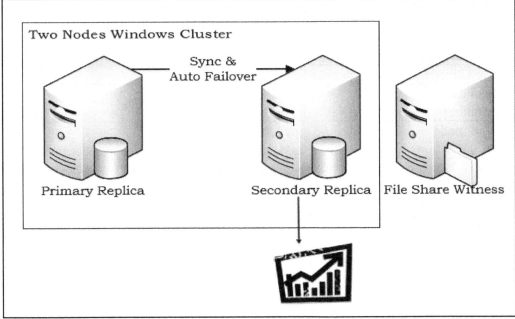

Figure 12.2 Two node standalone SQL instance on Windows Cluster with File Share Witness and readable secondary.

Advantage(s):

- Due to standalone instances there is no cost of shared storage.

- This is no single point of failure in terms of storage since there are two copies of all the database files (one on each node).

- The additional advantage of this topology as (compared to previous one) is that we have the ability to offload the reporting workload to a secondary replica. This provides the capability for analysts to create reports from close to real-time data without impacting the primary workload.

Disadvantage(s):

- In case of a data center level disaster, there is no recovery possible.

Pattern 3: Three Node with Readable and Failover separated

This configuration is a superset of the previous two designs. We have an asynchronous secondary replica for readonly reporting and a synchronous secondary replica for failover. The following is an overview of this configuration:

Number of Nodes	3
Quorum Model	Nodes Majority
Nodes are in same data center	Yes
Automatic failover	Yes
Any Clustered SQL Instances	No
Read capability from secondary	Yes
Sync mode	synchronous for Failover. asynchronous for ReadOnly connections.

Table 12.3 Overview of the "Three Node with Readable and Failover separated" configuration.

Figure 12.3 is the visual representation of this configuration.

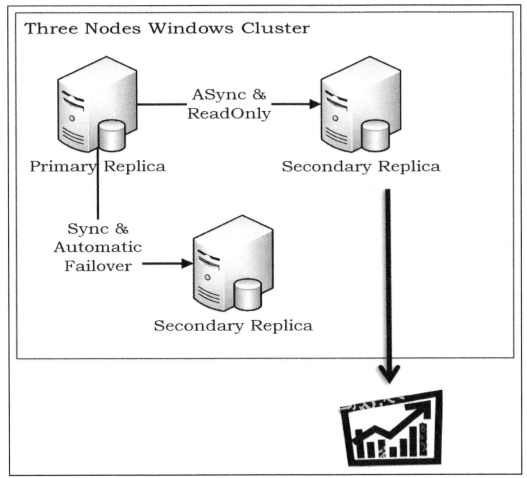

Figure 12.3 Three node configuration with asynchronous Readable and synchronous configuration for Failover.

Advantage(s):

- The advantage of this configuration is that we have taken the previous two configurations and made sure the failover node is separate as compared to the readable secondary for the reporting infrastructure.

Disadvantage(s):

- In case of a data center level disaster, there is no recovery possible.

Pattern 4: Two Node across Data Centers

In the earlier three designs we stated that there is no High Availability in case of a complete data center level failure because we have all three servers in same data center. If the data centers are not far away from each other (the same geographic location) we can go with a secondary replica in a separate data center. We are scaling out distance but in reality we need to consider the network latency between the data centers when considering this configuration. The following is an overview of this configuration:

Number of Nodes	2
Quorum Model	Nodes and File Share Majority
Nodes are in same data center	No
Automatic failover	Yes
Any Clustered SQL Instances	No
Read capability from secondary	Yes
Sync mode	synchronous

Table 12.4 Overview of the "Two Node across Data Centers" configuration.

Figure 12.4 is the visual representation of this configuration.

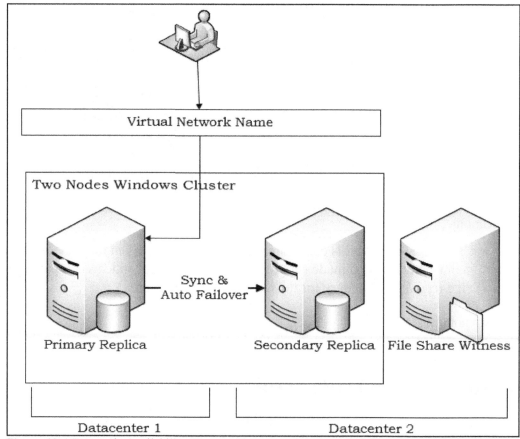

Figure 12.4 Two node Availability Group with sync and Automatic failover across data centers.

Advantage(s):

- We have made sure the failover node is separate and will not be subject to data center level failure.

Disadvantage(s)

- Since the File Share Witness and the secondary replica are in the same data center, there would be no availability if the second data center is down. What would make this group go down? In this situation we would have only one vote out of three which means loss of quorum. Ideally, we should have a File Share Witness in a third data center.

Pattern 5: Two Node Async mode across Data Centers

This pattern is similar to the previous configuration. In this configuration we have made the secondary in the asynchronous mode when compared to Pattern #1 or Pattern #3. With data centers far apart and network latency a problem, administrators can resort to an asynchronous mode of synchronization. The following is an overview of this configuration:

Number of Nodes	2
Quorum Model	Nodes and File Share Majority
Nodes are in same data center	No
Automatic failover	No
Any Clustered SQL Instances	No
Read capability from secondary	Yes
Sync mode	Asynchronous

Table 12.5 Overview of the "Two Node Async mode across Data Centers" configuration.

Figure 12.5 is the visual representation of this configuration.

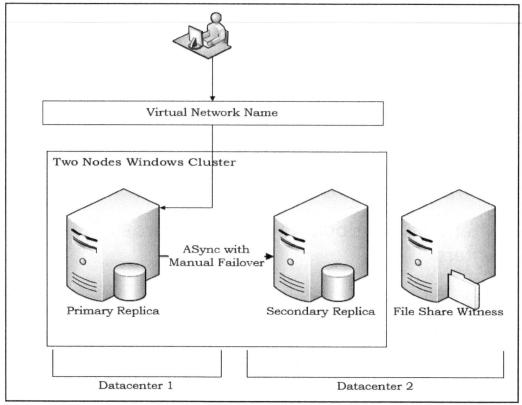

Figure 12.5 Two node Async mode synchronization with manual failover across data centers.

Advantage(s):

- We have made sure the failover node is separate and is asynchronous when compared to the previous pattern. If the latencies are high between the data centers it is better to use an asynchronous replica with manual failover between the data centers.

Disadvantage(s):

- Since the File Share Witness and the secondary replica are in one data center, there would be no quorum if the second data center goes down. In this situation we would have only one vote out of three. This means the loss of quorum. Ideally, we should have a File Share Witness in a third data center.

Pattern 6: Four Node with Sync across Data Centers

In a scenario where the two data centers are not too far apart (also means having good network bandwidth) and we want multiple synchronous secondary replicas. The following is an overview of this configuration:

Number of Nodes	4
Quorum Model	Nodes and File Share Majority
Nodes are in same data center	No
Automatic failover	Yes (in same data center)
Any Clustered SQL Instances	No
Read capability from secondary	Yes
Sync mode	Sync within same data center Sync and Async across data center's

Table 12.6 Overview of the "Four Node with Sync across Data Centers" configuration.

Figure 12.6 is the visual representation of this configuration.

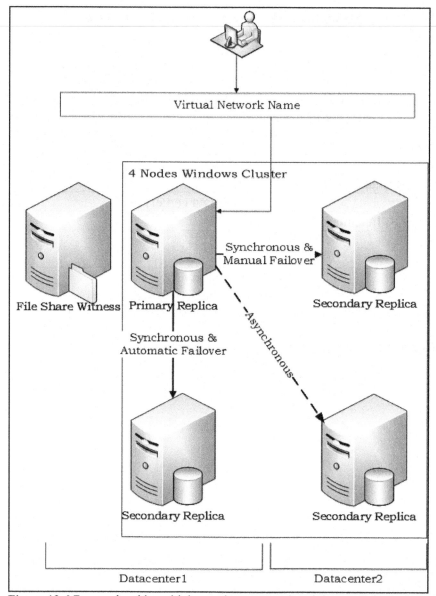

Figure 12.6 Four node with multiple synchronous copies giving availability from data center disaster.

We are using a virtual network name (the Listener name) in this configuration. This gives an advantage to the application to connect to the unique name without needing to worry about which node is owner of the Availability Group.

Advantage(s):

- We have two synchronous copies of the databases. One of them is in a separate data center. This gives us High Availability as well as Disaster Recovery.

- We can utilize a readable secondary for reporting and backup purposes.

Disadvantage(s):

- Having three out of five servers in Datacenter 1, we will not have quorum if Datacenter 1 fails.

- If Datacenter 1 fails, we will need to do manual failover because we don't have Automatic failover to Datacenter 2.

Pattern 7: Four Node with Sync across 2 Data Centers with separate Fileshare

This is another topology which can be used to achieve reliable automatic failover between two data centers. In our earlier pattern the automatic failover partner was in the same data center. The only way to achieve a reliable automatic failover between two data centers (for Disaster Recovery) is to put the File Share Witness in a third data center. If one data center is down, the tie-breaker (from third data center) would decide which data center should take over as the primary replica. The majority can be guaranteed in this configuration. The following is an overview of this configuration:

Number of Nodes	4
Quorum Model	Nodes and File Share Majority
Nodes are in same data center	No (Witness in 3rd data center)
Automatic failover	Yes (to other data center)
Any Clustered SQL Instances	No
Read capability from secondary	Yes
Sync mode	Sync within same data center Sync and Async across data centers

Table 12.7 Overview of the "Four Node with Sync across 2 Data Centers with separate Fileshare" configuration.

Figure 12.7 is the visual representation of this configuration.

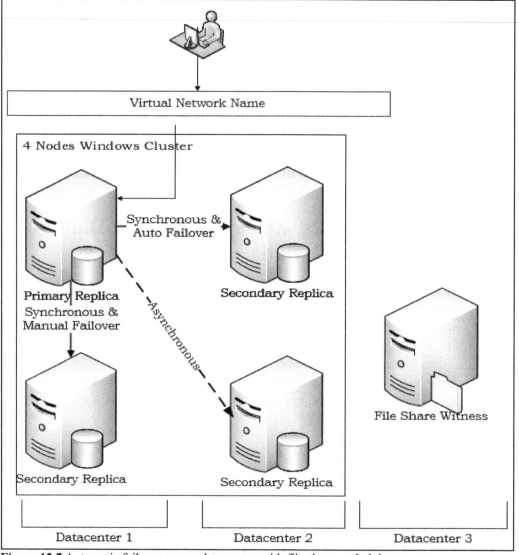

Figure 12.7 Automatic failover across data center with file share on 3rd data center.

Advantage(s):

- We have two synchronous copies of the databases. One of them is in separate data center, which gives us High Availability as well as Disaster Recovery.

- We can utilize a readable secondary for reporting and backup purposes.

- Also having the File Share on a separate data center protects us from Datacenter 1 failure which is the disadvantage in previous pattern.

Disadvantage(s):

- This will not work if we only have one data center.

Pattern 8: Four Node with Async across Data Centers

A slight variation of the earlier pattern would be to still have three data centers and make a secondary replica in the local data center for automatic failover. This means that replicas in the second data center would be asynchronous replicas and will not participate in automatic failover. The following is an overview of this configuration:

The following is an overview of this configuration:

Number of Nodes	4
Quorum Model	Nodes and File Share Majority
Nodes are in same data center	No (Witness in 3rd data center)
Automatic failover	Yes (to same data center)
Any Clustered SQL Instances	No
Read capability from secondary	Yes
Sync mode	Sync within same data center Async across data centers

Table 12.8 Overview of the "Four Node with Async across Data Centers" configuration.

Figure 12.8 is the visual representation of this configuration.

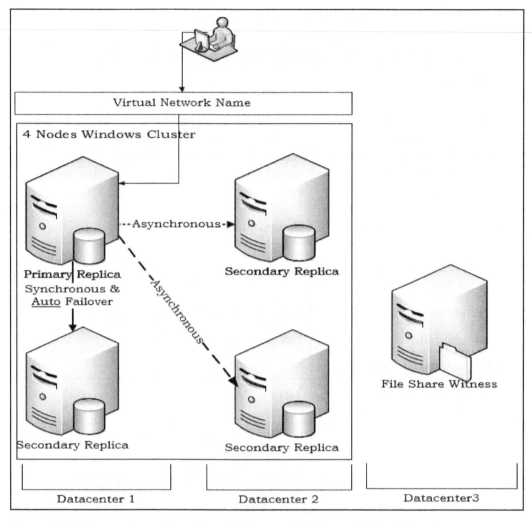

Figure 12.8 3 Data center configuration with Automatic failover only in primary data center.

In this configuration we can always use the secondary replicas for reporting needs or for backups. Prior to SQL Server 2012, a similar pattern can be deployed using a combination of Database Mirroring and Log Shipping together. Database Mirroring in the synchronous mode can be used to get a local secondary server and Log Shipping can be used to add a remote secondary server. As we discussed earlier, the Availability Group provides both High Availability and Disaster Recovery in a single configuration.

Advantage(s):

- We get all the advantages of a previous configuration, but since the latencies are high between the data centers this configuration of asynchronous across data centers is advisable.

Disadvantage(s):

- With asynchronous replicas in Datacenter 2, there can be potential data loss during failover.
- There is no automatic failover across data centers, we need to use a forced failover to bring a server in Datacenter 2 the primary role.

Pattern 9: Three Node FCI with Availability Group

So far, we have used various patterns where standalone SQL instances were used for High Availability and Disaster Recovery in an AlwaysOn AG. Another set of patterns can be derived using SQL Server in a clustered configuration.

In the following pattern, a SQL Server Failover Cluster Instance (FCI) is primarily used for High Availability and Disaster Recovery. The important thing to remember is that if there are any FCIs involved in the Availability Group, then Automatic failover is not possible to an AG replica. Any automatic failover in the FCI would only be to another node within the FCI. We cannot failover from nodes within the FCI to nodes in an AG. Any attempt to do so would fail with error 19405.

```
Messages
Msg 19405, Level 16, State 1
Failed to create, join or add replica to Availability Group '%.*ls', because
node '%.*ls' is a possible owner for both replica '%.*ls' and '%.*ls'. If one
replica is a Failover Cluster instance, remove the overlapped node from its
possible owners and try again.
```

The following is an overview of this configuration:

Number of Nodes	4
Quorum Model	Disk Majority
Nodes are in same data center	Yes
Automatic failover	No
Any Clustered SQL Instances	Yes
Read capability from secondary	Yes
Sync mode	asynchronous AG

Table 12.9 Overview of the "Three Node FCI with Availability Group" configuration.

Figure 12.9 is the visual representation of this configuration.

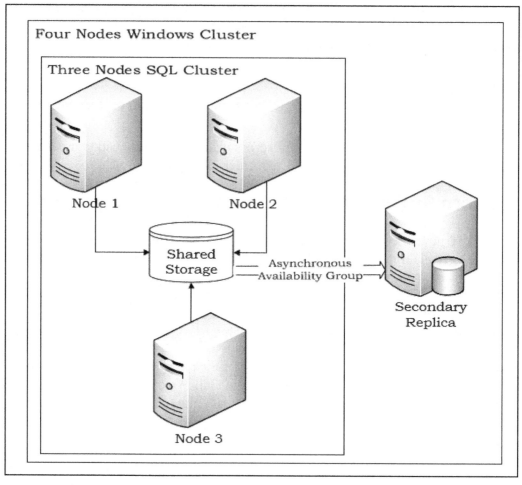

Figure 12.9 Combination of AlwaysOn Failover Cluster Instance and standalone instance to form an AlwaysOn Availability Group.

In this pattern the FCI is providing High Availability but the AlwaysOn Availability Group is not any providing High Availability or Disaster Recovery. The AlwaysOn Availability Group is providing a replica for a readable workload.

Advantage(s):

- The readonly workload from the production clustered instances can be redirected to the asynchronous secondary replica running on the standalone SQL Server.
- High Availability is provided by the cluster configuration.

Disadvantage(s):

- Shared storage is a requirement for this configuration. This disadvantage can be mitigated using Windows Server 2012 and the SMB 3.0 protocol.
- We still don't have a protection against a data center failure in this configuration.

Pattern 10: Six Nodes WSFC with two FCIs across Data Centers

When we have an FCI in one data center and an AG in another we don't have protection across data centers. Therefore, if we want the data replicated between the two data centers with High Availability using a SQL Server Failover Cluster Instance then this pattern can be used. The following is an overview of this configuration:

Number of Nodes	6
Quorum Model	Node and Disk Majority
Nodes are in same data center	No
Automatic failover	No
Any Clustered SQL Instances	Yes (both of them)
Read capability from secondary	Yes

Table 12.10 Overview of the "Six Nodes WSFC with two FCIs across Data Centers" configuration.

Figure 12.10 is the visual representation of this configuration.

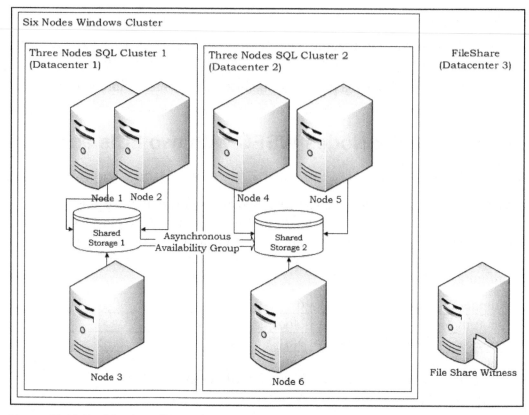

Figure 12.10 Combination of Two AlwaysOn Failover Cluster Instances across data centers to form single Availability Group.

Notice that we have one Windows Cluster running across two data centers because that is a prerequisite of the AlwaysOn Availability Group. Since both of the SQL FCIs would have their own storage, the key to this pattern would be the asymmetric storage. This means that nodes in the data center can see the storage only in their own data center. In this pattern we need to make sure that correct possible owners have been set for each resource.

In a typical multi-site cluster, each site has its own storage array as shown in Figure 12.10. This would also mean that not all nodes in the cluster would be able to see the same storage. Nodes in the first data center (Node1, Node2 and Node3) would see only shared storage 1. Node4, Node5, and Node6 (from the second data center) would be able to see only shared storage 2. Since some nodes can use one set of storage, and some nodes can use another, this is called "asymmetric storage". To support asymmetric storage in Windows Server 2008 and Windows Server 2008 R2, a hotfix was released via KB 976097.

Typically, whenever we create a WSFC (Windows Server Failover Cluster) we have symmetric storage. Symmetric storage means that all nodes in the cluster must be able to see the same storage. Since we have a share-nothing model, the disk can be owned by a single owner which can perform read/write operations. Anything written to the shared drive would be visible from the other nodes only after a failover to that node.

Let's assume a scenario where we have built Node1, Node2, and Node3 with shared storage 1. Later, we created a WSFC with three nodes and then installed SQL AlwaysOn FCI. At this point, we have used all the disks from shared storage 1 exposed to the cluster. Now if we attempt to add node 4, 5, or 6 in this cluster we may see the following error:

There was an error creating, configuring, or bringing online the Physical Disk resource (disk) 'Cluster Disk 1'.

We can also see the following warning:

Resource for 'Cluster Disk 1' has been created but will not be brought online because the disk is not visible from the node which currently owns the "Available Storage" group. To bring this resource online, move that group to a node that can see the disk. The possible owners list for this disk resource has been set to the nodes that can host this resource.

This is due to asymmetric storage because shared storage 2 can't be seen by Node1. To move the available storage group to the newly added nodes, we need to use the following command:

C:\>cluster.exe group "available storage" /moveto:Node4

As soon as we run the command, we would immediately see a message stating that it is moving the storage. The available storage will show a status of Online for Node4. We can also see the status of the disk under available storage in the Failover Cluster Manager UI.

In the asymmetric storage cluster, we will always have at least some disks that are offline, because the available storage group can be owned by only one node at a time and that node will not have access to the all disks.

There is another consideration which should be kept in mind while naming the instances in this topology. When we configure the Availability Group between two FCIs, we can't have the same instance name because both would be acting as a service in the Windows Cluster and we can't have a duplicate. Asymmetric storage provides the advantage of having the same drive letters for different drives on two clusters. It is recommended to keep the file on exactly the same path because adding a file later on the primary replica would perform the same "add file" action. If the drives are different than the replica it would go into a not-synchronizing state. This special case will be explained more in Chapter 17.

Pattern 11: Two Nodes with two Availability Groups

In all our earlier patterns we have been talking about having only one Availability Group. It is possible for us to have multiple Availability Groups in a single server instance. In this configuration we have taken two Availability Groups running across two servers.

The following is an overview of this configuration:

Number of Nodes	2
Quorum Model	Node and file share majority
Nodes are in same data center	Yes
Automatic failover	Yes
Any Clustered SQL Instances	No
Read capability from secondary	No (can be configured)

Table 12.11 Overview of the "Two Nodes with two Availability Groups" configuration.

Figure 12.11 is the visual representation of this configuration.

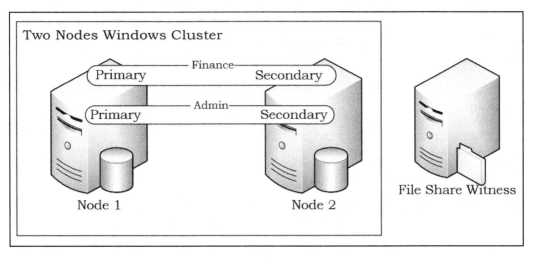

Figure 12.11 Shows a two node with two Availability Group configuration.

To maximize the investment we can make the secondary replicas readable. Another interesting way to utilize the secondary server hardware investment is to do a crisscross deployment as explained in the next pattern.

Advantage(s):

- Maximum use of hardware in this model.
- Logical grouping of application databases via multiple Availability Groups.

Disadvantage(s):

- If Node1 fails, all workload shifts to Node2 and this can become single point of failure.
- We are not utilizing the secondary node and it is in idle state.

Pattern 12: Two Node with Crossover Availability Group

In this pattern, we are using two Availability Groups and each one is running on separate nodes at any time. In case of a disaster, one node would be hosting both replicas in the primary mode. The following is an overview of this configuration:

Number of Nodes	2
Quorum Model	Node and file share majority
Nodes are in same data center	Yes
Automatic failover	Yes

Any Clustered SQL Instances	No
Read capability from secondary	No

Table 12.12 Overview of the "Two Node with Crossover Availability Group" configuration.

Figure 12.12 Overview of the "Two Node with Crossover Availability Group" configuration.

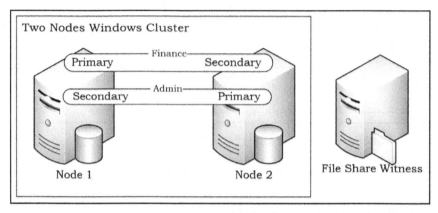

Figure 12.12 Two replicas configured in different roles on each node. Finance Availability Group is primary on Node1 and Admin Availability Group is secondary.

The advantage of this pattern is that we can couple application specific databases and make logical groups. This would help us in utilizing the instance, which is hosting the secondary replica for one Availability Group to perform read/write operations for the other Availability Group. This technique can be called a poor-man's load distribution technique.

Pattern 13: Three Node Balancing three Availability Groups

This pattern is an extension of an earlier pattern of multiple Availability Groups. This is generally categorized as a "brick pattern". In this diagram, we have a three node Windows Cluster, each running one standalone instance of SQL Server. The following is an overview of this configuration:

Number of Nodes	3
Quorum Model	Node majority
Nodes are in same data center	Yes
Automatic failover	Yes
Any Clustered SQL Instances	No
Read capability from secondary	Yes

Table 12.13 Overview of the "Three Node Balancing three Availability Groups" configuration.

Figure 12.13 is the visual representation of this configuration.

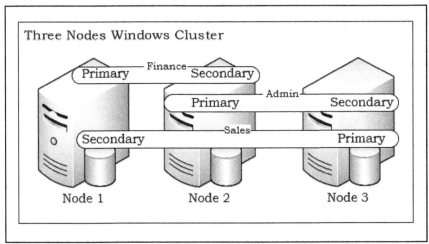

Figure 12.13 Brick architecture model with 3 nodes Windows Cluster.

In this pattern, we have used three SQL instances and three Availability Groups. On a closer look at any of the instances, we notice that each instance is hosting one primary replica and one secondary replica.

Advantage(s):

- We have tried to optimally utilize the hardware investments by placing secondary replicas on a server which is the primary for other Availability Groups.
- We can scale out in this crisscross configuration with more nodes too.

Disadvantage(s):

- It is quite possible that if a node goes down we could failover to another node that is already a primary. We might wind up having two Availability Groups hosting a primary replica on the same Node.

Pattern 14: Extended Brick Architecture across Multiple Nodes

In the earlier pattern we used only one synchronous secondary replica with automatic failover. To extend it further for a multi-site deployment scenario of

SQL Server, we can use multiple replicas and multiple Availability Groups. This pattern ensures High Availability as well as a fast minimal data loss failover to the second data center. The following is an overview of this configuration:

Number of Nodes	6 (three in each data center)
Quorum Model	Nodes and file share majority
Nodes are in same data center	No
Automatic failover	Yes (to local data center replica)
Any Clustered SQL Instances	No
Read capability from secondary	No

Table 12.14 Overview of the "Extended Brick Architecture across Multiple Nodes" configuration.

Figure 12.14 is the visual representation of this configuration.

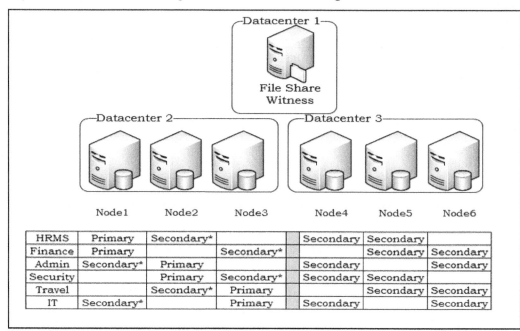

	Node1	Node2	Node3	Node4	Node5	Node6
HRMS	Primary	Secondary*		Secondary	Secondary	
Finance	Primary		Secondary*		Secondary	Secondary
Admin	Secondary*	Primary		Secondary		Secondary
Security		Primary	Secondary*	Secondary	Secondary	
Travel		Secondary*	Primary		Secondary	Secondary
IT	Secondary*		Primary	Secondary		Secondary

Figure 12.14 Pattern of deployment in multi data center, multiple Availability Groups (* represents synchronous copy).

To extend this pattern further, we can have six more Availability Groups running as the primary on data center #3. This can give us perfect utilization of hardware employed in the third data center if needed. We can also make the secondary as readable in case there is a business need to offload the reporting workload from the primary server.

Advantage(s):

- We have tried to optimally utilize the hardware investments by placing automatic failover replicas in the same data center while asynchronous replicas are on the far DR site.
- We can scale out in this crisscross configuration by adding more nodes.

Disadvantage(s):

- It is quite possible that if a node fails, we might have multiple Availability Groups with a primary replica hosted on the same node.

Pattern 15: Mix and Match Log Shipping

A closer look at all earlier patterns would reveal that they have been built by AlwaysOn technology (AGs alone or combined with FCIs). It is also a misconception that we cannot mix multiple HA / DR solutions to form a unified solution for deployment. In this pattern we have taken a simple two node Availability Group standard deployment in a HA mode. We have configured Log Shipping to a 3rd server which will be used extensively for readonly reporting queries. The following is an overview of this configuration:

Number of Nodes	2 for Availability Group, 1 for Batch
Quorum Model	Nodes and File Share Witness
Nodes are in same data center	Yes, including File Share
Automatic failover	Yes for AG
Any Clustered SQL Instances	No
Read capability from secondary replica	No for secondary replica Yes for Batch Server
Sync mode	synchronous

Table 12.15 Overview of the "Mix and Match Log Shipping" configuration.

Figure 12.15 is the visual representation of this configuration.

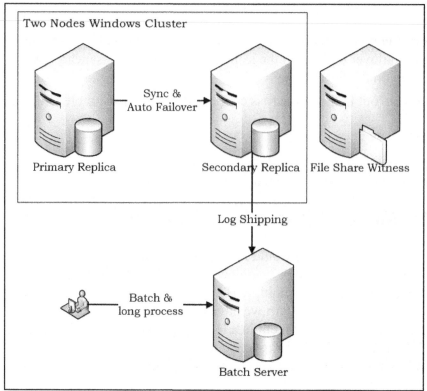

Figure 12.15 Mix and match Availability Group with Log Shipping for long batch processes.

Having seen this configuration, it is worthwhile to note that we can also use replication and other older techniques in combination with Availability Groups. Evaluate what the benefits are, limitations and additional overheads before getting into such configurations.

Pattern 16: Multi-Site Clustering

This is one of the patterns where we are not using AlwaysOn Availability Groups but only using AlwaysOn FCI. This is also called multi-site clustering where we have one SQL Server FCI spanning across two data centers. This pattern is used for both High Availability (local site) and remote Disaster Recovery (remote site). One important and additional (non-Microsoft) piece of hardware in this pattern is the "storage level replication". The following is an overview of this configuration:

Number of Nodes	4 (two on each site/data center)
Quorum Model	Nodes and File Share Witness
Nodes are in same data center	No
Automatic failover	No
Any Clustered SQL Instances	One. Spread across two data centers.
Read capability from secondary replica	No. Only one instance of SQL.
Sync mode	Disk level replication which is hardware vendor solution.

Table 12.16 Overview of the "Multi-Site Clustering" configuration.

Figure 12.16 is the visual representation of this configuration.

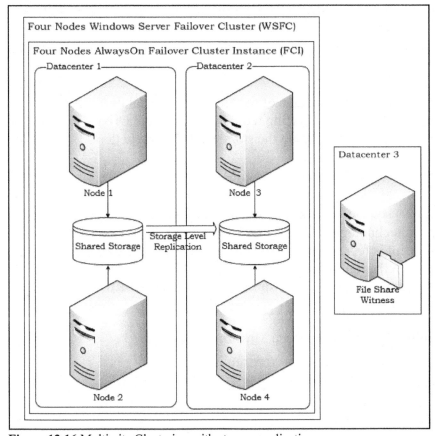

Figure 12.16 Multi-site Clustering with storage replication.

It would be important to note that all four nodes in the WSFC are not having the same shared storage. We already discussed asymmetric storage earlier. In this pattern we have used a File Share Witness from a third data center to achieve automated Disaster Recovery. This offers protection from data center level disasters.

The following are a few important notes on this pattern:

- Make sure that the storage vendor is engaged and best practices are followed as given by the storage vendor.
- If we are running a cluster validation tool we might get some errors about the storage because we are using asymmetric storage. Since we are using a multi-site FCI, it doesn't require passing the storage validation test. As per KB 943984 this solution is supported even if the storage test fails.
- If we check the Failover Cluster Manager, it would recommend using :Node and Disk Majority" as the quorum model. This recommendation can be ignored because we have different disk subsystems across both sites. We can go with "Node and File Share Majority" or "Node Majority" (based on number of nodes).

This pattern can take better advantage of the "tempdb on local disk" feature (explained earlier in Chapter 3 - Placing tempdb on the Local Drive). This would help in reducing the cost and utilizing the storage replication better.

Summary

This chapter shows some of the most common deployment scenarios for SQL Server AlwaysOn technologies. This is surely not an exhaustive collection of what is available but is representative of what can be achieved. Feel free to mix-and-match based on the requirements and SLA's set by businesses. Looking at the various deployments we would like to summarize by stating the following:

- AlwaysOn ≠ Availability Groups
- Availability Groups ≠ Database Mirroring
- Availability Groups ≠ Peer-to-Peer replication
- Availability Groups ≠ SQL Server Failover Cluster Instances
- AlwaysOn = SQL Server Failover Cluster Instances, Availability Groups

Points to Ponder – Deployment Variations of AlwaysOn

1. AlwaysOn Availability Groups support multiple secondary replicas with both synchronous and asynchronous modes.

2. The simplest configuration includes AlwaysOn Availability Group for High Availability within the same data center.

3. For scale out of reads, AlwaysOn Availability Groups can be used with a readable secondary replica.

4. A combination of the AlwaysOn Failover Cluster Instance (FCI) can be used for High Availability and the AlwaysOn Availability Group (AG) can be used for Disaster Recovery across data centers.

5. Multi-site AlwaysOn FCIs don't need third party solutions like stretch VLANs for implementation but SAN replication is still needed based on deployment architecture.

6. Reliable automatic failover across data centers can be achieved by having File Share Witness in a third data center.

7. Automatic failover to other replica is not possible when AlwaysOn FCI is involved in AlwaysOn Availability Group. So, availability replica that is hosted by an FCI can only be configured for manual failover.

8. Log Shipping can be combined along with an AlwaysOn Availability Group because Log Shipping backup jobs are aware of the backup preference of the Availability Group.

9. An asymmetric storage fix is needed for multi-site deployments where the Windows Cluster is stretched across sites.

Review Quiz - Chapter Twelve

1.) What is the fundamental building block for deploying AlwaysOn technologies?

O a. MSDTC
O b. Windows Cluster
O c. SQL Server Cluster
O d. All of the above

2.) What are the sync options available to work with secondary replicas?

☐ a. Synchronous
☐ b. Asynchronous

3.) Which of the following deployment scenarios requires a shared storage?

O a. AlwaysOn Availability Group for High Availability
O b. AlwaysOn Availability Group for High Availability and Disaster Recovery
O c. AlwaysOn Failover Cluster Instance for High Availability

4.) Which of the following sentences are incorrect? Choose all that apply.

☐ a. secondary Database replica can be a primary replica for another Availability Group.
☐ b. secondary Database replica can be configured for Log Shipping.
☐ c. secondary Database replica can be a principal of Database Mirroring.
☐ d. secondary Database replica can be a passive node in the cluster.

5.) What are the possible ways to move disks in an available storage group in a Windows 2008 R2 clustered environment?

☐ a. Failover Cluster Manager UI: Right of disk and move group.
☐ b. PowerShell CmdLet: Move-ClusterGroup "Available Storage"
☐ c. Command-line cluster.exe: cluster group "Available Storage" /Move

Answer Key

1.) Options (a) MSDTC, (c) SQL Server Cluster, (d) All of the above are all wrong. (b) Windows Cluster is the correct answer.

2.) The secondary replicas can be configured in both sync and async mode. Options (a) synchronous and (b) asynchronous are the correct answers.

3.) (a) AlwaysOn Availability Group for High Availability and (b) AlwaysOn Availability Group for High Availability and Disaster Recovery are wrong. The correct answer is (c) AlwaysOn Failover Cluster Instance for High Availability.

4.) Correct options are (a) secondary Database replica can be a primary replica for another Availability Group, (c) secondary Database replica can be a principal of Database Mirroring and (d) secondary Database replica can be a passive node in the cluster. All these sentences are incorrect and not possible in Availability Group configuration which makes them the correct answer.

5.) Options (b) PowerShell Cmdlet: Move-ClusterGroup "Available Storage" and (c) Command-line cluster.exe: cluster group "Available Storage" /Move are the correct.

[NOTES]

Chapter 13. AlwaysOn Common Issues

Have you ever gone to a cell phone provider's location for some problem with your phone? It is surprising to see how they solve the problem with just couple of questions or with a few clicks on the phone. There is no substitute for experience. This makes the staff an expert in everything they do when it comes to phones. In this chapter we will talk about a few common problems which we might face while working with AlwaysOn technologies. We will cover some of the problems and see the approach to solve these common scenarios.

Unable to join the Availability Group

To configure an AlwaysOn Availability Group, a DBA has performed a backup and restore of the database from primary replica to secondary replica. Later the DBA uses the following command on the secondary replica to join the Availability Group:

```
ALTER DATABASE [MyAdventureWorks] SET HADR AVAILABILITY
GROUP = [MyAvailabilityGroup];
ALTER DATABASE [MyNorthwind] SET HADR AVAILABILITY GROUP =
[MyAvailabilityGroup];
```

We might get the following error message:

```
Messages
Msg 35250, Level 16, State 7, Line 1
The connection to the primary replica is not active. The command cannot be
processed.
```

READER NOTE: *There is a very bad bug in build 3000 or SP1 of SQL Server 2012 which will cause the registry to fill. This is a major issue for clusters to the point where the entire cluster needed to be rebuilt. You need to at least be on build 3128 (which is the GDR hotfix for SP)1, or better yet be on CU3 or higher or build 3349 or higher.* http://support.microsoft.com/kb/2793634p

The Object Explorer for this scenario looks like the Figure 13.1.

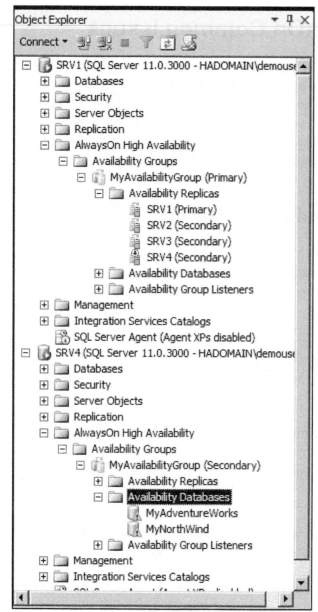

Figure 13.1 SRV4 is not able to get an active connection to the primary.

If we investigate the errorlog we can see an interesting message on the primary replica (SRV1).

```
Database Mirroring login attempt by user 'HADOMAIN\SRV4$.'
failed with error: 'Connection handshake failed. The login
'HADOMAIN\SRV4$' does not have CONNECT permission on the
endpoint. State 84.'. [CLIENT: 192.168.1.12]
```

In the error message, HADOMAIN is the domain name and SRV4 is the server name of the secondary replica. The error message means that SRV4 is trying to communicate to SRV1 via the machine account rather than a domain user account. If we look at the errorlog of the secondary server and look at the service account we can see the below message.

```
The service account is 'NT SERVICE\MSSQLSERVER'. This is an
informational message; no user action is required.
```

There are two ways we can to solve the problem. One way is to allow the machine account to connect to all the endpoints in the group. Add the machine account as a login and provide connect permission to the endpoint. The following query can be executed on SRV1 (which is the current primary replica).

```
CREATE LOGIN [HADOMAIN\srv4$] FROM WINDOWS;
GRANT CONNECT ON ENDPOINT::HADR_Endpoint TO
[hadomain\srv4$];
```

SRV4 may need to communicate with SRV2 and SRV3 as well. The following command needs to be executed on SRV2 and SRV3 to avoid login failures when these servers become the primary because of failover:

```
CREATE LOGIN [HADOMAIN\srv4$] FROM WINDOWS;
GRANT CONNECT ON ENDPOINT::HADR_Endpoint TO
[hadomain\srv4$];
```

A better approach would be to use a consistent domain account as a service account between the servers. In our example it will be the [hadomain\Demouser] domain user account.

Automatic Failover not working

Let's pretend that a DBA had decided to test the capability of the automatic failover after creating an AlwaysOn Availability Group that has only two nodes. She stops the primary replica SQL instance (SRV1). As expected the Availability Group failover takes place and the secondary replica (SRV2) switched its role and became the primary replica. Now she starts SRV1 and stops SRV2. After a certain restart sequence, they notice that the Availability Group is not failing over. The AlwaysOn Dashboard shows the role of the replica as "resolving" and the Failover Cluster Manager shows the Availability Group resource in failed state.

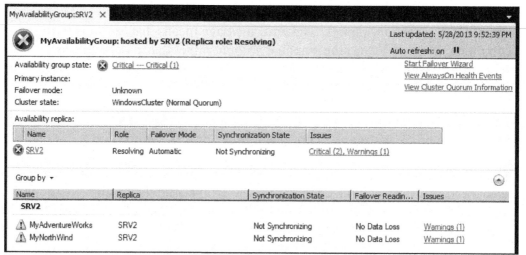

Figure 13.2 "Resolving" role of replica while testing automatic failover.

At this point, we can use the following command to perform a failover to the SRV1:

```
ALTER AVAILABILITY GROUP [MyAvailabilityGroup] FAILOVER;
```

Alternatively, we can use the Dashboard to move the replica by using the "Start Failover Wizard" (Figure 13.2 top right-hand corner).

It is human nature to want to know why the automatic failover happened. If we ever tell a kid not to do something, their first reaction is to ask why and if we fail to convince them and they are bound to do that and learn from their mistakes. This is one of the most common behaviors we see in humans.

In our scenario the question is yet to get answered – Why didn't it perform the automatic failover after a few attempts? Let's go back to our environment which has four replicas. In our environment, it has three successful automatic failovers. After that we were able to perform only a manual failover. Looking into the Windows Cluster logs can provide us with a much needed hint. To generate the cluster log we can run the **cluster log /g** command from command-line and the log will be generated on each node's **%SystemRoot%\Cluster\Reports** folder. The following error will be seen in the log:

```
INFO [RCM] rcm::RcmGroup::UpdateStateIfChanged: (AG GROUP,
Pending --> Failed)
```

```
WARN [RCM] Not failing over group AG GROUP, failoverCount 4,
failover threshold 4294967295, nodeAvailCount 3.
```

INFO [RCM] Will retry online of <u>AG RESOURCE</u> in 3600000
milliseconds.

Looking at the error, we understand that there must be a setting in the cluster
which is causing this behavior. Check the property of the group by going to the
Properties of the group and clicking the **Failover** tab.

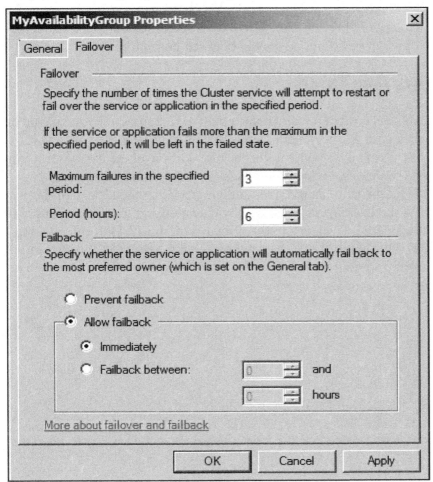

Figure 13.3 Property of group which might cause "no automatic failover" behavior after a few
attempts.

Why do we see the value of 3 was initially set for the number of failures allowed
in 6 hours? We have four replicas. The default value for the maximum number of
automatic failovers is n-1 (where n is the number of nodes in the AG). We have
four nodes in our environment. This sets a ceiling on the number of online failure
events a group can incur before the cluster service ceases to attempt another
automatic failover.

This policy is in place to prevent the cluster service from having a ping pong effect. This is an unbounded attempt by the cluster service to bring the resource online among the various participating nodes. This means that if an Availability Group goes offline for the $(n-1)^{th}$ time, the cluster service will not attempt to bring the resource back online automatically. While this value may be sufficient for production environments, this policy may result in unexpected behavior during testing of automatic failover. Though we can change the value, it is recommended to keep this at a relatively low number. This way if multiple node failures occur, the application or service will not be moved between nodes forever.

No Backups Available

Let's say the DBA has created a maintenance plan for a transaction log backup on the primary replica with all the default values. A few days later, they receive a call from the boss asking to see one of the backups for one of the databases. Upon investigation they realize that none of log backups were taking place on the primary replica. Did the maintenance plan fail? In checking the history of the maintenance plan, the backup was successfully executed and there is no history of any errors. But there are no backups in the primary (Figure 13.4). Upon clicking the **View T-SQL** link (Figure 13.4), they get some hints about this Availability Group backup configuration.

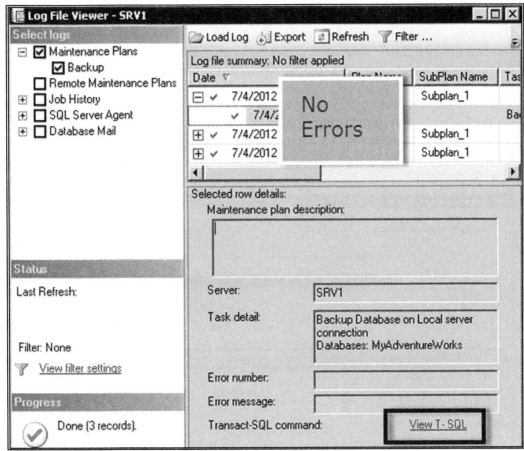

Figure 13.4 No Errors, backups still not available!

DECLARE @preferredReplica int
SET @preferredReplica = (SELECT
[master].sys.fn_hadr_backup_is_preferred_replica('MyAdventureWorks'))
IF (@preferredReplica = 1)
BEGIN
  BACKUP LOG [MyAdventureWorks] TO DISK = N'C:\Program
Files\Microsoft SQL
Server\MSSQL11.MSSQLSERVER\MSSQL\Backup\MyAdventureWorks_back
up_2012_07_04_062401_6530946.trn' WITH NOFORMAT, NOINIT, NAME =
N'MyAdventureWorks_backup_', SKIP, REWIND, NOUNLOAD, STATS = 10
END

Looking at the T-SQL it is clear that the maintenance plan is taking a backup
preference for the Availability Group into consideration before executing the
actual backup command. The default value of the backup preference is set to

"Prefer secondary". If we choose log backup task in the maintenance plan wizard (Figure 13.5) there is a checkbox which says "For availability databases, ignore Replica Priority for Backup on primary Settings". This can be ignored but the default value while creating a maintenance plan is this box is unchecked.

The end effect of these two would be that if we create a default maintenance plan for the backup only on the primary then no backups will happen. This is something to watch out for in a database that is part of an Availability Group. Below is the screenshot with default values when we create a maintenance plan in SQL Server 2012.

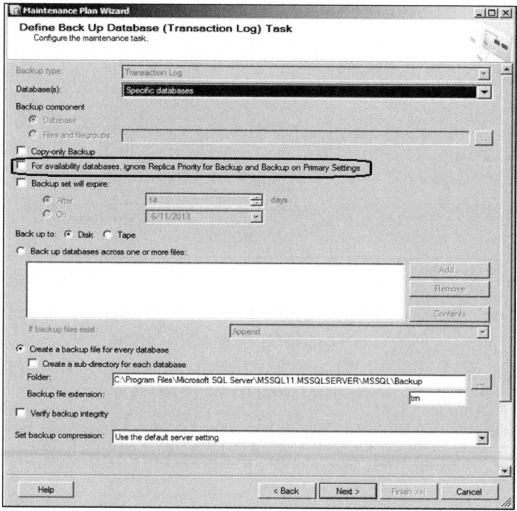

Figure 13.5 Maintenance plan UI with default setting for Availability Database.

Is the DBA who did not know this technique in trouble? What if the manager wanted a point-in-time restore to take the database to where it was 2 hours ago?

318

The DBA can run a transaction log backup right now and still do a point-in-time restore as per the managers requirement.

Readonly Routing not working

The Readonly routing not working dilemma is one of the common problems we see in Availability Group configurations. One of the reasons is that DBAs only do some of the needed steps to set this up. They set the secondary with Read-Intent and connect to Listener with read-intent. Doing only those two steps causes their connection to go to the primary replica for resolution where the routing list is not defined. Without a routing list the Listener fails to route the read-request and just sends all traffic to the primary. Even if the routing URL is set we should check that it is correct. In one of the situations, we found that routing URL was typed in wrong so the Readonly routing did not work.

We need to know what the endpoint is and if the endpoint is healthy. Even if the endpoint is healthy we need to make sure that the endpoint is set up as a readable secondary. The following is the query which can show most of the settings and help us in troubleshooting the routing problem:

```
SELECT ag.name 'Group Name',
 ar.replica_server_name 'Replica Name',
 ars.role_desc 'Role',
 ars.operational_state_desc 'op_State',
 ars.connected_state_desc 'conn_State',
 ars.synchronization_health_desc 'sync_Health',
 drs.synchronization_state_desc 'sync_State',
 ar.secondary_role_allow_connections_desc
  'secondaryAllowRead',
 ar.read_only_routing_url 'rorUrl'
FROM sys.availability_replicas ar
 INNER JOIN sys.availability_groups ag
 ON ar.group_id = ag.group_id
 INNER JOIN sys.dm_hadr_availability_replica_states ars
 ON ar.replica_id = ars.replica_id
 INNER JOIN sys.dm_hadr_database_replica_states drs
 ON ar.replica_id = drs.replica_id
ORDER BY ars.role_desc
```

	Group Name	Replica Name	Role	op_State	conn_State	sync_Health	sync_State	secondaryAllowRead	rorUrl
1	MyAvailabilityGroup	SRV1	PRIMARY	ONLINE	CONNECTED	HEALTHY	SYNCHRONIZED	NO	TCP://SRV1.hadomain.com:1433
2	MyAvailabilityGroup	SRV1	PRIMARY	ONLINE	CONNECTED	HEALTHY	SYNCHRONIZED	NO	TCP://SRV1.hadomain.com:1433
3	MyAvailabilityGroup	SRV2	SECONDARY	NULL	CONNECTED	HEALTHY	SYNCHRONIZED	ALL	TCP://SRV2.hadomain.com:1433
4	MyAvailabilityGroup	SRV2	SECONDARY	NULL	CONNECTED	HEALTHY	SYNCHRONIZED	ALL	TCP://SRV2.hadomain.com:1433
5	MyAvailabilityGroup	SRV3	SECONDARY	NULL	CONNECTED	HEALTHY	SYNCHRONIZED	READ_ONLY	TCP://SRV3.hadomain.com:1433
6	MyAvailabilityGroup	SRV3	SECONDARY	NULL	CONNECTED	HEALTHY	SYNCHRONIZED	READ_ONLY	TCP://SRV3.hadomain.com:1433
7	MyAvailabilityGroup	SRV4	SECONDARY	NULL	CONNECTED	HEALTHY	SYNCHRONIZING	ALL	NULL
8	MyAvailabilityGroup	SRV4	SECONDARY	NULL	CONNECTED	HEALTHY	SYNCHRONIZING	ALL	NULL

Figure 13.6 Query 1 output to verify Readonly routing.

Looking at the last four columns on the right of Figure 13.6 we can see all endpoints are healthy. We can also see that SRV2, SRV3, and SRV4 are setup as readable secondary replicas. SRV4 does not have an endpoint for readonly traffic in the routing list (no RoR URL). This means traffic sent to SRV2 or SRV3 would work. If the Listener was told to send readonly traffic to SRV4 then ROR would not be working.

If SRV1 is the primary, the listener gets ROR traffic, which replica will get this routed connection? What about if SRV2 was the primary, who should get the ROR traffic? The following query shows what server gets routed for readonly traffic:

```
SELECT ag.name 'AG Name',
ar_Primary.replica_server_name 'Primary',
ar_secondary.replica_server_name 'Route_to',
ror.routing_priority 'Priority'
FROM sys.availability_read_only_routing_lists ror
  INNER JOIN sys.availability_replicas ar_Primary
 ON ror.replica_id = ar_Primary.replica_id
  INNER JOIN sys.availability_replicas ar_secondary
 ON ror.read_only_replica_id = ar_secondary.replica_id
  INNER JOIN sys.availability_groups ag
 ON ag.group_id = ar_Primary.group_id
ORDER BY 1, 3
```

	AG Name	Primary	Route_to	Priority
1	MyAvailabilityGroup	SRV1	SRV3	1
2	MyAvailabilityGroup	SRV2	SRV3	1

Figure 13.7 The Routing list for MyAvailabilityGroup.

We don't want to be surprised by failure so what can be done ahead of time to maximize our changes? The following is a simple checklist that we can use:

S. No.	Item to Verify	Status
1.	Verify that we are connecting to Listener Name.	☐
2.	Verity that the initial catalog is provided in connection string.	☐
3.	Verify that the Readonly routing list (READ_ONLY_ROUTING_LIST) is defined. (output of second query)	☐
4.	Verify that the Routing URL (READ_ONLY_ROUTING_URL) of each instance has a proper FQDN and port combination.	☐
5.	Verify that ApplicationIntent is specified in the connection string.	☐
6.	Verify that the Sync_State is SYNCHRONIZED or SYNCHORNIZING in the query output for the replica (output of the first query).	☐
7.	Verify that the secondary replicas are set to allow connections (secondaryAllowRead is in the query output).	☐

Table 13.1 Checklist for Readonly routing troubleshooting.

Rather than testing via an application, we can first check the routing using SQLCMD on the routing server. In SQLCMD there is a new switch, -K (upper case), which can mimic the behavior of an ApplicationIntent parameter in a connection string. The following is a sample command for reference:

```
SQLCMD -S MyListener -K ReadOnly -d MyAdventureWorks -
Q"select @@servername"
```

If routing works fine, then our request would be sent to the next server in the priority list. If none of the replicas are available then we would receive the below error:

```
Sqlcmd: Error: Microsoft SQL Server Native Client 11.0 :
Unable to access the 'MyAdventureWorks' database because no
online secondary replicas are enabled for readonly access.
Check the Availability Group configuration to verify that at
least one secondary replica is configured for readonly
```

access. Wait for an enabled replica to come online, and retry your readonly operation.

In one of the cases, we were able to connect to the primary replica and the secondary replica separately but when we tried using the Listener name, we received the following error.

```
C:\Windows\system32>SQLCMD -S MyListener -K ReadOnly -d
MyAdventureWorks -Q"select @@servername"

Sqlcmd: Error: Microsoft SQL Server Native Client 11.0 : TCP
Provider: No such host is known.

Sqlcmd: Error: Microsoft SQL Server Native Client 11.0 :
Login timeout expired.

Sqlcmd: Error: Microsoft SQL Server Native Client 11.0 : A
network-related or instance-specific error has occurred
while establishing a connection to SQL Server. Server is not
found or not accessible. Check if instance name is correct
and if SQL Server is configured to allow remote connections.
For more information see SQL Server Books Online.
```

We followed the checklist defined earlier and found that the routing URL was defined for the wrong port. In our case the routing URL was defined by using a HADR_Endpoint port of 5022 rather than a SQL Server listening port of 1433. Due to that connection going to port 5022 it raised a generic connectivity error.

Replica in a Resolving State

When we see the role of a replica as "Resolving", it means that SQL Server was not able to decide if this server should be in the primary role or the secondary role state. This state can be seen in the Object Explorer and the Dashboard of SSMS (as shown in Figure 13.8). As we can see on the Dashboard, the primary instance is blank.

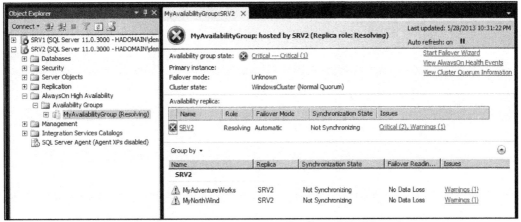

Figure 13.8 Resolving role of replica in Management Studio and Dashboard.

At this point, if the application tries to connect to the database, it would fail with error 983 as follows:

```
Messages
Msg 983, Level 14, State 1, Line 1
Unable to access database 'MyNorthwind' because its replica role is RESOLVING
which does not allow connections. Try the operation again later.
```

When a primary goes down and one of the secondary takes over during an automatic failover this takes some time for the new primary to be online. There is a short period of time where this server is no longer a secondary but is not yet a running primary. This state is called resolving. Resolving often means this is an intermittent state where if there is a role transition of any replica from the primary to the secondary or vice versa. In other words, in the middle of a failover there is short time period where there is no online primary. If role reversal fails, the replica role would stay in the resolving state.

To troubleshoot, start by checking the state of the clustered resource in the Failover Cluster Manager. In most of the cases, it would be in a failed state (Figure 13.9) or an offline state. If the cluster resource is not online, there is no node owning the AG and the cluster cannot decide who is the primary or secondary. This is the reason why we get a resolving state for the Availability Group in SQL Server.

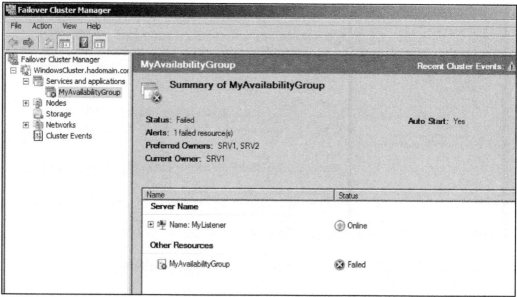

Figure 13.9 Failed state of resource caused resolving state in Figure 13.5.

Let's try to find out why or how this happened and what are the steps to recover from this state. From the SQL Server perspective, we need to identify a time when this role transition happened. This can be found from the AlwaysOn_health session, errorlog, or the application event log. Most of the events from the AlwaysOn_health sessions are logged into the errorlog and the application event logs. To look at the latest AlwaysOn_health log we have connected to Management Studio (on error node – SRV2). We did this by going to Object Explorer and expanding **Management** > **Extended Events** > **Sessions** > **AlwaysOn_health** > and then right-clicking **package0.event_file** > and selecting **View Target data**. In the health session, we found Error 1480 which happened at 22:28 Hrs. (Figure 13.10, also highlighted).

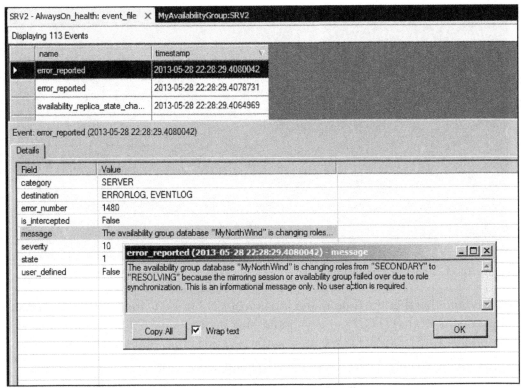

Figure 13.10 AlwaysOn_health session shows state change of replica.

The tooltip gives us vital information of the state. It was trying to switch roles and it failed in the process (therefore we have a resolving state). To move forward in troubleshooting of the clustered resource failure, we need to start from system event log, application event log, and the cluster logs. The cluster logs are not available by default. To generate cluster logs, we need to run a "Cluster log /generate" command from the command prompt. The logfile name Cluster.log would be generated in C:\Windows\Cluster\Reports\ location.

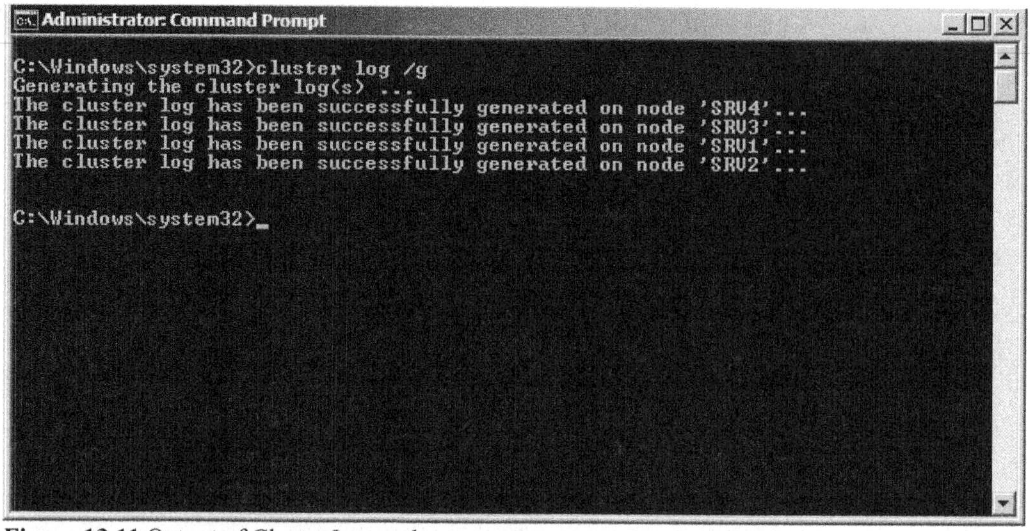

Figure 13.11 Output of Cluster Log code.

Please note that that the time in the log is recorded in UTC time. Our environment time zone is PDT (UTC-7) so we should look at around 05/29/2012 - 05:28 UTC (05/28/2013 - 22:28 PDT). We have surpassed our limit of automatic failovers.

2013/05/28-05:28:11.164	INFO	HandleMonitorReply: TERMINATERESOURCE for 'MyAvailabilityGroup', gen(3) result 0.
2013/05/28-05:28:11.164	INFO	TransitionToState(MyAvailabilityGroup) [Terminating to Failed]-->Failed.
2013/05/28-05:28:11.164	INFO	rcm::RcmGroup::UpdateStateIfChanged : (MyAvailabilityGroup, Pending --> Failed)
2013/05/28-05:28:11.195	WARN	**Not failing over group MyAvailabilityGroup, failoverCount 3, failover threshold 1, nodeAvailCount 1.**
2013/05/28-05:28:11.195	INFO	**Will retry online of MyAvailabilityGroup in 3600000 milliseconds.**

Table 13.2 Series of events seen in cluster log around the time of failure.

This error looks familiar as we have discussed the steps required earlier in this chapter. Another possible reason of the resolving state would be that the quorum is lost. This can be simulated by stopping the cluster service on at least 50% of the nodes and therefore reducing the voter count to not reach a quorum. Once we have less than the majority, the cluster would fail and replica state would become resolving.

Summary

We have all heard the phrase "To err is human" and we do make mistakes unknowingly during configuration. In this chapter we have called out some of the common mistakes we have seen while configuring an AlwaysOn Availability Group. Some of the errors (like Unable to join Availability Group, Readonly Routing not working, and automatic failover not working) can be annoying when we are in the setup stage or testing stage. Having no backups available and forced failover causing data loss can be very critical to business. Knowing the distinctions and fine points is critical as a seasoned DBA.

Points to Ponder – AlwaysOn Common Issues

1. If we get an error message number of 41158 while joining an Availability Group, check for the permissions and accounts used to connect.

2. A Failover can be initiated using T-SQL like:
   ALTER AVAILABILITY GROUP [MyAvailabilityGroup] FAILOVER;

3. The default value for the maximum number of failures is n-1 in the Cluster Failover resource property, where n is the number of nodes.

4. If the maintenance plan is using backup preferences for an Availability Group in consideration before executing backup command then make sure the maintenance plans are in place in all the replicas.

5. Readonly routing doesn't work when we have the wrong URL or when the routing URL is not set.

6. When we get the role of replica a as resolving, it means that SQL Server is not able to decide if that server is in the primary role or the secondary role state.

7. Resolving is also an intermittent state when there is a role transition of any replica from the primary to the secondary or the secondary to primary. If role reversal fails, the replica role would stay in the Resolving state.

8. In the case of an Availability Group join failure, the first place to look is the SQL ERRORLOGs.

9. One of the common causes of the automatic failover not working is testing with incorrect cluster group settings.

10. In Windows 2008 and onwards, we need to generate a cluster log using the "cluster log /g" command.

Review Quiz - Chapter Thirteen

1.) As a DBA you wanted to utilize the backup on the secondary configuration and have it set as the preferred backup location. After a week you realize that the backups are not happening and there are no logs created. What could be the possible problem?

   O a. Failed to create maintenance jobs on primary.
   O b. Failed to create maintenance jobs on secondary.
   O c. Listener was not configured.

2.) As a DBA you are told by the application team that Readonly routing is not working on our AlwaysOn Availability Group configuration. What could be the possible causes?

   □ a. Routing URL not configred.
   □ b. Incorrect Routing URL.
   □ c. Application not using Listener.
   □ d. Connection String doesn't have the ReadOnly attribute.

3.) When will the replica be in "Resolving state"? Choose all that apply.

   □ a. Role transition of any replica from primary to secondary.
   □ b. Role transition of any replica from secondary to primary.
   □ c. When IO error of 823 occurs on the server.
   □ d. When Backups are taken.

4.) Which catalog view provides us information about Readonly Routing?

   O a. sys.availability_read_only_routing_lists
   O b. sys.availability_db_routing_lists
   O c. sys.dm_hadr_routing_lists
   O d. sys.dm_hadr_db_routing_lists

Answer Key

1.) Options (a) Failed to create maintenance jobs on primary and (c) Listener was not configured are wrong. This makes (b) the correct answer.

2.) Readonly Routing does not happen when any of the options are met. Hence the correct answer is (a) Routing URL not configured, (b) Incorrect Routing URL, (c) Application not using Listener, (d) Connection String doesn't have the Readonly attribute.

3.)   The correct answer is (a) Role transition of any replica from primary to secondary and (b) Role transition of any replica from secondary to primary.

4.)   We can get Readonly routing information from (a) sys.availability_read_only_routing_lists. All other options (b) sys.availability_db_routing_lists, (c) sys.dm_hadr_routing_lists and (d) sys.dm_hadr_db_routing_lists are incorrect.

[NOTES]

Chapter 14. Availability Group Failover

When we buy a new vehicle like an SUV, we get three sets of keys from the manufacturer. The importance of these keys never comes to our mind when we buy the vehicle. One fine day, when we accidentally misplace one set of our keys, is when these duplicate keys come to our rescue. In our lives, having a duplicate copy is something we do regularly. A duplicate copy can be useful when we lose our original copy. Similarly, in the SQL Server world, the need for a duplicate is to secure the business from any disaster or from a machine level failure. In this chapter we will look at the various Availability Group failover mechanisms and how to achieve them.

Similar to Database Mirroring and SQL Server Clustering, Availability Groups provide a mechanism for High Availability by allowing the Availability Databases to failover from one machine to another. In the world of Availability Groups, failover is defined as a process where any secondary would change its role to the primary. If it's an automatic failover, then the current primary replica should change its role to secondary (unless it just went down). The benefits provided by Availability Groups compared to Database Mirroring are:

- More than one database can fail over at the same time.
- More than one possible failover partner (we can have more than one secondary replica).
- The secondary replica can be made available for readonly workloads while in it's in the secondary Role.
- Simplified connectivity from clients based on their connection string.

The benefits provided by Availability Groups compared to SQL Server Clustering are:

- No requirement to purchase specialized shared disk.
- Secondary replicas can be utilized for other tasks while in secondary role (like readonly workloads).

This chapter outlines the various modes of failover available with the Availability Groups.

Performing Automatic Failovers

Our offices (and these days even our homes) use one or more UPS units (Uninterruptible Power Supply). The function of these devices is to make sure the power is always available for our computers, lights, and other work machines. The UPS automatically takes over when there is a power outage. This is (for most cases) not known to our electrical devices because it is seamlessly done.

In an AlwaysOn Availability Group world, an automatic failover would be performed automatically when the primary replica is lost. We can define only one pair of replicas for automatic failover. In our topology we have four replicas but only SRV1 and SRV2 are set up as a pair for automatic failover.

It is important to recall that we can only set the automatic failover to a synchronous replica. This would mean that automatic failover will not cause data loss. Here is the list of prerequisites which must be met for automatic failover to be ready:

- There must be an automatic failover replica defined.

- The automatic failover replica must be in a healthy synchronized state.

- The failover condition level defined in the availability resource property must be met when the primary replica becomes unavailable (must not have already exceeded the limit on automatic failovers).

- The Windows Cluster should have the needed votes to form quorum.

As the name says, this is an automatic failover, there are no manual steps that need to be performed. If SRV1 is the primary replica and the service stops then a failover should happen. For testing purposes, we can simply stop the SQL Server Service on the current primary replica and check if automatic failover works. We need to be aware of one common issue described in the last chapter (*Chapter 13- Automatic Failover not working*).

Performing Manual Failovers

In our previous section we talked about the use of a UPS. In some heavy machinery setup it is not possible to have a battery UPS run the equipment. We have seen organizations that use generators that run on fuel instead of electricity. The only drawback of using these generators is that it needs human intervention to get started and to switch over to. This is a typical case of manual failover.

During the configuration of Availability Groups, it is not mandatory to have an automatic failover replica. Additionally, automatic failover can be defined as only one pair of replicas (like between SRV1 and SRV2). Due to these factors, there could be situations when we need to perform a manual failover to a secondary replica. If a primary replica is not available and any of the following are true then we might need to perform a forced failover:

- An automatic failover replica is not available.

- An automatic failover replica is not defined.

- An automatic failover replica is not in healthy state.

Other possible situations could be that we want to perform some maintenance on a node which is hosting the primary replica. It is also possible that we are patching the nodes with a service pack and as a part of the process a failover is needed to one of the synchronous replicas.

This failover is also referred as a "planned manual failover" or a "manual failover with no-data loss". Unlike an automatic failover, this needs some manual intervention to perform the failover to a synchronous secondary replica. Here are the conditions which must be met for a successful manual failover:

- There must be at least one secondary replica which is set for synchronous data movement.

- The upcoming primary replica (failover target secondary replica) must be in a synchronized state.

In our test environment, we have SRV1 and SRV2 as an automatic failover pair. Currently SRV3 is another synchronous replica and SRV4 is an asynchronous replica. To perform any failover, it is recommended to use either the "Start Failover Wizard" from management studio or use a T-SQL or a PowerShell command. The Failover Cluster Manager interface should not be used. We will now cover various ways to perform the planned manual failover.

Using Management Studio Wizard:

1. Launch the AlwaysOn Availability Group Dashboard using Management Studio.

2. Click on the **Start Failover Wizard** link from top right corner

3. Go to **Select New primary replica** screen and choose the replica where we want to failover. In this example we are using SRV3. Notice that we are seeing a warning message that says the following:

```
Failing over to this replica will result in
changing the failover mode for the primary replica
of this Availability Group.
```

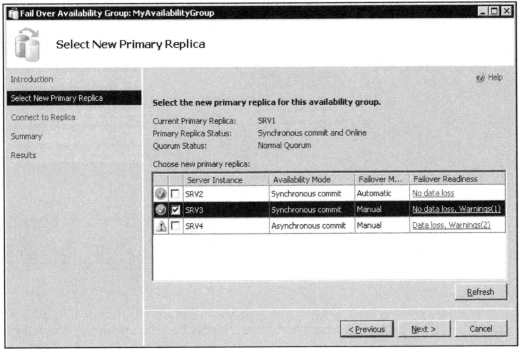

Figure 14.1 Fail Over Availability Group screen from SSMS.

4. Choose SRV3 and click **Next**. In the next screen (called **Connect to Replica**), we need to provide credentials to connect to the new primary replica (which is SRV3 in our scenario).

5. In the last screen (the **Summary** screen), we need to click **Finish** to make these changes.

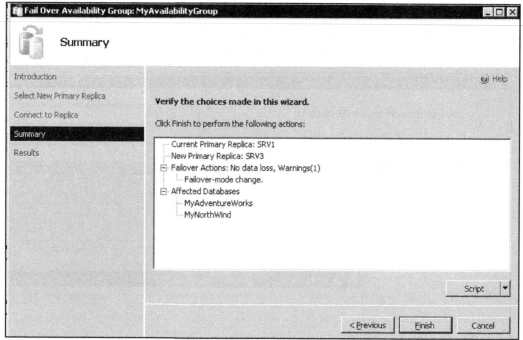

Figure 14.2 Summary screen for Fail Over Availability Group via SSMS.

An important part of the Summary screen is the Script button. This can help us in getting a T-SQL command which would be executed on the upcoming secondary (SRV3 in our case).

```
--- YOU MUST EXECUTE THE FOLLOWING SCRIPT IN SQLCMD MODE.
:Connect SRV3
```

```
ALTER AVAILABILITY GROUP [MyAvailabilityGroup] FAILOVER;
```

We can run the command directly by connecting to SRV3 or we can use SQLCMD mode while on one of the other replicas.

READER NOTE: *To start a query with SQLCMD mode go to the SSMS Menu and choose **Query >SQLCMD mode**.*

Once the failover is complete, we can launch the Dashboard on SRV3 and verify that it has taken the primary role. Notice there is no automatic failover pairing for SRV3. That was the warning given earlier on that link.

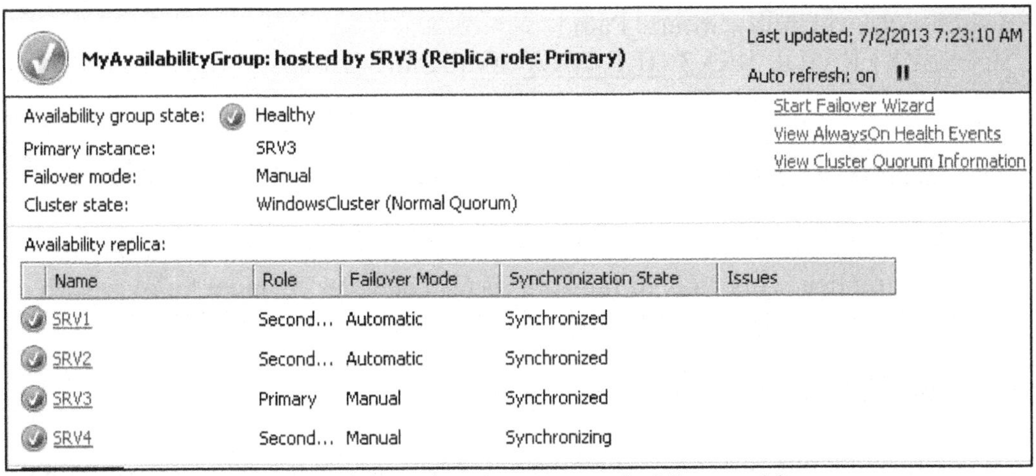

Figure 14.3 With SRV3 as the primary, there is no automatic failover pairing.

Using T-SQL:

Here is the command which we need to run on the new primary replica (SRV3) which is synchronous with the current primary replica.

```
ALTER AVAILABILITY GROUP [MyAvailabilityGroup] FAILOVER;
```

If we attempt to run the above command on a secondary replica which is not in a synchronized state (SRV4 in our scenario is asynchronous), we would get the following error:

```
Messages
Msg 41142, Level 16, State 34, Line 1
The availability replica for Availability Group 'MyAvailabilityGroup' on this
instance of SQL Server cannot become the primary replica. One or more
databases are not synchronized or have not joined the Availability Group, or
the WSFC cluster was started in Force Quorum mode. If the cluster was started
in Force Quorum mode or the availability replica uses the asynchronous-commit
mode, consider performing a forced manual failover (with possible data loss).
Otherwise, once all local secondary databases are joined and synchronized,
you can perform a planned manual failover to this secondary replica (without
data loss). For more information, see SQL Server Books Online.
```

Using PowerShell:

To do this we need to use the Switch-SqlAvailabilityGroup cmdlet and provide the new secondary replica details along with the Availability Group name. Here is the PowerShell equivalent of the same scenario (a manual failover to SRV3) which we have done earlier using the UI and T-SQL.

Switch-SqlAvailabilityGroup –Path
SQLSERVER:\SQL**SRV3****DEFAULT**\AvailabilityGroups**MyAvailabilityGro up**

Performing Forced Failovers (Quorum Available)

In certain situations, we might need to perform a failover to an asynchronous secondary replica. This "forced failover" is also called a "manual failover with data loss". The steps are similar to the failover that was done earlier with one major difference. This is a failover with data loss. Due to data loss, it is strictly performed only for Disaster Recovery purposes.

To demonstrate this, we have failed back to SRV1 as the primary so our topology matches that of the start of this chapter. SRV4 is an asynchronous secondary replica. This time, we will failover to SRV4.

Using Management Studio Wizard:

To perform this failover in Management Studio we can do the following steps:

1. Launch the AlwaysOn Availability Group Dashboard using Management Studio.

2. Click on the **Start Failover Wizard** link from top right corner.

Once the **Failover Wizard** is up, get to the **Select New Primary Replica** screen and choose the replica to failover to. In this example we are using SRV4. Notice that we are seeing the following two warnings for SRV4:

```
This replica has one or more databases that are not
synchronized. Failing over to this replica could result in
data loss for any transactions that did not reach this
secondary replica prior to failing over.
```

```
Failing over to this replica will result in changing the
failover mode for the primary replica of this Availability
Group.
```

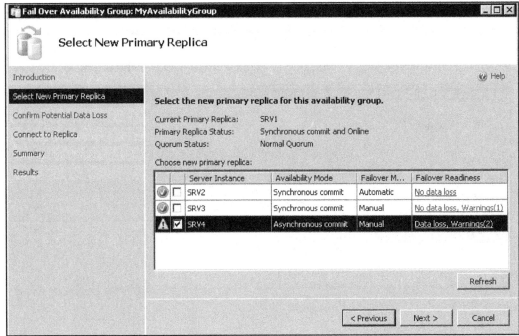

Figure 14.4 Forced failover via SSMS.

3. Choose the checkbox next to **SRV4** and click **Next**. On the next screen (**Confirm Potential Data Loss**), we need to acknowledge our decision to perform this forced failover.

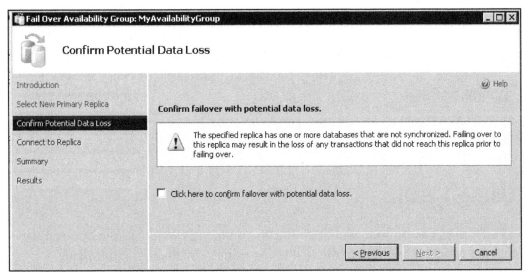

Figure 14.5 Confirmation for possible data loss in UI.

4. In the next screen (**Connect to Replica**) we need to provide the credentials to connect to the new primary replica (which is SRV4 for this scenario).

5. In the **Summary** screen we need to click **Finish** and see the changes.

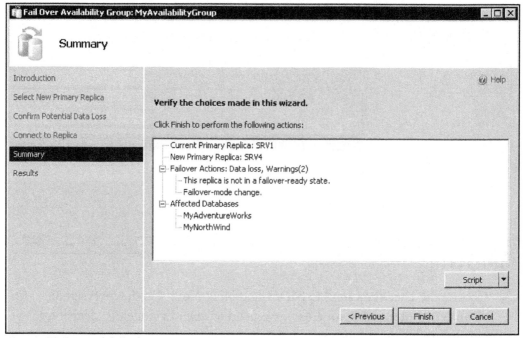

Figure 14.6 Forced failover summary screen.

Notice the Script button is an option. The following is the output by clicking the **Script** button:

```
--- YOU MUST EXECUTE THE FOLLOWING SCRIPT IN SQLCMD MODE.
:Connect SRV4

ALTER AVAILABILITY GROUP [MyAvailabilityGroup]
FORCE_FAILOVER_ALLOW_DATA_LOSS;
GO
```

Using T-SQL:

The failover can be done with T-SQL code on the new replica. The new replica is the one which needs to be promoted to the primary replica. The following example will be using this T-SQL code on SRV4 to promote it as our new primary replica with data loss:

```
ALTER AVAILABILITY GROUP [MyAvailabilityGroup]
FORCE_FAILOVER_ALLOW_DATA_LOSS;
GO
```

The only difference in the command between the failover to a synchronous copy vs. an asynchronous copy, is the allowance for data loss. If we use the earlier command (**FAILOVER** vs. **FORCE_FAILOVER_ALLOW_DATA_LOSS**), we would get the following error message:

```
Messages
Msg 41142, Level 16, State 34, Line 2
The availability replica for Availability Group 'MyAvailabilityGroup' on this
instance of SQL Server cannot become the primary replica. One or more
databases are not synchronized or have not joined the Availability Group, or
the WSFC cluster was started in Force Quorum mode. If the cluster was started
in Force Quorum mode or the availability replica uses the asynchronous-commit
mode, consider performing a forced manual failover (with possible data loss).
Otherwise, once all local secondary databases are joined and synchronized,
you can perform a planned manual failover to this secondary replica (without
data loss). For more information, see SQL Server Books Online.
```

Using PowerShell:

With PowerShell we need to use the same Switch-SqlAvailabilityGroup cmdlet as before and provide the new secondary replica details and the AG name. Since we are failing over to an asynchronous copy, we need to add the –AllowDataLoss parameter as seen in the following code example:

```
Switch-SqlAvailabilityGroup –Path
SQLSERVER:\SQL\SRV4\DEFAULT\AvailabilityGroups\MyAvailabilit
yGroup -AllowDataLoss
```

This code would prompt us for **Yes**, **No** or **Suspend**. To avoid the prompt, we can add **–Force** parameter.

```
Switch-SqlAvailabilityGroup –Path
SQLSERVER:\SQL\SRV4\DEFAULT\AvailabilityGroups\MyAvailabilit
yGroup –AllowDataLoss -Force
```

Once the failover with data loss is complete, we would notice that all other replicas (SRV1, SRV2, and SRV3) are no longer synchronizing (Figure 14.7).

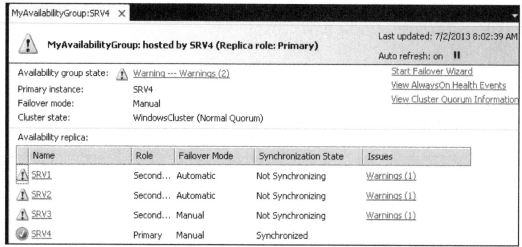

Figure 14.7 After a forced failover the secondary replicas are no longer synchronizing.

We need to take the steps mentioned in Books Online to bring the other replicas back online. http://msdn.microsoft.com/en-us/library/ff877957.aspx

Performing Forced Failovers (Quorum not Available)

The forced failover we just performed was done while the windows quorum was available. We were able to perform the manual failover since the Availability Group was online in the Failover Cluster Manager and the primary and secondary roles were defined. Another situation where we need to perform a forced failover will be when the Windows Cluster has lost its quorum and all the replicas go to a resolving state. In this situation we would not be able to perform a normal forced failover. If we try to use the SSMS failover wizard, we will see the error in Figure 14.8.

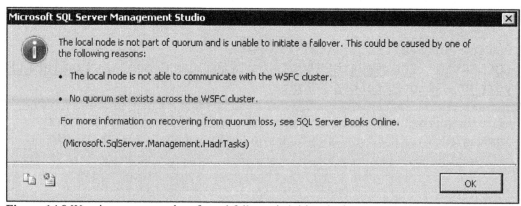

Figure 14.8 Warning message when forced failover is initiated when quorum is lost.

The quorum needs more than 50% of the votes to function. We will simulate this failure in our lab by stopping the cluster service on two out of four nodes. Since the cluster will not have more than 50% of the votes the quorum is lost and the cluster service shuts down automatically on all the rest of the nodes. The following message in the system event log shows the cause.

```
The Cluster service is shutting down because quorum was
lost. This could be due to the loss of network connectivity
between some or all nodes in the cluster, or a failover of
the witness disk.

Run the Validate a Configuration wizard to check your
network configuration. If the condition persists, check for
hardware or software errors related to the network adapter.
Also check for failures in any other network components to
which the node is connected such as hubs, switches, or
bridges.
```

At this point, since quorum is not available, we need to follow these steps:

1. Choose the node where we need to start the cluster service in forced quorum mode. We will do this for SRV4.

2. Start the cluster service using /fq switch (Refer to KB http://support.microsoft.com/kb/947713 - The implications of using the /forcequorum switch to start the cluster service in Windows Server 2008). In our example, we have started the cluster service on the SRV4 node.

```
net start clussvc /fq
```

Figure 14.9 shows what we see in the Failover Cluster Manager interface:

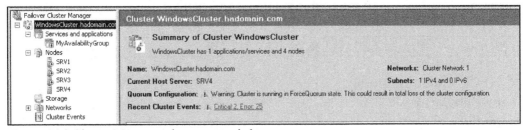

Figure 14.9 Cluster Manager when quorum is lost.

SQL Server Management Studio would also show forced quorum in Dashboard (Figure 14.10).

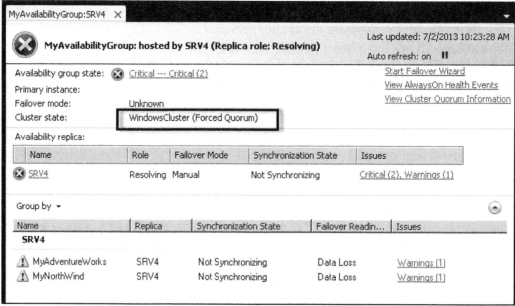

Figure 14.10 AlwaysOn SSMS Dashboard when the quorum is lost.

The same status can be views from the sys.dm_hadr_cluster_members and sys.dm_hadr_cluster DMVs. The following queries when run on SRV4 will give a diagnosis result for our cluster members and the state of the quorum:

```
SELECT member_name,
 member_type_desc,
 member_state_desc,
 number_of_quorum_votes as Vote
FROM sys.dm_hadr_cluster_members
```

member_name	member_type_desc	member_state_desc	Vote
SRV1	CLUSTER_NODE	DOWN	1
SRV2	CLUSTER_NODE	DOWN	1
SRV3	CLUSTER_NODE	DOWN	1
SRV4	CLUSTER_NODE	UP	1

```
SELECT cluster_name,
 quorum_type_desc,
 quorum_state_desc
FROM sys.dm_hadr_cluster
```

cluster_name	quorum_type_desc	quorum_state_desc
WindowsCluster	NODE_MAJORITY	FORCED_QUORUM

3. If the Availability Group is part of a multi-subnet cluster and we are performing steps during a data center disaster, then we need to adjust the votes of each voter, if needed. The unrecovered nodes should be set offline or have their node votes set to zero. In a prior version of Windows Server 2012, it has to be done via commands (PowerShell or cluster.exe).

```
# Setting NodeWeight to 0 for SRV2

Import-Module FailoverClusters
$node = "SRV2"
(Get-ClusterNode $node).NodeWeight = 0

# Returns the vote setting for each node in the cluster
# Our Cluster Name is Windowsluster.hadomain.com
Import-Module FailoverClusters
$nodes = Get-ClusterNode -Cluster WindowsCluster

$nodes | Format-Table -property NodeName, State,
NodeWeight
```

We have done the same thing for all the other nodes except SRV4.

4. Now, to bring the database to an available state, we need to run:

```
ALTER AVAILABILITY GROUP [MyAvailabilityGroup]
FORCE_FAILOVER_ALLOW_DATA_LOSS;
```

5. At this point it looks like the database is up and running but we need to take care of the other replicas too. Data synchronization is not currently happening. If we resume data movement at this point, we will lose the data which was not sent to the replica that we brought online. To salvage the data, we can create a Database Snapshot to compare the data with the current primary.
Refer to http://msdn.microsoft.com/en-us/library/hh270277.aspx for a more detailed explanation.

6. Windows Cluster quorum votes, Availability Group synchronization model, and replica state all needs re-evaluation after a forced failover is complete.

Summary

Understanding business needs is critical when we plan our AlwaysOn deployments. As the deployment happens we need to plan out each step of how various modes of failovers can happen in our environment. Detailing each of the failovers is important because when disasters happens, we really don't have control of who might actually do the restore process. Finally, testing the documentation from time-to-time with various team members is also an important step. In this chapter we discussed the possible failover mechanisms which can be used as a starting guide.

Points to Ponder – Availability Group Failover

1. In the world of Availability Groups, failover is defined as a process where any secondary would change its role to the primary. This failover could be automatic or it could be done manually.

2. We can define only one pair of availability replicas for automatic failover.

3. Manual failover is required when we want to perform some maintenance on a node which is hosting the primary replica or we are patching the nodes with the service pack.

4. A manual failover can be done using no-data loss on a synchronous replica or the failover can be done with data loss on an asynchronous replica (also called a forced failover).

5. In a forced failover with data loss, it is strictly performed for Disaster Recovery purposes only.

6. We can use SQL SSMS, T-SQL, or PowerShell for various modes of Failover.

7. If a quorum is not formed then the cluster service won't start on any of the nodes. In such situations, we must bring up the cluster service with force quorum to perform data recovery.

8. Performing manual failover to a non-automatic replica will result in changing the failover mode for the primary replica of the Availability Group. The AG will no longer use automatic failover.

9. Once the quorum is lost, we need to start the cluster service in a forced quorum mode using the command of **net start clussvc /fq** in a command window.

Review Quiz - Chapter Fourteen

1.) How many synchronous secondary replicas can we configure for automatic failover?

   O a. One
   O b. Two
   O c. Three
   O d. Four

2.) When can we have a forced failover?

   □ a. When quorum is available.
   □ b. When quorum is not available.

3.) Which command would we use for perform manual failover?

   O a. **ALTER AVAILABILITY GROUP [MyAvailabilityGroup] FAILOVER;**
   O b. **ALTER AVAILABILITY GROUP [MyAvailabilityGroup] MANUAL FAILOVER;**
   O c. **ALTER AVAILABILITY GROUP [MyAvailabilityGroup] FORCE FAILOVER;**
   O d. **ALTER AVAILABILITY GROUP [MyAvailabilityGroup] AUTO FAILOVER;**

Answer Key

1.) Option (a) One, is the correct answer. We can have only one pair of synchronous replica configured as automatic failure.

2.) Forced failover can be configured on both modes of quorum available or not. Hence options (a) When quorum is available and (b) When quorum is not available are the correct answers.

3.) Option (a) ALTER AVAILABILITY GROUP [MyAvailabilityGroup] FAILOVER; is the correct syntax. Hence options (b), (c) and (d) are wrong options.

[NOTES]

Chapter 15. Migrating from Previous High Availability Scenarios

There will always be a little "kid" in all of us. Living rooms these days are filled with a PlayStation or Xbox to keep the entertainment factor high. Even with these toys we always look for something new to try. If you have become addicted to the Halo series of games, you will always look forward to the next version to come out. As soon as a new release comes home we give most of our time and attention to it and are excited to spend hours playing it.

In a similar way, sometimes we get excited with new features and plan to migrate or upgrade our infrastructures. We all know that there are fundamental differences between toys and our company's production environment. So, before moving to the steps of migration, we want to emphasize that the testing of an application on a new platform is necessary and critical. We should have proper plans and processes in place for a successful migration and get ready for using the new features in production environments. Sometimes, we need to go through a very tough process called unlearn-and-learn because the new version might bring-in new processes. In this chapter we take a tour of migration from a prior High Availability solution to the new AlwaysOn Availability Groups.

Migrating from Log Shipping

There are two situations where we want to move from Log Shipping to SQL Server 2012 AlwaysOn Availability Groups.

1. We are currently using SQL Server 2008 R2 (or 2008 or 2005) and have Log Shipping configured.
2. We are currently using SQL Server 2012 and have Log Shipping configured.

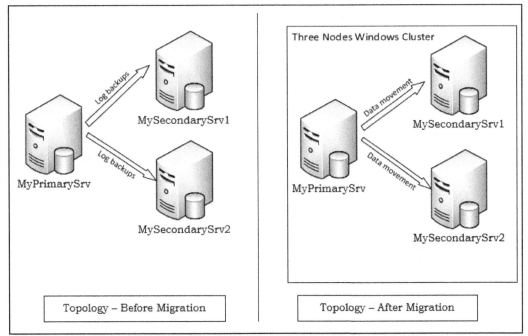

Figure 15.1 Typical topology from Log Shipping configuration to AlwaysOn Availability Group.

In the first scenario, we need to migrate to SQL Server 2012 and then meet all the prerequisites for an Availability Group. After the upgrade to SQL 2012 we perform step 2. If a database on the secondary server is not having the same name as the primary then we need to perform a complete backup and restore of the database with the same name as the primary. We also need to keep in mind that Log Shipping can also work in bulk-logged recovery model but for Availability Groups it need to be in full recovery model. It must be set to full.

Here is the high level overview for the first scenario where we are using Log Shipping with SQL 2005, 2008, or 2008R2.

a. If Log Shipping is configured for a standby secondary then we might want to change it to the "in recovery" mode because backups taken from a lower version can't be restored to a higher version of SQL while in Standby Mode. Here is the error message for the restore log operation in such a scenario:

```
Messages
Msg 3180, Level 16, State 1, Line 1
This backup cannot be restored using WITH STANDBY because a database upgrade
is needed. Reissue the RESTORE without WITH STANDBY.
```

Messages
Msg 3013, Level 16, State 1, Line 1
RESTORE LOG is terminating abnormally.

This also means that as soon as the Log Shipping secondary migration starts from SQL 2008 R2 to SQL 2012, the secondary can't be used for reporting the latest data (either the No Recovery Mode or the Standby Mode while no restores happening).

b. Migrate the secondary servers (MysecondarySrv1 & MysecondarySrv2) to SQL Server 2012.

c. Disable the Log Shipping backup job on the primary server (MyPrimarySrv) and then run the job manually. This will create the log backup in the shared location.

d. On the secondary servers, disable the copy jobs and the restore jobs. Run the copy job manually and once that completes, run the restore job manually. This will ensure that the latest log backup that was taken from the primary has been restored to the secondary servers. Check the history of the jobs to make sure they have successfully completed.

e. Migrate the primary server (MyPrimarySrv) to SQL Server 2012.

At this point, we have migrated Log Shipping on the primary server and the secondary servers to SQL Server 2012 and have Log Shipping configured with the jobs disabled. If we are in scenario 2 then the following are the steps which are common for both scenarios:

a. Enable the Windows Clustering feature and create a Windows Server Failover Cluster. Add all three nodes to the Windows Cluster.

b. Enable the AlwaysOn Availability Groups feature for each instance of SQL Server using the Failover Configuration Manager or PowerShell. Doing this needs restart of SQL Service

c. Configure the AlwaysOn Availability Group for the databases. Since we already have databases restored on the secondary replicas, we need to use the **Join only** option in the **Select Initial Data Synchronization** page of the **New Availability Group Wizard**. (Figure 15.2)

d. Once the wizard has completed, we can get the status of each of the replicas on the **Results** page of the wizard.

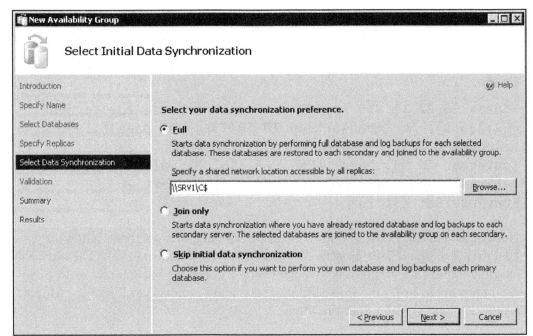

Figure 15.2 Since we already have databases restored on the secondary replicas, we need to use the Join only option.

In case of failure, we need to take action based on the error we get. Several known errors and solutions to look for will be covered now.

Failure 1

If we have missed changing the Standby Mode to NoRecovery Mode (step a), then we would get the following error:

```
Messages
Msg 1466, Level 16, State 2, Line 1
Database "MyAdventureWorks" is readonly on one of the server instances which
is incompatible with participating in Database Mirroring or in an
Availability Group. Set the database to read-write mode, and retry the
operation.
```

Cause: The Database was in Standby Mode.

If we try to change the secondary node in log shipping to the "in recovery" mode, we would run into the following error (in the Errorlog during the restore):

```
<date> 06:22:11.020 Backup    Log was restored. Database:
MyAdventureWorks, creation date(time): 2013/02/07(17:12:29),
first LSN: 31:160:1, last LSN: 31:236:1, number of dump
devices: 1, device information: (FILE=1, TYPE=DISK:
```

```
{'C:\LS\MyAdventureWorks_20130210141112.trn'}). This is an
informational…
```

```
<date> 06:22:11.460 spid67      Error: 3456, Severity: 16,
State: 1.
```

```
<date> 06:22:11.460 spid67      Could not redo log record
(31:236:3), for transaction ID (0:752), on page (1:9),
allocation unit 6488064, database 'MyAdventureWorks'
(database ID 9). Page: LSN = (31:162:2), allocation unit =
6488064, type = 13. Log: OpCode = 4, context 20,
PrevPageLSN: (31:231:
```

Notice that page 1:9 (file 1, Page 9) is a special page of a database called the "database boot page" (refer to Books Online for more information). The only way to come out of this situation is by performing a complete backup and restore. So it's important to bring the Log Shipping secondary database to Recovery Mode rather than leaving it in Standby Mode.

Failure 2

There could be other reasons why the database is unable to join the Availability Group. Based on our testing, we found that sometimes the log chain may get broken if the steps are not followed properly. We can run the backup, copy, and restore jobs in sequence again, and try to join the database to the Availability Group. The following is the error message we could get:

```
Messages
Msg 1478, Level 16, State 211, Line 1
The mirror database, "MyAdventureWorks", has insufficient transaction log
data to preserve the log backup chain of the principal database. This may
happen if a log backup from the principal database has not been taken or has
not been restored on the mirror database.
```

Cause: There was a log backup that happened between the last backup which was restored and the Join only option in the wizard.

Solution: Run the backup, copy, and restore jobs in sequence and try again. If some manual backup happened in between then use the errorlog or backup history to locate the backup files and restore them manually to the secondary.

After a successful configuration of an AlwaysOn Availability Group, we can safely remove Log Shipping from the primary server. It would be important to configure a transaction log backup job because the removal of Log Shipping would also cause the removal of regular transaction log backups of the database.

This is one of the most common causes of uncontrolled transaction log growth. In Availability Groups backups can be configured at any replica (see Chapter 6).

Migrating from Database Mirroring

The basics of migration still remain same. Data can't flow from a higher version to a lower version of SQL Server. Here we can consider two scenarios:

1. Database Mirroring between instances of SQL Server 2008 R2 (or 2008 or 2005)
2. Database Mirroring between instances of SQL Server 2012

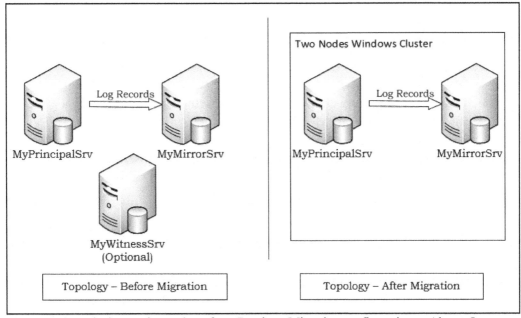

Figure 15.3 Typical upgrade topology from Database Mirroring configuration to AlwaysOn Availability Group.

In Figure 15.3, we have assumed that we are using a witness server. The witness server is an optional component for the Database Mirroring topology, only required for automatic failover.

Here are the steps to migrate in scenario 1.

1. Based on the migration strategy, we can either migrate the witness sever to SQL Server 2012 or remove it from the topology. If the plan is to perform a phased migration (taking days) then the witness is needed to give us automatic failover capability. If we plan to perform a complete migration of all the instances then we can remove the mirror server. We can perform

an in-place upgrade for the witness to migrate from SQL Server 2008 R2 to SQL Server 2012.

2. The next step would be to perform an in-place upgrade of the mirror (MyMirrorSrv) to SQL Server 2012. Before doing that, we need to remove the witness from the topology until the upgrade is complete. This is needed because the principal database would not be accessible if two out of three voters are down. We can add the witness server back to the topology once the mirror is upgraded.

3. The last upgrade step of the SQL version migration would be to migrate the principal server. To have less application downtime, we need to manually failover the principal to the current mirror server (which is now running SQL 2012). Once the failover is performed, the Database Mirroring session would go to a suspended state because data movement can't happen from MyMirrorSrv (the current principal on SQL 2012) to MyPrincipalSrv (the current mirror on SQL Server 2008 R2).

4. Once the migration is complete, add the witness again and failback the mirroring topology to MyPrincipalSrv.

Once the above steps are completed, we have all the SQL instances running on SQL Server 2012 and with Database Mirroring configured. This is the same starting point as scenario 2.

1. Enable the Windows Clustering feature and create a Windows Server Failover Cluster. Add two nodes (Principal and Mirror) to the Windows Cluster.

2. Enable the AlwaysOn Availability Group feature for each instance of SQL Server (this needs a restart of the SQL Service). It would be advisable to do it on the mirror first and then the principal.

3. The roles might have been changed due to a restart in the last step. Bring the principal role back to MyPrincipalSrv by doing a manual failover.

4. If there are transaction log backup jobs configured, disable them.

5. Remove the Database Mirroring.

6. Configure Availability Groups for the database(s). Create an Availability Group by adding Availability Databases. Since we already have databases restored on the secondary replicas we need to use the **Join only** option in the **Select Initial Data Synchronization** page of the **New Availability Group Wizard**. We are using the **Join only** option because the database on MyMirrorSrv is already available due to the previously configured Database Mirroring.

7. Once the wizard has completed, we can get the status of each replica on the Results page of the wizard.

8. Enable the transaction log backup jobs, which we disabled in one of the previous steps.

If most of the cases the Listener would also be configured. We need to remember to make changes to the application connection string to incorporate the Listener.

Migrating from Replication

Replication technology has been in the SQL Server product suite for the past 15+ years. Many customers have solved their business problems (like read scale out, write scale out, heterogeneous replication, change tracking and distributed systems) using various topologies of replication. SQL Server Replication is generally used for *selected* objects in a database, not *all* objects in database. Replication also provides filtering of data sent to a subscriber and different schemas at the subscriber. Since these are not possible in an Availability Group, it is quite likely that we may not perform a direct upgrade to an AlwaysOn Availability Group as we did earlier in this section with Log Shipping and Database Mirroring. If we want to achieve High Availability with Replication, we might want to have multiple copies of the publisher and may want to use Replication and Availability Groups together.

In rare situations, a few of us may want to use the new AlwaysOn feature and do away with Replication. There are no special steps needed if we want to remove Replication and configure an AlwaysOn Availability Group. To remove Replication we can refer to SQL Server documentation later. We can then use what we learned earlier in this book to configure the Availability Group for the databases. In this section we will discuss having replication and Availability Groups together.

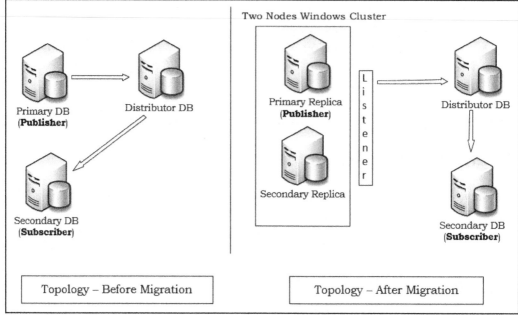

Figure 15.4 Replication topology before and after the migration.

Based on the supportability of replication and AlwaysOn Availability Groups together, here is the tabular format for easy reference.

Server Role in Replication	Publisher	Supported
	Subscriber	Supported
	Distributor	Not Supported
Type of Replication	Snapshot	Supported
	Transactional	Supported
	Merge	Supported
	Change Data Capture	Supported
	Change Tracking	Supported
	Peer-to-Peer, Bi-directional	Not Supported
	Queued/Immediate Updating subscriber	Not Supported

Table 15.1 Supportability matrix of AlwaysOn Availability Group and Replication.

Another limitation is that a republishing scenario (subscriber also acting as publisher) is not supported in Availability Groups. Since the secondary replica is readonly in nature, to configure Replication we must write some information to the publisher. We can't have a secondary replica as a publisher in the Availability Group. In case of a disaster, we need to perform a manual failover for a subscriber whereas the publisher failover can be automatic.

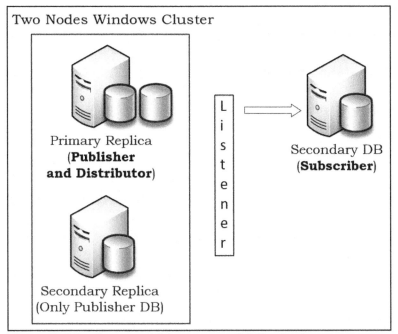

Figure 15.5 Configure a publisher as an availability database.

Here is the high level summary of steps to configure a publisher as an availability database.

1. Configure the remote distributor. It is not a requirement but a recommendation. We can configure the distributor on the same instance as the publisher but it won't provide High Availability if hosting instances go down.
2. Complete the prerequisites for an AlwaysOn Availability Group for all servers which might take the publisher role.
3. Create an Availability Group and add replicas.
4. Create a Listener.
5. As a last step, we need to provide details to Replication agents that the publisher instance may go down and it should connect to next publisher replica. Execute sp_redirect_publisher with the parameter @redirected_publisher as the Listener name in a distribution database.

Using the previous steps, we can provide High Availability to a publisher in Replication. There are no special steps needed for adding a subscribed database to the Availability Group. We must remember that automatic failover is not available when a subscriber is part of an Availability Group. The list of actions needed will depend on the type of Replication. Please refer to the Books Online topic "Replication Subscribers and AlwaysOn Availability Groups" for detailed information about recovering subscribers.

Migrating from Clustering

The SQL Server AlwaysOn Failover Cluster Instance has fewer new features as compared to the previous version of SQL Clustering.

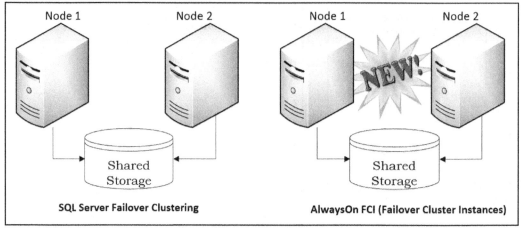

Figure 15.6 SQL Server FCI has fewer new features than the previous version of SQL Clustering.

There could be various paths to upgrade. If we think a little deeper, there would be three possibilities of migration.

In Place Upgrade

If we only want to upgrade SQL Server Clustering from the older version to SQL Server 2012 then we can perform an in-place upgrade. This is a risky option because we can't back-out of the old version easily. To have minimal downtime, we should first upgrade the passive nodes. Once that is complete, perform a failover to an upgraded node and upgrade the pending one. This can all be done by choosing "Upgrade from SQL Server 2005, SQL Server 2008, or SQL Server 2008 R2" from the SQL Server Installation Center (Figure 15.7). This technique is known as a rolling upgrade.

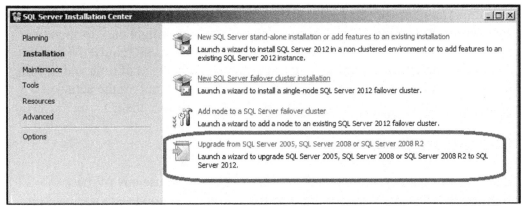

Figure 15.7 The "Upgrade from SQL Server 2005, SQL Server 2008, or SQL Server 2008 R2" option from the SQL Server Installation Center.

Side by Side Upgrade

The fundamentals of this approach are to install a SQL Server 2012 FCI on the same Windows Cluster which has another instance of an older version. We need additional shared disks for the new instance because we can't use the disks which are already in use. It can be considered risky to the live environment because an earlier version (SQL Server 2008) and the latest version (SQL Server 2012) would be on the same machine. Application connection strings need a modification.

Migrate to a new Server

This has the lowest risk but a higher cost due to the need for new hardware. We also have a choice to back off to an older version. This provides us the flexibility to perform load testing on the new machine or environment without affecting current production.

The basic difference of this approach as compared to the previous two approaches is pretty self-explanatory based on its name. In this approach, we need to purchase a new server, install a fresh operating system, and install SQL Server 2012 and some other applications. Once everything is installed we need to move the database from the old server to the new server. User databases can be moved with detach/attach or backup/restore methods. Since system databases can't be moved across instances of SQL, we need to put forth efforts to generate a script to duplicate the objects in the system databases (i.e. jobs, alerts, operators, logins, permissions and server level settings).

One important note of this approach would be that the backup and restore process can be time consuming. If it is a huge database then we might end up spending most of the time doing a full backup and restoration. We can reduce the amount of downtime due to the migration by doing a full backup ahead of time and keeping it restored on new server (in the NoRecovery state). Just before the actual migration, we can take transaction log backups and restore them.

Migration Overview

Based on our budget, testing, and comfort level, we can use any of these approaches. Be sure to prepare for a rollback to the last good state and backup everything possible.

Summary

Migrating and upgrading from older versions are inevitable because we want to capitalize on the fantastic new features. The flow path of migration would change based on answers to the following key questions:

- Are we going to migrate only SQL Server, or do we want to migrate the operating system as well at the same time?
- Are we going to reuse the hardware or do we want to move to new hardware?
- How much downtime can we have to perform the migration?
- Do we want to migrate in phases or all at once? If we are using SQL 2012 and using Log Shipping + Database Mirroring we can keep Log Shipping for now and migrate it later?

Use these as guidelines and not something written in stone. For the environment and deployment scenarios there will be a few more questions that need to get answered before a potential migration can happen.

Points to Ponder – Migrating from Previous High Availability Scenarios

1. Before converting Log Shipping to AlwaysOn Availability Group, make sure that the databases are in the NoRecovery mode (restoring state), not the Standby mode (readonly state).

2. Backups taken from lower versions of SQL Server can be restored to higher version of SQL Server. It can't be done while in Standby Mode.

3. If the secondary database is already initialized (Log Shipping or mirroring) then we can use the Join only option in the Availability Group wizard.

4. To migrate an existing Log Shipping environment, below are the important considerations.

    *   Log Shipping works for databases in the bulk-logged recovery model but the AlwaysOn Availability Group requires the full recovery model.
    *   Log Shipping can work if a database name is different on the primary and secondary but the AlwaysOn Availability Group requires the replica database to have the same name.
    *   Log Shipping works in workgroup environments but the AlwaysOn Availability Group does not. It needs a domain.

5. Database Mirroring works from a lower version of SQL Server to a higher version of SQL Server.

6. In Database Mirroring, once we failover to a higher version of SQL Server, data synchronization would go to a suspended state.

7. The distribution database can't be part of an AlwaysOn Availability Group.

8. All replication types are supported except Peer-to-Peer, Bi-directional, Queued/Immediate, and Updating subscriber.

9. Being "Ready to rollback" is one of the important pieces in planning to upgrade.

10. There are three possible ways to upgrade Failover Clustering.

    *   In Place.
    *   Side by Side.
    *   Migration to new server.

Review Quiz - Chapter Fifteen

1.) Which of the Replication roles is not supported in an Availability Group?

- O a. Publisher
- O b. Distributor
- O c. Subscriber
- O d. Both a and c

2.) Which of the Replication types is not supported for availability database?

- O a. Snapshot.
- O b. Merge.
- O c. Transactional – one way.
- O d. Transactional - Peer to Peer.

3.) Which of the below items need to change if we want to migrate from Log Shipping to AlwaysOn Availability Group?

- □ a. Bulk-logged Recovery Model.
- □ b. Database name mismatch in primary and secondary.
- □ c. Standby Mode of secondary database.
- □ d. Workgroup to Domain
- □ e. All of the above.

4.) Which one is the correct order of in-place migration from Database Mirroring to AlwaysOn Availability Group with lowest risk?

- O a. Break mirroring, create cluster, and create Availability Group.
- O b. Create cluster, break mirroring and create Availability Group.
- O c. Create Availability Group, create cluster, and break mirroring.

5.) What is the advantage of an in-place upgrade from SQL Server 2008 to SQL Server 2012?

- □ a. No need to script logins and password.
- □ b. Easy rollback in case something goes wrong.
- □ c. No need to script information from MSDB database.
- □ d. Cost effective solution.

Answer Key

1.) Options (a) Publisher, (c) Subscriber, and (d) Both (a) and (c) are incorrect. Since (b) Distributor is not one of them, this is the correct answer.

2.) The correct answer is /9c) Transactional .

3.) As we migrate from Log Shipping to AlwaysOn Availability Group we need to do (a) Bulk-logged Recovery Model, /9b) Database name mismatch in primary and secondary, /9c) Standby Mode of secondary database and /9d) Workgroup to Domain, therefore the option /9e) All of the above, is the correct option.

4.) The correct order is /9b) Create cluster, break mirroring and create Availability Group.

5.) The advantage of doing an in-place upgrade from SQL Server 2008 to SQL Server 2012 are /9a) No need to script logins and password, (c) No need to script information from MSDB database and (d) Cost effective solution. Option (b) Easy rollback in case something goes wrong is incorrect and the rollback can be a problem. We highly recommend taking a backup before performing an in-place upgrade.

[NOTES]

Chapter 16. AlwaysOn Availability Group Maintenance Activities

Ask a homemaker how difficult it is to run a family and keep the home clean with kids running all over the place. Every day there has to be time taken to make sure the home gets back to a normal state before the next day's routine gets underway. In the same way, the chapters so far have shown the various installation, deployment, and troubleshooting of an AlwaysOn Availability Group in detail. This chapter takes an unconventional yet important part of the AlwaysOn Availability Group where we look at various options to exclude databases, exclude secondary replicas, remove primary replicas, remove Availability Groups, suspend Availability Groups, and many more.

Suspending an Availability Database

DBAs have an option to suspend data movement for one or more databases that are a part of an Availability Group. One of the most common reasons to suspend a secondary database is to increase performance of the primary replica database. This is because it no longer has to sync that database with the secondary replicas. The drawback is having fewer secondary replicas means less redundancy and less availability. It is critical to understand that the availability and redundancy agreement with our company (the SLA) can be broken if we have suspended the secondary. A typical T-SQL statement to do this is seen in the following code example:

```
ALTER DATABASE MyAdventureWorks SET HADR SUSPEND;
```

Notice this did not specify which server should suspend the database. If we run the code on SRV1 then it will suspend the database on SRV1. To suspend a database, the command needs to be run from the context of the respective machine. If we suspend the database from the primary then the database goes into a NOT SYNCHRONIZING state for the entire group. Suspending a database on the secondary replica would not affect the entire group. It would send the database into a NOT SYNCHRONIZING state just for that one replica.

Why does a suspended database cause the entire database to stop all synchronization traffic for the whole group? If we suspend the database from the primary replica then all of the log movement to the secondary is stopped. The database is still available on the primary replica. We can suspend the database using the SSMS UI from the Availability Database folder.

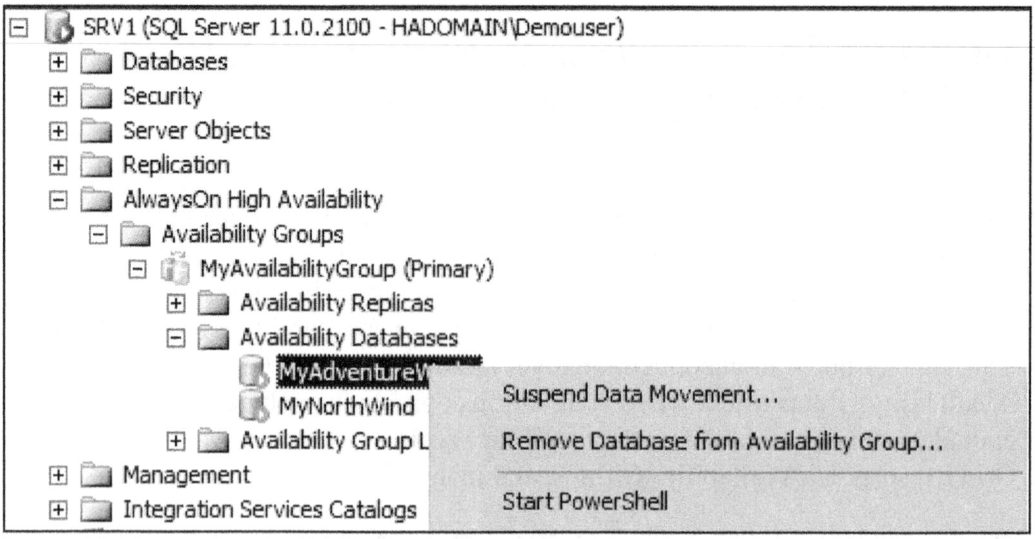

Figure 16.1 Suspend an Availability database.

We can also use PowerShell to achieve the same thing. The PowerShell cmdlet to suspend data movement is Suspend-SqlAvailabilityDatabase.

The following code is an example of how to use this PowerShell cmdlet to suspend the MyAdventureWorks database:

PS SQLSERVER:\> Suspend-SqlAvailabilityDatabase -Path
SQLSERVER:\SQL**SRV1****DEFAULT**\AvailabilityGroups**MyAvailabilityGro
up**\AvailabilityDatabases**MyAdventureWorks**

A small trivia tidbit to note here is that when any of the databases on the secondary replicas get suspended, the transaction log on the primary does not get truncated even after a log backup. This behavior can easily fill up the space and is something we need to be aware off. Suspending the databases is not the same as removing the database from the group. It is comparable to a pause and then play button we are used to in music players.

Resuming an Availability Database

If we suspend an Availability Group database (either explicitly on a secondary or on the primary) the data movement can be brought back using the RESUME command. The following is the T-SQL command to resume a suspended database:

```
ALTER DATABASE MyAdventureWorks SET HADR RESUME;
```

Just like the suspend command, the resume command needs to be executed locally on the server. The resume operation can also be executed using the SSMS UI from the "Availability Databases" folder.

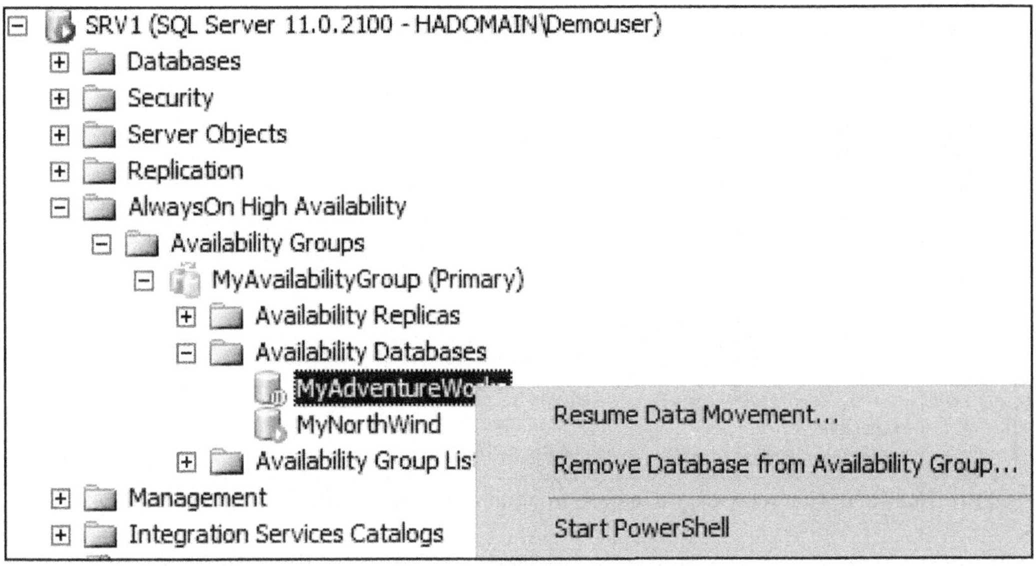

Figure 16.2 Resume data movement for an Availability Database.

If a database has been suspended, the SSMS icon will display a pause symbol as in Figure 16.2.

We can also use PowerShell commands to resume the data movement. The PowerShell cmdlet to resume the data movement is Resume-SqlAvailabilityDatabase.

```
PS SQLSERVER:\> Resume-SqlAvailabilityDatabase -Path
SQLSERVER:\SQL\SRV1\DEFAULT\AvailabilityGroups\MyAvailabilit
yGroup\AvailabilityDatabases\MyAdventureWorks
```

Removing a Secondary Database from an Availability Group

Making complete use of the hardware available in the data center is one of the important tasks that a DBA has on their mind. As part of this planning process, DBAs might want to remove a database from a secondary replica in the Availability Group. This can be achieved with the following command run on the secondary to be removed.

```
ALTER DATABASE MyAdventureWorks SET HADR OFF;
```

This step does not delete or remove the existing database on the secondary but it logically removes this database from the synchronization from the primary. The same task can be achieved using SSMS as shown in Figure 16.3.

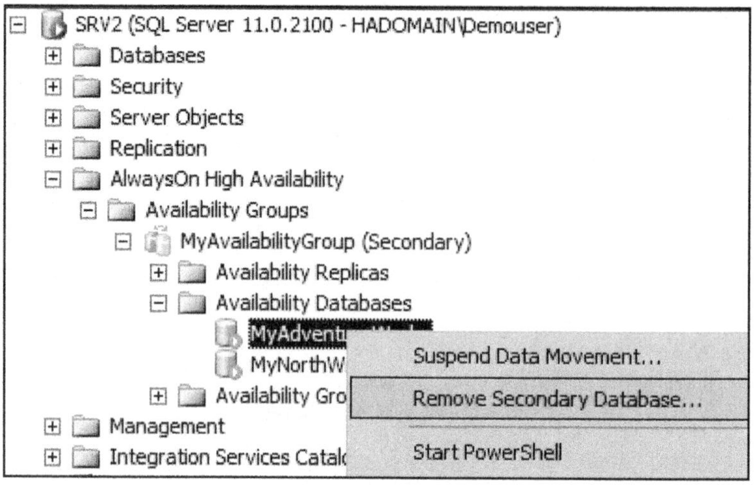

Figure 16.3 Remove a secondary database from an Availability Group using SSMS.

The same action can also be performed by the PowerShell cmdlet Remove-SqlAvailabilityDatabase as shown in the following code sample:

```
PS SQLSERVER:\> Remove-SqlAvailabilityDatabase -Path
SQLSERVER:\SQL\SRV2\DEFAULT\AvailabilityGroups\MyAvailabilit
yGroup\AvailabilityDatabases\MyAdventureWorks
```

Removing a Database from an Availability Group

Just like we removed a database from the Availability Group of the secondary replica, we can also remove the database from the Availability Group on the primary replica. This step is similar to our previous activity but it has a small difference. When a database is removed from the Availability Group on the primary it also removes it from the Availability Group on all the secondary replicas.

```
ALTER AVAILABILITY GROUP MyAvailabilityGroup REMOVE DATABASE
MyAdventureWorks;
```

This task can be achieved using the SSMS UI as shown on the primary replica.

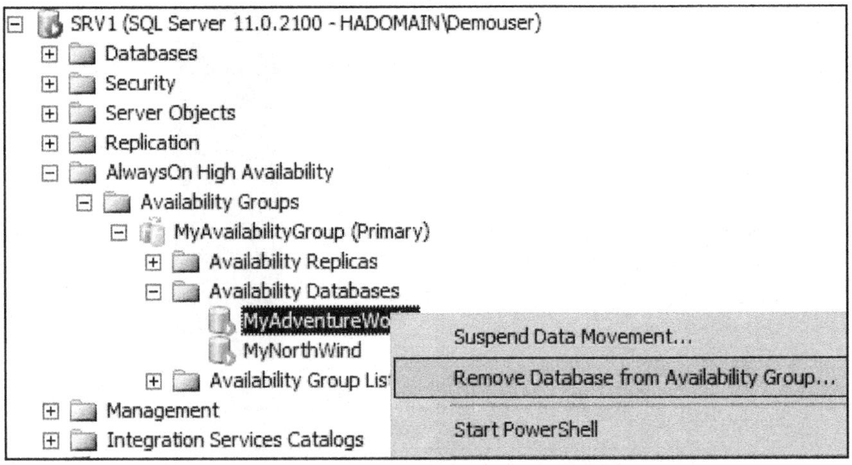

Figure 16.4 Remove a primary database from an Availability Group.

The PowerShell cmdlet to perform the same change is Remove-SqlAvailabilityDatabase. If we compare it with the last section of removing a database from the secondary replica, the cmdlet is exactly the same.

```
PS SQLSERVER:\> Remove-SqlAvailabilityDatabase -Path
SQLSERVER:\SQL\SRV1\DEFAULT\AvailabilityGroups\MyAvailabilit
yGroup\AvailabilityDatabases\MyAdventureWorks
```

Once a database is removed from an Availability Group on the primary, it will be in a restoring state on all the secondary replicas. If needed, the database on the secondary replica can be dropped or brought online.

Removing a Secondary Replica from an Availability Group

We know the limitation of the number of replicas an Availability Group can have (five including the primary). From time-to-time organizations get some new hardware and we have a requirement to remove an older active secondary replica. This can be achieved using the following command:

```
ALTER AVAILABILITY GROUP MyAvailabilityGroup REMOVE REPLICA
ON 'SRV3';
```

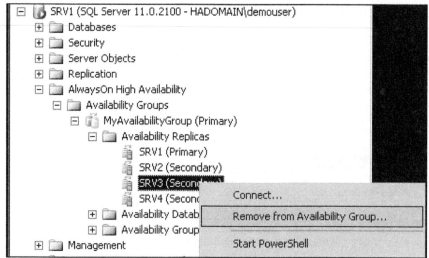

Figure 16.5 Removing a secondary replica from an Availability Group.

Removal of a secondary replica can only be performed from the primary replica. In Management Studio, a right-click on the Availability Replicas folder from a secondary would not provide such option on a secondary replica. Also, running the equivalent T-SQL command would fail with the following error:

```
Messages
Msg 41190, Level 16, State 10, Line 1
Availability Group 'MyAvailabilityGroup' failed to process remove-replica
command. The local availability replica is not in a state that could process
the command. Verify that the Availability Group is online and that the local
availability replica is the primary replica, then retry the command.
```

If we want to use PowerShell to remove SRV3 from the group, it too needs to initiate the action on the primary (SVR1). The following is the PowerShell equivalent of the command to remove SRV3 from the Availability Group:

`PS SQLSERVER:\>` Remove-SqlAvailabilityReplica -Path SQLSERVER:\SQL**SRV1****DEFAULT**\AvailabilityGroups**MyAvailabilityGroup**\AvailabilityReplicas**SRV3**

If we want to drop the database which is part of the Availability Group then we need to first follow the steps in our earlier section about how to drop the Availability Group. After that, we can drop the database. Removing the Availability Group doesn't drop the database from any replica. If we attempt to drop any database which is part of an Availability Group, we would get the following error message:

Messages
Msg 3752, Level 16, State 1, Line 1 The database 'MyAdventureWorks' is currently joined to an Availability Group. Before you can drop the database, you need to remove it from the Availability Group.

Dropping the Listener

As we know, at any point in time there can be only one Listener defined for an Availability Group. There are times when we would like to drop the Listener defined. This can only be done from the primary replica. The following T-SQL will drop the Listener (MyListener) from the Availability Group (MyAvailabilityGroup):

```
ALTER AVAILABILITY GROUP MyAvailabilityGroup REMOVE LISTENER
'MyListener';
```

The Listener can be dropped from the Object Explorer while connected to the primary replica. Find the name of the listener and right-click it and there will be an option to delete. Figure 16.6 shows we are on SRV1 and the Listener called MyListener has the delete option for the context menu.

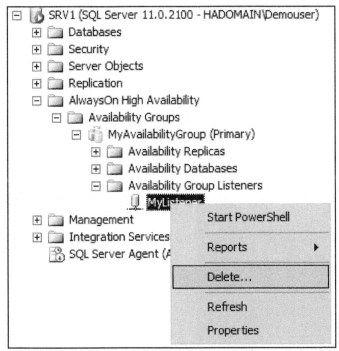

Figure 16.6 Dropping an Availability Group Listener using SSMS.

Dropping the Listener will cause all applications using our Availability Group (via the Listener) to stop working. This step needs to be done in consultation with the application owners using these databases. If we drop the Listener we are either getting ready to create a new one or are planning on having the applications connect to a server by its name. In either case it is quite possible that the application connection strings needs to be changed and therefore needs to be done with care. The removal of the Listener can be done only from the primary replica.

Taking an Availability Group Offline

The next command we will demonstrate can only be run on systems running SQL Server 2012 SP1 and above. Do not try this on a production environment without knowing the implications of taking an Availability Group offline. Once the Availability Group is taken offline this operation cannot be reversed. This operation also makes all the databases inaccessible and is suggested only for a cross-cluster migration of the Availability Group resources. The following T-SQL command will take the Availability Group (MyAvailabilityGroup) offline:

```
ALTER AVAILABILITY GROUP MyAvailabilityGroup OFFLINE;
```

Dropping an Availability Group

If we need to remove an Availability Group we can run the following command from the primary replica:

```
DROP AVAILABILITY GROUP MyAvailabilityGroup;
```

The previous T-SQL command will make sure the Availability Group is removed from all the replicas. The same thing can be done with the UI in the Object Explorer. While on the primary replica simply right-click the Availability Group and choose **Delete**.

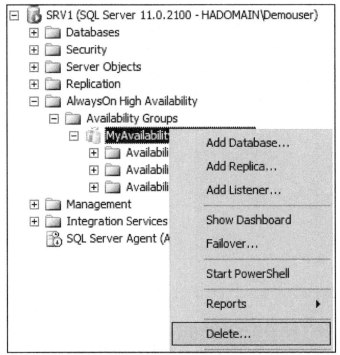

Figure 16.7 Drop an Availability Group using SSMS.

Upon choosing to delete the group in the UI we get a confirmation window. From here we can either click **OK**, **Cancel**, or choose to generate a script by click the **Script** button at the top of the window.

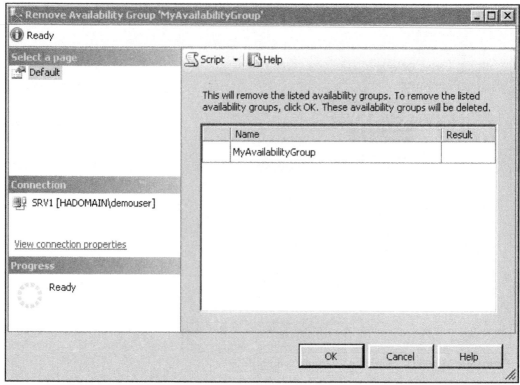

Figure 16.8 Drop an Availability Group using SSMS.

The PowerShell command to remove an Availability Group is seen in the following code sample:

```
PS SQLSERVER:\> Remove-SqlAvailabilityGroup -Path
SQLSERVER:\SQL\SRV1\DEFAULT\AvailabilityGroups\MyAvailabilit
yGroup
```

This command must be run on the primary replica. Avoid running this command from any of the secondary replicas because this can send the database on the primary replica into a RESTORING state. The reason is, the primary never knows the reason why the secondary went into an OFFLINE state.

Summary

In a SQL Server AlwaysOn Availability Group deployment, the need to add nodes or remove nodes is a common occurrence because a hardware refresh or a hardware procurement happens over a period of time. Administrators need to know how to remove nodes, add nodes (to scale reporting needs), and plan for

Disaster Recovery. This chapter covered how to do clean up or how to run commands to extend the existing infrastructures.

Points to Ponder – AlwaysOn Availability Group Maintenance Activities

1. All the maintenance related to an AlwaysOn Availability Group can be done using SSMS UI, T-SQL, or PowerShell.

2. When data movement is suspended, the transaction log on the primary does not get truncated even after a log backup.

3. Taking an Availability Group offline can be done by T-SQL after SQL 2012 Service Pack 1. This command can't be reversed.

4. The removal of a secondary replica can only be performed from the primary replica.

5. To make any Availability Group related change (such as dropping the Listener) it is always preferred to do this within SQL Server rather than doing it from the Failover Cluster Manager.

6. To drop an availability database, we need to take it out of the Availability Group.

Review Quiz - Chapter Sixteen

1.) What is the T-SQL command to pause data movement?

   O a.   ALTER DATABASE <DatabaseName> SET HADR PAUSE;
   O b.   ALTER DATABASE <DatabaseName> SET HADR SUSPEND;
   O c.   ALTER DATABASE <DatabaseName> SET MOVEMENT PAUSE;
   O d.   ALTER DATABASE <DatabaseName> SET MOVEMENT SUSPEND;

2.) What is the PowerShell cmdlet to resume data movement?

   O a.   Resume-SqlAvailabilityDatabase
   O b.   Resume-SqlAvailabilityDB
   O c.   Resume-SqlHADRDatabase
   O d.   Resume-SqlHADRDB

3.) What is the T-SQL command to remove replica SRV2 from Availability
     Group MyAvailabilityGroup?

   O a.   ALTER AVAILABILITY GROUP MyAvailabilityGroup REMOVE
          REPLICA AT 'SRV4';
   O b.   ALTER AVAILABILITY GROUP MyAvailabilityGroup REMOVE
          REPLICA ON 'SRV4';
   O c.   ALTER AVAILABILITY GROUP MyAvailabilityGroup AT 'SRV4'
          REMOVE REPLICA;
   O d.   ALTER AVAILABILITY GROUP MyAvailabilityGroup ON SRV4'
          REMOVE REPLICA;

4.) What is the PowerShell cmdlet to delete an Availability Group?

   O a.   Remove-SqlAvailabilityDatabase
   O b.   Delete-SqlAvailabilityDatabase
   O c.   Remove-SqlAvailabilityGroup
   O d.   Delete-SqlAvailabilityGroup

Answer Key

1.) The command to pause data movement is (b) ALTER DATABASE <DatabaseName> SET HADR SUSPEND; therefore options (a), (c) and (d) are incorrect.

2.) The PowerShell cmdlet to resume data movement is (a) Resume-SqlAvailabilityDatabase. Options (b) Resume-SqlAvailabilityDB, (c) Resume-SqlHADRDatabase and (d) Resume-SqlHADRDB are incorrect.

3.) The command to remove replica SRV2 from Availability Group is (b) ALTER AVAILABILITY GROUP MyAvailabilityGroup REMOVE REPLICA ON 'SRV4'; so options (a), (c) and (d) are wrong.

4.) The options (b) Delete-SqlAvailabilityDatabase, (c) Remove-SqlAvailabilityGroup, and (d) Delete-SqlAvailabilityGroup are all incorrect. The PowerShell cmdlet to delete an Availability Group is (a) Remove-SqlAvailabilityDatabase.

[NOTES]

Chapter 17. AlwaysOn - FAQs

Have you ever tried to spend time with a child? There are a number of things we can learn from a child. One of the important traits is the need to keep questioning everything they see. At times it can get annoying but the need to find answers is something we have had in our DNA for ages. If we analyze the questions properly then it can be quite a learning experience for us too. We are so into learning the internals and trying to learn advanced topics that we forget to understand the basics. It is answering these basics that help us in discovering the advanced topics.

In this chapter we have a collection of questions which we commonly see over various forums, user group meetings, sessions, and customer visits. This is an attempt to keep the repeated questions in a single place so that we can easily refer to this list to get answers.

Common FAQs

1. Do I need to replicate my login to all replicas?

Answer: Yes, we need to. The AlwaysOn Availability Group provides user database level protection and logins are part of the master database. So, a database administrator has to move or replicate the logins across to other replicas. On a side note, the contained database feature can be used where the login would be stored within the database and this has no dependency on the master database for logins. To find out more on sp_help_revlogin and contained databases see these web addresses:

- http://support.microsoft.com/kb/918992
- http://technet.microsoft.com/en-us/library/ff929071.aspx

2. What are the minimum permissions I need to play around with Availability Groups?

Answer: We can divide the permissions based on the actions taken. The following is the list for quick reference:

- *Creating an Availability Group:* We require the CREATE AVAILABILITY GROUP permission and the ALTER ANY AVAILABILITY GROUP permission. The CONTROL SERVER permission by itself can do this.

- *Altering or Dropping an Availability Group:* We require the ALTER AVAILABILITY GROUP permission on the Availability Group, the

CONTROL AVAILABILITY GROUP permission, and the ALTER ANY AVAILABILITY GROUP. The CONTROL SERVER permission by itself can do this.

- *Joining a database to an Availability Group:* We need to be part of the db_owner fixed database role.

3. **I have followed all the permission advice but still am having problems connecting to the database on the secondary replica. I performed the following steps on the primary:**

   1. Created SQL Login **Morpheus** with some password.
   2. Added User **Morpheus** in my availability database called **MyAdventureWorks** and mapped it to the **Morpheus** login.

Now when I am adding the SQL login on the secondary server and while mapping to the user in the database, I am getting the following error:

```
Messages
Msg 15023, Level 16, State 1, Line 1
User, group, or role 'Morpheus' already exists in the current database.
```

What is wrong with my steps?

Answer: When a user is created under the availability database, it would transfer this user to all the secondary replicas. We would be able to see the **Morpheus** user in SSMS under **databases** > **MyAdventureWorks** > **Security** > **Users**. Now, even if we create a SQL login called **Morpheus** on the secondary replica, it would not be mapped to the user due to a SID mismatch. The following is the query output to explain this:

```
USE Master;
GO
SELECT * FROM sys.syslogins WHERE name = 'Morpheus';
GO
--0x0B25347008DB754CB56D476A878F6D51

USE MyAdventureWorks;
GO
SELECT * FROM sys.sysusers WHERE name = 'Morpheus';
--0xD200F8A90B1B03428A7F071CC89A1533
```

To overcome this situation, we need to take a little care while creating the login on the secondary replica. Since we know the SID of the user in our availability database, we can create the login with the same SID using the following command:

```
CREATE LOGIN [Morpheus] WITH PASSWORD=N'VeryStrongPwd123',
SID = 0xD200F8A90B1B03428A7F071CC89A1533,
```

With this command, the SID value is the same as the output from the second query (sys.sysusers). We can also follow the following KB which shows how to transfer logins and passwords between instances of SQL Server: http://support.microsoft.com/kb/918992

4.   Database Mirroring is marked as a deprecated feature in SQL Server 2012. What does that mean?

Answer: Any feature which is marked as deprecated would be available for at least one (or at most two) future release of the product. There would be no enhancement made to the feature by the product development team. In this scenario, we highly recommend to start by exploring SQL Server 2012 AlwaysOn Availability Group capability before upgrading blindly from an older version of SQL Server that was implemented using Database Mirroring.

5.   My application doesn't support the compatibility level of 110. Is it possible to use the AlwaysOn Availability Group feature in a lower compatibility level?

Answer: Yes, we can place any database within an AlwaysOn Availability Group. It can be in any compatibility mode supported by SQL Server 2012.

6.   I have an application which uses two databases for its complete functionality. I would like to create an Availability Group for these two databases but they have different compatibility levels (one is 100 and another is 110). Is there any limitation of compatibility mode?

Answer: No, there is no such limitation. Technically, compatibility modes affect the way the optimizer works and doesn't affect the transaction logging to the transaction logfile of the database. It is safe to configure the Availability Group for any compatibility level available in SQL Server 2012.

7.   Do we have any writeable secondary replicas?

Answer: In this current release of SQL Server 2012, it is not possible to have a writable secondary replica.

8.   Can I deploy an AlwaysOn Availability Group on Windows Server 2003?

Answer: The minimum operating system requirement for installing SQL Server 2012 is Windows Server 2008, so, an AlwaysOn Availability Group needs to have a minimum of Windows Server 2008 SP2 or Windows Server 2008 R2 SP1 or Windows Server 2012.

9.   How can I connect my older SQL Server 2008 clients to the Availability Group Listener?

Answer: To use all features of the AlwaysOn technology, we need .Net 4.02 or SQL Native Client 11.0. If we want to use .Net 3.5 then we need to apply the patch available at KB 2654347.

10.   I am doing testing and need a minimal number of machines to create and test Availability Groups. How many machines will I need?

Answer: Since we need a cluster, we need a minimum of two machines. If we need a new domain controller then it would be on a third machine. If we try to enable the AlwaysOn Availability Group feature in the configuration manager on the machine which is the domain controller, we would see the following error:

READER NOTE: The AlwaysOn Availability Group feature requires the x86(non-WOW) or x64 Enterprise Edition of SQL Server 2012 (or later version) running on Windows Server 2008 (or later version) with WSFC hotfix KB 2494036 installed. This SQL Server edition and/or Windows Server System does not meet one or more of the requirements.
For more information about prerequisites, restrictions and recommendations for AlwaysOn Availability Groups, see SQL Books Online.

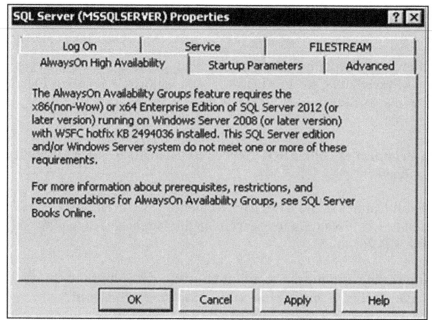

Figure 17.1 Error message when we go to AlwaysOn High Availability tab in SSCM on a SQL Server running on domain controller. Error message is not very intuitive.

Alternatively, the number of machines still remains as 3 even in a virtual environment.

11. Can I create a demo environment for learning on a single machine just like what I did for SQL Server to have Database Mirroring?

Answer: AlwaysOn Availability Group cannot be deployed between multiple instances of SQL Server running on a single machine since we need two nodes to do a failover in Windows Cluster. An alternate way to achieve this is to create virtual machines and configure the Availability Group between those virtual machines. If we try to configure the AlwaysOn Availability Group from SSMS using the Availability Group wizard and choose two replicas on same machine then we will get the following error during connection phase:

READER NOTE: *SQL Server instance SRV1\ALWAYSON is installed on the same computer as server instance SRV1, which is already selected for this Availability Group. Each Windows Server Failover Clustering (WSFC) node can host only one availability replica per Availability Group. Specify a server instance on a different WSFC node.*
(Microsoft.SqlServer.Management.HadrTasks)

This error is raised by SSMS. If same configuration is tried using T-SQL, we would also get errors. The following shows the create availability attempt for SRV1 and the SRV1\AlwaysOn instances and the error:

```
/*------------------------
CREATE AVAILABILITY GROUP [MyAvailabilityGroup1]

WITH (AUTOMATED_BACKUP_PREFERENCE = SECONDARY)

FOR DATABASE [OneNode]

REPLICA ON N'SRV1' WITH (ENDPOINT_URL =
N'TCP://SRV1.hadomain.com:5022', FAILOVER_MODE = AUTOMATIC,
AVAILABILITY_MODE = SYNCHRONOUS_COMMIT, BACKUP_PRIORITY =
50, SECONDARY_ROLE(ALLOW_CONNECTIONS = NO)),

N'SRV1\AlwaysOn' WITH (ENDPOINT_URL =
N'TCP://SRV1.hadomain.com:5023', FAILOVER_MODE = AUTOMATIC,
AVAILABILITY_MODE = SYNCHRONOUS_COMMIT, BACKUP_PRIORITY =
50, SECONDARY_ROLE(ALLOW_CONNECTIONS = NO));

GO

------------------------*/
```

Messages
Msg 35235, Level 15, State 1, Line 5 The system name 'SRV1' was specified more than once in the REPLICA ON clause of this command. Reenter the command, specifying a different instance of SQL Server for each replica.

If we created an Availability Group on one replica and added another instance from same machine, we would get the following error:

```
ALTER AVAILABILITY GROUP [MyAvailabilityGroup1]

ADD REPLICA ON N'SRV1\AlwaysOn' WITH (ENDPOINT_URL =
N'TCP://SRV1.hadomain.com:5022', FAILOVER_MODE = AUTOMATIC,
AVAILABILITY_MODE = SYNCHRONOUS_COMMIT, BACKUP_PRIORITY =
50, SECONDARY_ROLE(ALLOW_CONNECTIONS = NO));

----------------------*/
```

```
Messages
Msg 19405, Level 16, State 17, Line 2
Failed to create, join or add replica to Availability Group
'MyAvailabilityGroup1', because node 'SRV1' is a possible owner for both
replica 'SRV1' and 'SRV1\AlwaysOn'. If one replica is Failover Cluster
instance, remove the overlapped node from its possible owners and try again.
```

12. To extend the previous situation, we need to do testing of the failover of the availability replica between the standalone instance and the Failover Cluster Instance (FCI). Do I need more machines?

Answer: Yes. We need one machine for the domain controller, two for the Failover Cluster Instance (FCI) and one more for the standalone instance of SQL Server. If we attempt to create an Availability Group between a clustered instance and a standalone instance (which is running on one of the nodes of the cluster), we will be presented with the following error message:

```
Messages
Msg 19405, Level 16, State 1
Failed to create, join or add replica to Availability Group
'MyAvailabilityGroup', because node 'SRV2' is a possible owner for both
replica 'SRV2\INSTANCE1' and 'SRV2\INSTANCE2'. If one replica is Failover
Cluster instance, remove the overlapped node from its possible owners and try
again.
```

13. Can I implement Failover Cluster Instances (FCI) and Availability Groups (AG) using the same SQL Server nodes?

Answer: No, this is not possible. Please refer to the previous explanation for a possible configuration.

14. Can AlwaysOn Availability Groups give me read and write scale out?

Answer: Availability Groups don't provide write scale out because there is only one write replica (the primary replica). Read scale out is possible due to multiple secondary (read) replicas.

15. Is there any way to specify a few databases to be in Readonly mode on a secondary replica within an Availability Group?

Answer: No. The setting is defined on the Availability Group at the replica level. There is no way to specify only database X of Availability Group Y are readable on this secondary.

16. Can one of the databases in an AG be a readonly database and be set by using the database level property?

Answer: No, we cannot have readonly databases using this database property. Doing so will yield the following error message:

```
USE [master]
GO
ALTER DATABASE [MyNorthwind] SET READ_ONLY WITH NO_WAIT
GO
```

Messages
Msg 1468, Level 16, State 1, Line 1 The operation cannot be performed on database "MyNorthwind" because it is involved in a Database Mirroring session or an Availability Group. Some operations are not allowed on a database that is participating in a Database Mirroring session or in an Availability Group.

Messages
Msg 5069, Level 16, State 1, Line 1 ALTER DATABASE statement failed.

17. **Are there objects that are not part of an Availability Group that as a DBA I need to be aware of when designing applications with the Availability Group?**

Answer: Yes, the Availability Group cannot guarantee all the SQL Server objects that an application might require. Some of these objects include SQL Server Agent Jobs, Linked Servers, SQL Server Integration Services Packages, and CLR stored procedures. Additional synchronization of these objects must be performed on all the nodes if the application requires them in the event of failover.

Availability Group Related FAQs

18. **Is there any limitation on the number of databases per Availability Group?**

Answer: SQL Server does not have a hard limit on the number of databases per Availability Group. As per Books Online, the recommendation is up to 100 databases and that's a soft recommendation limit.

19. **I am taking a backup of the availability databases to a network location. I have noticed that after the role change my backups are not available in the share. What could be the possible cause?**

Answer: One of the possible causes of this behavior is that the maintenance plan was not created on the secondary replica. This is with the assumption that the Availability Group would create it on all secondary replicas. It is important to note that maintenance plans, jobs, logins, and other system database objects must be created on all the replicas for smooth functionality after failover.

20. **Can I have one database in two Availability Groups? Or can I have two Availability Groups with same name?**

Answer: One database can't be part of two Availability Groups. Any attempt would fail with error 35244.

Messages
Msg 35244, Level 16, State 1, Line 1 Database 'MyAdventureWorks' cannot be added to Availability Group 'MyNewAvailabilityGroup'. The database is currently joined to another Availability Group. Verify that the database name is correct and that the database is not joined to an Availability Group, then retry the operation.

We also can't have two Availability Groups with the same name. If we try to create a duplicate Availability Group name then we get error 41171.

Messages
Msg 41171, Level 16, State 2, Line 2 Failed to create Availability Group 'MyAvailabilityGroup', because a Windows Server Failover Cluster (WSFC) group with the specified name already exists. The operation has been rolled back successfully. To retry creating an Availability Group, either remove or rename the existing WSFC group, or retry the operation specifying a different Availability Group name.

21. **In Management Studio, we are unable to see the AlwaysOn Availability Group replica status as shown in Figure 17.2. Is this normal?**

Answer: Yes, the right place to get all the information about the Availability Group is the primary replica. The secondary replica talks to only the primary replica whereas the primary replica can talk to all secondary replicas. On any secondary, we can get its primary replica name but we cannot get complete information about other secondary replicas.

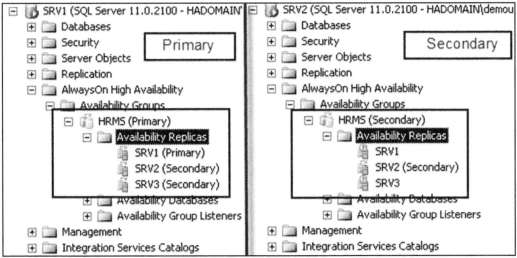

Figure 17.2 Availability Replica status not shown for others on secondary replica.

22. What is the patching strategy in an AlwaysOn Availability Group topology?

Answer: The way we need to do patching for Availability Groups is similar to how we would deal with patches in Database Mirroring. That means patching the secondary replicas first. The key point in patching is that the version, patch level, or service pack level of the server which is hosting the secondary replica must be on or above the server hosting primary replica.

In the steps mentioned, we have asked DBAs to change the mode to synchronous. This is to make sure that we don't have any data loss during failover. The following is an overview of the steps:

1. Apply a patch to all servers holding the secondary replicas. Even after the patch, the data movement would continue.

2. When we are ready to patch the server holding the primary replica, make sure that there is at least one synchronous secondary. If all secondary replicas are asynchronous, change at least one to synchronous.

3. Perform a failover using Management Studio to a synchronous secondary (made in step b). Make sure the failover wizard says no-data loss.

4. Now, we need to patch the previous old primary server. Note that at this point data movement to this secondary would be suspended because it is on a lower version than the primary replica.

5. Once patching is complete, we can failback to the previous primary after making sure that the previous primary (now the current secondary) is in a synchronized state.

6. If we have made any change to the topology (step b) then revert back those changes.

After patching the secondary replicas we need to failover the Availability Group to one of the patched instances. Once all of the instances in the Availability Group have been patched, fail the Availability Group back to the original primary replica.

23. Is it possible to change the availability mode of a replica from asynchronous to synchronous and vice versa?

Answer: Yes, it is possible. This is one of the steps explained in the previous question. The following are the various ways to do this:

- **SSMS**: Go to the Properties page of given Availability Group under AlwaysOn High Availability > Availability Groups.
- **T-SQL**: We can use the ALTER AVAILABILITY GROUP command as seen in the following T-SQL code example:

```
USE [master]
GO
ALTER AVAILABILITY GROUP MyAvailabilityGroup
MODIFY REPLICA ON N'SRV2' WITH (AVAILABILITY_MODE =
SYNCHRONOUS_COMMIT);
GO
```

It is important to note here that this can only be done from the primary replica. If we attempt to do it from the secondary replica then we would get the following error:

```
Messages
Msg 41140, Level 16, State 6, Line 1
Availability Group 'MyAvailabilityGroup' cannot process the ALTER
AVAILABILITY GROUP command, because the local availability replica is not the
primary replica. Connect to the server instance that is currently hosting the
primary replica of this Availability Group, and rerun the command.
```

- **PowerShell** : We can use the Set-SqlAvailabilityReplica cmdlet and modify the availability mode as shown in the following code example:
```
Set-SqlAvailabilityReplica -AvailabilityMode
"synchronousCommit" -Path
SQLSERVER:\Sql\SRV1\DEFAULT\AvailabilityGroups\MyAvailabi
lityGroup\AvailabilityReplicas\SRV2
```

Using this, we have modified the SRV2 replica to synchronous. The command was executed on the default instance of SRV1.

24. **SQL Server Books Online documentation recommends doing Availability Group related details via T-SQL command. Is there any operation which cannot be done by T-SQL construct?**

Answer: The Availability Group resource property, the Listener name, the IP, and many more can be changed by using T-SQL. The cluster level properties can't be changed using T-SQL commands. These properties include:

- Configure Cluster Quorum
- Force Quorum when necessary
- Configure Cluster Failover Policies

25. **Can I have automatic failover on an asynchronous secondary replica?**

Answer: No. Automatic failover is designed for no data loss scenarios which can only be guaranteed with synchronous data movement.

26. **I have configured one synchronous replica for my database. When I am running the select statement on the secondary, there is a lag as compared to the primary. Is that expected even with synchronous data movement?**

Answer: Yes. It is an expected behavior. Synchronous data movements guarantee the hardening of the log record on the secondary transaction log. The redo thread working behind the scenes would pick the log record and replay it. Once the record is replayed, the queries would be able to read the record. So there is a small lag before the redo thread can finish its processing. This is done to provide a faster transaction commit response for the primary.

27. **I have two databases in the Availability Group. One of the databases went into a SUSPECT state because the drive containing the datafile was lost. Shouldn't there be a failover to the other replicas in this situation?**

Answer: There would be no failover in this situation. If we recall our explanation about health detection in Availability Groups, the sp_server_diagnostics doesn't have any output for database level health.

28.   When running the Availability Group script, I am getting the following error:

```
Messages
Msg 35250, Level 16, State 7, Line 3
The connection to the primary replica is not active. The command cannot be
processed.
```

Answer: Refer to the "Unable to join the Availability Group" section in Chapter 13 for troubleshooting this particular error.

29.   What would happen if my secondary replica is down for many days? Is there any impact on the primary replica?

Answer: Unless all the secondary replicas have received the data, the truncation of the transaction log cannot happen on the primary. This means if a secondary is not available, the transaction log on the primary would keep on growing until the disk becomes full.

30.   I want to add a new file (data or log) on the primary replica, before doing so do I need to take any precautions?

Answer: We need to make sure that the path exists on all the secondary replica(s). If a path doesn't exist then the data movement would go to a suspended state. The following is a quick code demonstration:

```
ALTER DATABASE [MyNorthwind]
ADD FILE ( NAME = N'FolderOnPrimary',
FILENAME = N'C:\FolderOnPrimary\NewFile.mdf')
TO FILEGROUP [PRIMARY]
GO
```

We have added a file called NewFile.mdf on the location of C:\FolderOnPrimary. This location does not exist on the secondary.

This caused the database movement to go to a suspended state and we could see the following message in the AlwaysOn_health session.

AlwaysOn Availability Groups data movement for database 'MyNorthwind' has been suspended for the following reason: "system" (Source ID 2; Source string: 'SUSPEND_FROM_REDO'). To resume data movement on the database, you will need to resume the database manually. For information about how to resume an availability database, see SQL Server Books Online.

This previous message indicated that something went wrong when the redo thread was trying to replay the transaction. Therefore the data movement went to a suspended state. The following are the messages in the errorlog file on the secondary replica:

```
2012-12-29 16:50:55.810 spid29s   Error: 5123, Severity: 16,
State: 1.
```

```
2012-12-29 16:50:55.810 spid29s   CREATE FILE encountered
operating system error 3(The system cannot find the path
specified.) while attempting to open or create the physical
file 'C:\FolderOnPrimary\NewFile.mdf'.
```

```
2012-12-29 16:50:55.86 spid29s   Error: 5183, Severity: 16,
State: 1.
```

```
2012-12-29 16:50:55.86 spid29s   Cannot create the file
"C:\FolderOnPrimary". Use WITH MOVE to specify a usable
physical file name. Use WITH REPLACE to overwrite an
existing file.
```

```
2012-12-29 16:50:55.87 spid29s   AlwaysOn Availability
Groups data movement for database 'MyNorthwind' has been
suspended for the following reason: "system" (Source ID 2;
Source string: 'SUSPEND_FROM_REDO'). To resume data movement
on the database, you will need to resume the database
manually. For information about how to resume an
availability database, see SQL Server Books Online.
```

```
2012-12-29 16:50:55.91 spid29s   Error: 3313, Severity: 21,
State: 2.
```

```
2012-12-29 16:50:55.91 spid29s   During redoing of a logged
operation in database 'MyNorthwind', an error occurred at
log record ID (29:2321:1). Typically, the specific failure
is previously logged as an error in the Windows Event Log
service. Restore the database from a full backup, or repair
the database.
```

To come out of this, we have created the same folder on the secondary and executed the following T-SQL command:

```
ALTER DATABASE [MyNorthwind] SET HADR RESUME;
```

This caused the database movement to resume and we were able sync the replica. The can be proven by the following informational message in the errorlog.

```
AlwaysOn Availability Groups data movement for database
'MyNorthwind' has been resumed. This is an informational
message only. No user action is required.
```

31. Can I pause the synchronization to my synchronous secondary? If so, what will be the impact on the primary? Will the transactions get committed on the primary in this case?

Answer: Pausing (technically suspending) data movement to the synchronous replica is possible. There are a few points to remember:

- Transactions would continue and the primary replica would continue to be sending data to the other secondary replicas.
- The transaction log on the primary would continue to accumulate the data which has not yet been sent to any of the suspended replicas.
- In case we have only one synchronous secondary replica which is suspended, a manual or forced failover would cause data loss.

32. What will happen when my synchronous secondary fails or is not accessible because of hardware failure? Will the primary still work and will the application work for me in this case?

Answer: The primary would run in an exposed state, which means that transactions on the primary replica are not sent to the secondary replica. Any failover to those replicas would cause data loss. If a secondary replica would never come back then it would be advisable to remove that replica from the Availability Group. We will use the example of removing the secondary replica SRV4 from our MyAvailabilityGroup. The following command has to be executed on the primary replica to achieve this:

```
ALTER AVAILABILITY GROUP [MyAvailabilityGroup]
REMOVE REPLICA ON N'SRV4';
```

33. Can we install the SQL Server 2012 Availability Group on a Windows Server Core machine? If so, are we supposed to do anything special?

Answer: The AlwaysOn Availability Group feature is completely supported on the Windows Server Core. PowerShell is a great way to deploy a complete solution in such scenarios.

34. **Can I have the Availability Group created on two servers that are in different domains?**

Answer: No. This is the limitation of the Windows Cluster. All of our WSFC nodes must be part of the same domain. If we are trying to move from Database Mirroring or a Log Shipping solution to an Availability Group, this is one of the limitations to watch for.

FCI Related

35. **What is the "MultiSubnetFailover=True" parameter in the connection string?**

Answer: This keyword in the connection string provides a faster connection time. Note that this is also recommended when we have multiple IP addresses, but not necessarily multiple subnets. In earlier versions of the SQL Server client library, there was a parameter called "failover partner" which used to send a request to all servers one by one to check who is in the principal role. In SQL 2012, the MultiSubnetFailover parameter unwraps all the IP addresses and connects to all of them in parallel. While connecting to the Listener in the Availability Group (or the Virtual Server Name in FCI), it is recommended to use this parameter.

36. **What is the maximum number of nodes supported by a SQL Server 2012 AlwaysOn Failover Cluster Instance (FCI)?**

Answer: SQL Server supports the nodes supported by the underlying operating system. On Windows 2008 R2, it supports 16 nodes. Refer to KB Article 288778 for "Maximum number of supported nodes in a cluster". On Windows Server 2012 this limit has been increased to 64 nodes.

37. **We are getting the following warning in the Create Availability Wizard and the Failover Wizard. What should we do**?

"The current WSFC cluster quorum vote configuration is not recommended for this Availability Group. For more information, see the following topic in SQL Server Books Online: http://go.microsoft.com/fwlink/?LinkId=224159."

Answer: To summarize the information in the link provided, the warning is displayed if:

- The node hosting the primary replica doesn't have a vote.
- The secondary replica is configured for automatic failover and its node doesn't have a vote.
- The Windows Cluster (KB 2494036) is not installed.

In SQL Server 2012 Service Pack 1, the warning has been removed if the secondary replica was configured for manual failover and its node had a vote.

38. **I am not able to perform failover to an asynchronous secondary using the Failover Cluster Manager but I am getting the following error:**

```
The action 'Move to node SRV4' did not complete.
System error 5016 has occurred (0x00001398). The
operation failed because either the specified cluster
node is not the owner of the group, or the node is not
a possible owner of the group.
```

Answer: We should not use Failover Cluster Manager to perform the failover (even to synchronous replica). If we take a close look at the Failover Cluster Manager Interface and look at the preferred owners for the Availability Group resource, it is evident that the value is set to automatic failover pair. Otherwise it would be set to the current owner node. We might work around this manually by overriding the setting (which is not recommended). SQL Server knows better about the Availability Group failover. It can take corrective actions once the T-SQL command is run. In short, we should do a failover only using the T-SQL command or Failover Wizard from the Dashboard in SSMS. SQL Server internally does modifications of the resource owner in a failover cluster once we perform Availability Group failover via SQL Server.

39. **Can I change the properties of the Availability Group via the Failover Cluster Manager?**

Answer: We should not change the properties of the Availability Group via the Failover Cluster Manager. For almost all the properties seen in the Failover Cluster Manager, there is an equivalent parameter in the ALTER AVAILABILITY GROUP statement (These parameters are HEALTH_CHECK_TIMEOUT, and FAILURE_CONDITION_LEVEL)

Routing Related

40. I am unable to find the user interface for creating a Readonly Routing list. Am I missing something?

Answer: No, you are not missing anything. Even with SQL Server 2012 SP1, there is no user interface available to define the Readonly Routing list. It has to be done using T-SQL commands.

41. I have configured Readonly Routing for the secondary replica. Do we have any options for load balancing the connections to the readonly replicas?

Answer: No. There is no built-in feature for load balancing. Once we define the routing list and connect to the Listener with the Readonly intent, the connection would go to the first secondary replica eligible in the priority list. There are a few workarounds that can be used:

- Run a SQL Agent job on the servers periodically to modify the routing list and change the priority order in the background.

- Use a hardware switch among the secondary replicas that would redirect the connections. The other option is to use DNS round robin to achieve redirection.

- Define your own logic to redirect the connections among secondary replicas and directly connect to the secondary. In this workaround, we would not be using the Listener so after a failover, the Readonly traffic could end up on the primary. The applications need to be aware of that. This is often called application based routing.

42. I have configured Readonly Routing, the routing list, and the Listener to redirect readonly connections to a secondary replica. It was working fine before the role reversal (a failover). After the failover, my connections are not going to the secondary via the Listener. These read connections are getting sent to the primary. What could be the problem?

Answer: The most likely cause of such behavior could be that we have missed a configuring Readonly Routing list for the current primary. During the routing list configuration we need to specify a list of the secondary servers for each server for when it would be in the primary role. For a detailed troubleshooting section, please refer to the "Readonly Routing not working" section in Chapter 13.

43. When we add the "Application Intent=ReadOnly" parameter to an embedded data source connection string in the report, it fails with a "Keyword not supported" error. What should we do?

Answer: In the keyword there is no space, and must be written as "ApplicationIntent=ReadOnly". Also we need to ensure the .NET Framework update to 4.0.2 or later is installed on the Reporting Services host. We can get it working with normal ADO.NET connections (instead of using OLEDB) by installing the .NET Framework Update 4.0.3.

Troubleshooting Related

44. I have dropped the AlwaysOn_health session. How can I create it again or should I need to reinitialize it via the Availability Group wizard?

Answer: The AlwaysOn health session script can be found in the u_tables.sql script which is located under the Install folder of our instance. In our environment, it is in the following location:

```
C:\Program Files\Microsoft SQL
Server\MSSQL11.<InstanceID>\MSSQL\Install\
```

45. We have mentioned that sp_server_diagnostics takes a persisted connection to the server. If there are multiple Availability Groups configured on a single instance, how many server diagnostics procedures would be run?

Answer: There would be only one sp_server_diagnostics running to handle all the Availability Groups. Some groups might be using a different interval. The interval parameter passed would be one third of minimum of the HealthCheckTimeout across all Availability Groups.

46. I have some SQL Agent jobs which need to run only on the primary replica. How can I make sure they are running properly?

Answer: First, we need to create the jobs on all the servers because this information is not part of the user databases. Within the job, we need to define the logic to identify the current primary replica. Based on the replica state, move forward in the job or exit gracefully. We can use the sys.dm_hadr_availability_group_states DMV to get the state of the replica.

- http://msdn.microsoft.com/en-us/library/hh710053.aspx

47. Is there any difference if I suspend data movement on the primary or the secondary?

Answer: Yes, there are little differences we should be aware of. What we know so far is the ALTER DATABASE ... SUSPEND command needs to be done on the replica which hosts the database to be suspended. We should also remember that if we suspend the data movement on a readable secondary, new connections are not allowed although existing ones will succeed returning data as of the point of time of suspension. The following error message will be given to the new connections:

```
Messages
Msg 976, Level 14, State 2, Line 1
The target database, 'MyAdventureWorks', is participating in an Availability
Group and is currently not accessible for queries. Either data movement is
suspended or the availability replica is not enabled for read access. To
allow readonly access to this and other databases in the Availability Group,
enable read access to one or more secondary availability replicas in the
group. For more information, see the ALTER AVAILABILITY GROUP statement in
SQL Server Books Online.
```

If we perform the same ALTER DATABASE ... SUSPEND command on the primary replica, a new connection would be allowed to the primary replica as well as the readable secondary replicas.

48. I am performing testing of the synchronous mode and the asynchronous mode for my data centers which are a few miles apart. I found that for a batch of 500 rows the transaction took 3 seconds to finish in the asynchronous mode. When I switched to the synchronous mode, the transaction took 8 minutes (480 seconds). Is that expected?

Answer: We know that the synchronous mode is slower than the asynchronous mode but the numbers stated here are not acceptable. In testing environments, make sure that we start the test with a minimally sized transaction to ensure that transactions are replicating as expected and then increase the batch size. If we are running RTM versions of SQL Server 2012, then make sure that KB 2723814 (2723814 = "You experience slow synchronization between primary and secondary replicas in SQL Server 2012") is applied. As per the knowledge base article, the known issue occurs when the availability mode for a replica is changed from asynchronous commit to synchronous commit.

49. In theory, I read that transaction log backups on all replicas form a chain and can be restored in sequence. Is it possible to get the information from the errorlog?

Answer: Yes, it is possible to get this information from the errorlog. Whenever any backup is successful, informational messages are logged in the SQL Server errorlog. For demonstration purposes, we have taken backups from the secondary, the primary and then the secondary. The following entries in the log have been highlighted and we have underlined the same numbers to demonstrate the chain:

secondary
2013-01-01 16:35:02.540 Backup Log was backed up. Database: MyAdventureWorks, creation date(time): 2011/12/13(01:13:46), first LSN: 35:12891:1, last LSN: 35:12913:1, number of dump devices: 1, device information: (FILE=1, TYPE=DISK: {'NUL'}). This is an informational message only. No user action is required.

primary
2013-01-01 16:36:03.800 Backup Log was backed up. Database: MyAdventureWorks, creation date(time): 2012/12/18(05:12:19), first LSN: 35:12913:1, last LSN: **35:12923:1**, number of dump devices: 1, device information: (FILE=1, TYPE=DISK: {'NUL'}). This is an informational message only. No user action is required.

secondary
2013-01-01 16:36:09.140 Backup Log was backed up. Database: MyAdventureWorks, creation date(time): 2011/12/13(01:13:46), first LSN: **35:12923:1**, last LSN: 35:12929:1, number of dump devices: 1, device information: (FILE=1, TYPE=DISK: {'NUL'}). This is an informational message only. No user action is required.

Miscellaneous

50.   Is Microsoft SharePoint 2010 supported on Availability Groups?

Answer: Yes. We need to install Service Pack 1 (SP1) for Microsoft SharePoint Server 2010 to deploy SharePoint Server on SQL Server 2012 and use the AlwaysOn Availability Group feature.

51.   Can I configure an AlwaysOn Availability Group for SharePoint 2013 databases?

Answer: SharePoint 2013 has many databases for various functionalities. Not all databases are supported to be configured as availability databases. Most of the databases are supported for synchronous commit mode but a few databases are not supported for asynchronous commit mode. To know the complete list, please refer to http://technet.microsoft.com/en-us/library/jj841106.aspx (Supported High Availability and Disaster Recovery options for SharePoint databases (SharePoint 2013)).

52. In Database Mirroring, cross database transactions were not supported. Does the same hold true for multiple databases added in AlwaysOn Availability Group as well?

Answer: Yes. Cross database transactions are not supported in AlwaysOn Availability Groups. Distributed transactions are also not supported as in the documentation at: http://msdn.microsoft.com/en-us/library/ms366279.aspx

53. In the Database Mirroring feature, there was a third server needed for automatic failover called a witness. Do I still need that?

Answer: In contrast to Database Mirroring, we don't need a witness role in AlwaysOn Availability Groups. Back in Database Mirroring the witness was needed to form a quorum and make failover decisions. This has been replaced by the Windows Server Failover Cluster quorum.

54. Can we encrypt the availability database using TDE (Transparent Data Encryption)?

Answer: Yes. The only restriction here is that the service master key for creating and decrypting the other keys must be the same across all the replicas. Therefore; we need to import the keys on each secondary replica after the restore.

55. I already have Database Mirroring configured in my environment. Can I deploy an Availability Group solution on top of it?

Answer: Yes. We need to follow these steps:
1. First, make sure that you have completed all operating system and SQL Server prerequisites (versions, editions, and hotfixes).
2. Install the Windows Clustering feature and create a Windows Cluster.
3. Enable the AlwaysOn Availability Group feature for all SQL Server instances. This would cause a restart of the SQL Server service. This means there could be application downtime if done during business hours.
4. Disable transaction log backup jobs, if any.
5. Remove Database Mirroring, either by the UI or a T-SQL command.
6. Create the Availability Group and add the database. These databases were part of mirroring topology earlier.

7. Enable the SQL Agent jobs which we disabled in step d.
8. We might need to change the connection string to use the Listener name.
9. Bring the application up.

It is important to emphasize here that testing is one of the key steps for any migration or upgrade activity. Test all the steps in a simulated environment before attempting this on production boxes. This scenario is explained in detail under Chapter 15: "Migrating from Database Mirroring" section.

56. What are the considerations and limitations of using Replication with AlwaysOn?

<u>**Answer**</u>: In replication topology, publisher and subscriber databases can be part of an Availability Group, with some limitations. For more details, refer to the topic "Replication, Change Tracking, Change Data Capture, and AlwaysOn Availability Groups (SQL Server)" in Books Online.

57. Can I use the FileStream and FileTable features along with the AlwaysOn Availability Group?

<u>**Answer**</u>: FileStream is fully supported with Availability Groups. In FileStream, We can access the data from the primary as well as the readable secondary replicas (even after failover). On the other hand, FileTable is partially supported. After the failover, we can access the FileTable data from new primary but not from readable secondary replicas.

58. My application uses Service Broker; can I go ahead with Availability Group deployment?

<u>**Answer**</u>: It is possible to use Service Broker with the Availability Group with a few prerequisites, such as the Listener should be created for Availability Groups. For a complete list, please refer to this link: http://msdn.microsoft.com/en-us/library/hh710058.aspx

59. Can I configure Replication when my database is in an Availability Group?

<u>**Answer**</u>: Replication topology has multiple databases involved called publisher, distributor, and subscriber. Out of these, the distributor database is not supported to be used with an Availability Group. The publisher can be a part of an Availability Group (except peer-to-peer transactional replication and updateable subscribers). A subscriber can also be part of an Availability Group but the

failover will become a manual and complex procedure. Migrating from Replication topology to SQL Server AlwaysOn has been discussed earlier in Chapter 15.

60. Why is the bulk-logged recovery model not allowed in Availability Groups whereas with Log Shipping it works fine?

Answer: Log Shipping works on backup and restore technology and that is the fundamental cause of not allowing the bulk-logged recovery model in Availability Groups. In the bulk-logged recovery model some operations are minimally logged (for the list please see: http://msdn.microsoft.com/en-us/library/ms191244.aspx), so we can't send all the information necessary to a secondary replica because it is not in a transaction logfile. For the bulk-logged recovery model database, when the log backup is performed, the extents changed by the minimally logged (tracked using bitmap on bcm - bulk change map page) operation that are included in the log backup file. This happens even though the data is not present in the transaction logfile. This allows the restore operating to apply those changes on the secondary server in a Log Shipping topology.

61. Should I shrink the transaction log on the primary replica?

Answer: The database added in an Availability Group needs the same maintenance as a regular full recovery model database. One of the important maintenance is to take regular transaction log backups. If transaction log backups are regular, the transaction log would not keep growing and there is no need to shrink it. If your last option is to shrink, then you can go ahead and shrink the transaction log of the primary. The same operation would be performed on the secondary replica automatically.

62. I have already configured Log Shipping in my environment, should I move to an AlwaysOn Availability Group configuration after upgrading to SQL Server 2012? What is the advantage I get and are there pit falls to doing so?

Answer: One of the biggest advantages of moving over to the Availability Group is the almost instant availability of data in the secondary replica when compared to the delayed time in the case of "time bound" Log Shipping.

This is a double edged sword in some ways. We have seen administrators use the time interval configured in Log Shipping to recover from human errors of accidentally dropping a table.

Moving away from Log Shipping means we will miss the functionality of regular time bound backups of our transactional logs and the jobs are deleted. Care must be taken to create these jobs explicitly on the server to match the SLA of the business in case of recovery. For detailed steps, refer to Chapter 15 – Migrating from Log Shipping section.

63. Can I use Change Data Capture (CDC) and Change Tracking (CT) features with Availability Group?

Answer: Yes. Both features are supported with Availability Groups. One important thing which we should be aware of is that CDC would not harvest the changes unless they are hardened on the asynchronous secondary replica. Trace Flag 1448 can be used if we want to override this behavior.

64. Can I use any isolation levels on the primary replica including Snapshots?

Answer: Yes, the database on the primary is as good as any read/write database. A readable secondary does create some overheard of row versioning on the primary but the isolation level works as expected on the primary.

65. Can I use any isolation levels on the secondary including Snapshots?

Answer: A readable secondary is a Readonly copy of the database where the redo thread is working behind the scenes to apply the log records. To avoid blocking situations with this background thread, all isolation levels are internally mapped to the Snapshot isolation level. All locking hints provided in the query are ignored.

66. My reporting stored procedure needs to create a temporary table (#tables) as part of the logic. Is this allowed on my secondary server even though it is Readonly?

Answer: Temporary tables (#tables) are created in the tempdb database even if the create statement is executed under the context of an availability databases. So, it is perfectly fine to use those tables in the data retrieval logic in a stored procedure or an ad-hoc query on the readable replica.

67. I have extensively used many NOLOCK hints for reporting queries. Can I still use them when accessing a Readonly secondary?

Answer: All locking hints and isolation level settings are ignored when queries are run against the readable replicas. We are free to use locking hints but SQL internally would use the Snapshot Isolation level and no error or information is given to the end user.

68. Can 3rd party backup software run on my servers when my preferred backup location is the secondary for my configuration? Is there anything I need to be aware of?

Answer: It is important to understand that the preferred backup setting for the Availability Group only impacts the result returned by the function sys.fn_hadr_backup_is_preferred_replica. It doesn't prevent it from taking backups on any replica. We should check with the 3rd party product documentation whether it supports an AlwaysOn Availability Group.

69. Can I take filegroup backups on the primary or secondary?

Answer: The Copy Only database backup of any type (Database or File and filegroups) are supported on the secondary replicas and regular full backups are supported on the primary replica.

70. Can I restore a database over an existing availability database?

Answer: No. Any attempt to restore would generate error 3104:

Messages
Msg 3104, Level 16, State 1, Line 1 RESTORE cannot operate on database 'MyAdventureWorks' because it is configured for Database Mirroring or has joined an Availability Group. If you intend to restore the database, use ALTER DATABASE to remove mirroring or to remove the database from its Availability Group.

Messages
Msg 3013, Level 16, State 1, Line 1 RESTORE DATABASE is terminating abnormally.

71. Can I take the file offline for an availability database?

Answer: No. Any attempt to take file offline would generate error 1468.

Messages
Msg 1468, Level 16, State 1, Line 1 The operation cannot be performed on database "MyAdventureWorks" because it is involved in a Database Mirroring session or an Availability Group. Some operations are not allowed on a database that is participating in a Database Mirroring session or in an Availability Group.

Messages
Msg 5069, Level 16, State 1, Line 1
ALTER DATABASE statement failed.

72. I have run out of disk space for my transaction log on the primary replica. What should I do because it is in an Availability Group?

Answer: First thing to do in such a situation would be to see why the transaction log became full and take corrective action. We have discussed earlier that regular transaction log backups are a more common cause of this issue. We can look at sys.databases catalog view and look at the last_reuse_wait_dec column to know the cause of the transaction log not getting reused. Be aware that the action done on the primary would be replayed on the secondary as well.

73. Can we use the different port for Database Mirroring than in an Availability Group?

Answer: There is only one endpoint/port defined for both Database Mirroring and the AlwaysOn Availability Group. This information can be viewed by the catalog view sys.database_mirroring_endpoints. It is important to note that a database cannot be part of both Database Mirroring and an Availability Group.

74. While defining a routing URL for Readonly Routing, I have set up port 5022. Will I get any error messages while connecting?

The routing URL defined in Readonly Routing should have the port on which the SQL Server instance is listening, not the port of endpoint used by Availability Group. If we have provided a port where SQL is not listening then Readonly Routing will fail with an error message. This is the same error message which we would receive if we connected to the wrong the port. The following is the error message returned if you use port 5022 for ROR routing.

Sqlcmd: Error: Microsoft SQL Server Native Client 11.0 : TCP Provider: No such host is known.

Sqlcmd: Error: Microsoft SQL Server Native Client 11.0 : Login timeout expired.

Sqlcmd: Error: Microsoft SQL Server Native Client 11.0 : A network-related or instance-specific error has occurred while establishing a connection to SQL Server. Server is not found or not accessible. Check if instance name is correct

and if SQL Server is configured to allow remote connections.
For more information see SQL Server Books Online.

**75. Can I take the file offline when the database is in the Availability
Group?**

There are some alter database operations which cannot be executed if a database
is part of an Availability Group. Taking the database offline is one of them. We
would get the following error message if we execute such commands:

Messages
Msg 1468, Level 16, State 1, Line 1 The operation cannot be performed on database "MyAdventureWorks" because it is involved in a Database Mirroring session or an Availability Group. Some operations are not allowed on a database that is participating in a Database Mirroring session or in an Availability Group.

Messages
Msg 5069, Level 16, State 1, Line 1 ALTER DATABASE statement failed.

Summary

We are sure these common questions brought some interesting insights into how
some of the common areas of Availability Group, FCI, Routing, Troubleshooting,
and certain queries work. This overview can provide some great learning. This is
not an exhaustive list of all possible questions that can arise but were
representative of what we found from various newsgroups and customers of
AlwaysOn.

Error Messages Index

This book has a number of error messages mentioned in various sections. We
have consolidated them here for a quick reference.

Error Number	Chapter Number, Section
Msg 5191	Chapter 3, tempdb on local drive
Msg 5123	
Msg 17204	
Msg 5120	
Msg 1802	
Msg 976	Chapter 6, readable secondary
Msg 978	
Msg 3062	Chapter 6, How backups on secondary happens?
Msg 35221	Chapter 7, Step 4: Create Availability Group
Msg 41140	Chapter 7, Step 6: Adding Listener (Optional)
Msg 979	Chapter 8, ApplicationIntent section
Msg 824	Chapter 8, Automatic Page Repair
Msg 7934	Chapter 8, DBCC Checks on secondary
Msg 833	Chapter 10, sp_server_diagnostics - IO_Subsystem
Msg 35264	Chapter 11, Failover Troubleshooting
Msg 19405	Chapter 12, Patter 9 - Three node FCI with Availability Group
Msg 41158	Chapter 13, Unable to Join Availability Group
Msg 983	Chapter 13, My replica is in resolving state. What should I do?
Msg 41142	Chapter 14, Performing Manual Failover
Msg 41142	Chapter 14, Forced Failover with Quorum
Msg 3180	Chapter 15, Migrating from Log Shipping
Msg 1466	
Msg 1478	
Msg 41190	Chapter 16, Remove secondary replica from Availability Group
Msg 3752	
Msg 19405	Chapter 17, AlwaysOn : Common FAQ

Msg 1468	
Msg 5069	
Msg 15023	
Msg 41140	Chapter 17, AlwaysOn : Availability Group Related
Msg 35250	
Msg 3104	Chapter 17, AlwaysOn FAQ
Msg 3013	
Msg 1468	
Msg 5069	
Msg 1468	
Msg 5069	
Msg 35235	
Msg 19405	
Msg 35244	
Msg 41171	
Msg 976	

Table 17.1 Error Messages Index.

[NOTES]

Chapter 18. SQL Server 2014 - AlwaysOn Enhancements Teaser

Hollywood always has unique ways of entertaining audiences even if they serve an old wine in a new bottle. There are a number of movies that come to mind that show the old movies in the current new context. Some of the movies to mention include, 101 Dalmatians, Death Race, Footloose, Gone in 60 Seconds, The Karate Kid, Ocean's Eleven, I am Legend, Ransom, and many more. These old movies were added with a modern spin to the old flavor as they were re-shot. Each movie brought new concepts and a new screenplay to the same plot. In a similar way, the next version of SQL Server brings new enhancements and we bring a teaser in this chapter.

When we were completing this book, SQL Server 2014 CTP1 (Community Technology Preview) just released for public preview (this happened less than a month ago). Therefore this chapter doesn't contain all the enhancements that were introduced with the new SQL 2014 version. In this Chapter we bring a sneak peek to some of these enhancements. Though the list can expand by the time SQL Server 2014 officially releases, this is based on information we have at the moment.

Increased Secondary Replica

Starting with SQL Server 2014, AlwaysOn can have up to a maximum of eight replicas. In SQL 2012 the maximum is just four secondary replicas. The restrictions on the number of synchronous replicas and number of automatic failover replicas still remain the same as in SQL Server 2012 release.

Reliable Readable Secondary Replica

When the cluster loses the quorum or if the primary becomes offline the secondary replicas are not accessible in SQL Server 2012. In the SQL Server 2014 release, the secondary databases are still available for read workloads even when the replica changes to a "Resolving" state. This is a great addition for geo-distributed deployments.

Extend Replicas to Cloud

SQL Server 2014 introduces a new capability called "Add Azure replica" as part of the AlwaysOn Add Replica wizard. This is a great addition because enterprises might not have all the hardware resources on site all the time. Hence, using Windows Azure Virtual Machines as an extension to the DR strategy and a cold standby is always desirable to organizations.

Support for Clustered Shared Volumes (CSV)

Windows Server and Hyper-V environments have been supporting Clustered Shared Volumes (http://technet.microsoft.com/en-us/library/dd759255.aspx) for a while now. Until SQL Server 2012, this was not supported. SQL Server 2014 now adds support for clustered shared volumes where the same volume can be accessed by multiple cluster nodes provided they access different files. This also removes the limitation of the 24 drive letters in clustered storage. A new DMV called dm_io_cluster_shared_volumes gets added as part of the enhancement.

Backup to Azure

Taking backups to Windows Azure is a great asset to environments who have a replica on the cloud already. In this case, the backup can happen from an Azure VM directly to an Azure storage as a typical DR backup strategy. Since storage is cheap yet quite resilient on SQL Azure, it makes sense for customers to look at this as an option.

Improved Dashboard

In SQL Server 2012, there was no way to estimate how far behind the secondary replica is when compared to the primary replica. In SQL Server 2014, the Dashboard has additional information for each of the replica databases.

Enhancement to DMVs for AlwaysOn

At this moment we didn't find many additions, but we found some interesting functions added. The following is a list of some of these additions:

- DMF - fn_hadr_is_primary_replica: This helps to quickly identify if the current server is the primary replica.
- DMV - dm_hadr_database_replica_states: This has a new field called low_water_mark_for_ghosts.

There have been enhancements to DMVs which will show information for AlwaysOn FCIs. The following list shows the AlwaysOn FCIs that have been enhanced:

- sys.dm_hadr_cluster
- sys.dm_hadr_cluster_members
- sys.dm_hadr_cluster_networks

There are a number of other enhancements to AlwaysOn XEvents, the Failover Wizards, Error Messages, Error Logs, and Additional warning messages in the New Availability Group wizard. Many more changes are currently out of scope of this edition of this book.

Having said all this, the concepts of SQL Server 2012 still hold true for the SQL Server 2014 release. Be assured that we will make sure to add these additions to our second edition of this book.

[NOTES]

INDEX

418

419

CPSIA information can be obtained
at www.ICGtesting.com
Printed in the USA
BVOW09s0824231116
468743BV00006B/48/P